'This book is a must read for every supervisor
of chapters passionately and comprehensivel
intercultural elements in supervision and thera ̗
sors and Supervisees to explore and sensitively engage with the nuances and
clues of race and culture in the therapeutic process. This volume paves the
way for open conversations amongst clinicians in the supervision space.
A rich, deep and valuable work.'

Pınar Çakır, *trainee counsellor at Enfield Counselling Service*

'This comprehensive collection of writings is a rare invitation to envision a
supervisory space that embraces the often hidden and complex lived
experiences which touch the borders of race and culture. With candour
and honesty, the various authors offer the therapy profession supervisor
and supervisee perspectives that provide learning, challenge and, impor-
tantly, hope.'

Eugene Ellis, *author of* The Race Conversation:
An essential guide to creating life-changing dialogue

'The singular achievement of this volume is its presentation of trainee
chronicles within its multiple voices. It is an invitation to therapists in
training to understand the many perspectives within their supervision. The
book exposes the reader to a fuller realm of the experiential complexities
within the supervision encounter. The writings of these practitioners are
crucial, introducing us to a future generation of essayists in the clinical
supervision field of race and culture. Which is often missing from other
studies on supervision.'

Monika Schwartz, *Director of Better Practice Advisors
and former CEO of Women's Therapy Centre*

Intercultural Supervision in Therapeutic Practice

Intercultural Supervision in Therapeutic Practice extends the dynamics of intercultural principles beyond the scope of the therapy room to the supervisory relationship.

The book spotlights reflections from diverse cultural and 'racial' identities and modalities facilitating critical exchanges and conversations amongst the contributors without the constriction of rank. Trainee and qualified therapists who are not supervisors highlight the radical perspective of their placement supervision experience within intercultural settings and some pitfalls encountered in non-intercultural practice contexts. Chapters by experienced supervisors describe and review interventions with recommendations for practice. The themes covered include the supervision of trainees within agencies; multi-disciplinary women working with survivors of domestic violence; and the supervision of therapists working with refugees and asylum seekers.

At once contemporary and historical, this volume will serve as a reference for inquiring academics, and be of interest to students and clinicians undertaking supervision training, and supervisors and practitioners seeking to offer supervision to multi-disciplinary mental health practitioners.

Baffour Ababio is a psychoanalytic intercultural psychotherapist and clinical supervisor in private practice and at the Nafsiyat Intercultural Therapy Centre, where he is Clinical Lead. Baffour completed his psychotherapy training at University College London and his supervision training at the Guild of Psychotherapists, and is a member of UKCP and BAPPS. With Roland Littlewood, he has co-edited a volume on intercultural psychotherapy entitled *Intercultural Therapy: Challenges, Insights and Developments*.

Intercultural Supervision in Therapeutic Practice

Dialogues, Perspectives and Reflections

Edited by Baffour Ababio

Routledge
Taylor & Francis Group

LONDON AND NEW YORK

Designed cover image: © Charles 'Staché' daCosta

First published 2024
by Routledge
4 Park Square, Milton Park, Abingdon, Oxon OX14 4RN

and by Routledge
605 Third Avenue, New York, NY 10158

Routledge is an imprint of the Taylor & Francis Group, an informa business

© 2024 selection and editorial matter, Baffour Ababio; individual chapters, the contributors

British Library Cataloguing-in-Publication Data
A catalogue record for this book is available from the British Library

Library of Congress Cataloguing-in-Publication Data
Names: Ababio, Baffour, editor.
Title: Intercultural supervision in therapeutic practice : dialogues, perspectives and reflections / edited by Baffour Ababio.
Description: Abingdon, Oxon ; New York, NY : Routledge, 2023. |
Includes bibliographical references and index. |
Identifiers: LCCN 2023004479 (print) | LCCN 2023004480 (ebook) |
ISBN 9781032461342 (hardback) | ISBN 9781032461335 (paperback) |
ISBN 9781003380214 (ebook)
Subjects: LCSH: Psychotherapists--Supervision of--Cross-cultural studies. |
Psychotherapists--Training of--Cross-cultural studies. |
Psychotherapy--Study and teaching--Cross-cultural studies.
Classification: LCC RC459 .I58 2023 (print) | LCC RC459 (ebook) |
DDC 616.89/14--dc23/eng/20230428
LC record available at https://lccn.loc.gov/2023004479
LC ebook record available at https://lccn.loc.gov/2023004480

ISBN: 978-1-032-46134-2 (hbk)
ISBN: 978-1-032-46133-5 (pbk)
ISBN: 978-1-003-38021-4 (ebk)

DOI: 10.4324/9781003380214

Typeset in Times New Roman
by MPS Limited, Dehradun

Contents

PART 5
Ananse(sɛm)   243

Contributors

Ali Donat is an integrative psychotherapist currently working in private practice and at the Nafsiyat Intercultural Therapy Centre, alongside his role as an honorary psychotherapist at the Munro Centre as part of the South London and Maudsley NHS Foundation Trust. He received an MA and an advanced diploma in integrative counselling and psychotherapy from Regent's University in London. He is interested in how our feelings remain at the heart of our thoughts and how culture shapes our ways of being in the world. He was born and raised in Turkey and has lived in several countries before settling in London. Culture, he says provides a very rich reservoir of material in understanding others, and he has a sense of gratitude towards his clients and the stories they entrust him with in the therapy room (www.alidonat.com).

Angie Knorpel has over 20 years post-qualification experience as a counsellor and psychotherapist (Dip Psychodynamic Psychotherapy & Counselling, Regents College), is a senior accredited member of BACP, has almost 15 years post-qualification practice as a supervisor (Dip. SAP), is BAPPS-registered, is a qualified adult education tutor, and most recently completed his training in reflective practice with the IGA (Dip. RPiO). Angie has always sought to work in inclusive, representative, community-based organisations and has worked in the therapeutic field with a broad range of people in a wide variety of settings since the mid-1980s. She has worked in many public facing/serving roles from "shop-floor" to administration, management, and leadership, and has served on boards, latterly on the membership committee, and as co-chair and then chair, of BAPPS. As a lead counsellor in NHS primary care, she devised, developed, and led on a model of brief intensive counselling for inner-city GP surgeries that had no exclusions, and an urgent referral service that saw patients within three days. She has intentionally sought experienced intercultural supervisors whose supervision has massively influenced, shaped, and supported her: in particular Ali Zarbafi, who supervised her during her years in the NHS, and Priya

Commander, whose supervision she continues to benefit from. Angie currently supervises trainees and qualified counsellors and therapists, mixed modality groups, and youth and school counsellors. She has a private practice and also works as a counsellor and psychotherapist, a trainer, and reflective practice facilitator in the third sector.

Anna Chait is a psychodynamic psychotherapist and supervisor at Nafsiyat Intercultural Therapy Centre. She also works as an adult psychotherapist in CNWL NHS secondary care community service and in private practice. She is a registered member of the British Psychoanalytic Council (BPC) and the British Association of Counselling and Psychotherapy (BACP). Her experience includes working with clients from diverse cultural backgrounds and heritages, dealing with a range of issues such as trauma, anxiety, depression, bereavement, domestic violence, sexual abuse, issues of exclusion, marginalisation, and issues regarding identity.

Baffour Ababio is a mixed-ethnic Ghanaian-British psychoanalytic intercultural psychotherapist and clinical supervisor in private practice and at Nafsiyat Intercultural Therapy Centre, where he is also the clinical lead. He completed his psychotherapy training at University College London (UCL) and undertook his supervision training at the Guild of Psychotherapists, and is a member of the United Kingdom Council for Psychotherapy (UKCP) and the British Association for Psychoanalytic and Psychodynamic Supervision (BAPPS). Alongside his clinical role, he developed a career in managing mental health services, integrating a community-based response to support recovery from a broad range of mental health problems. He co-edited a volume on intercultural psychotherapy entitled *Intercultural Therapy: Challenges, Insights and Developments* (Routledge, 2019) with Roland Littlewood.

Caroline Adewole trained at the Bowlby Centre as an attachment-based psychoanalytic psychotherapist and sits on its Clinical Training Committee. She is also a training psychotherapist and training clinical supervisor, and has worked extensively with a wide range of post graduate students in group supervision in an intercultural setting for several years. Caroline also works in private practice with both individuals and couples. She is a parent facilitator and a trainer, and facilitates cultural competency training workshop at the Nafsiyat Intercultural Centre. Caroline has a special interest in working with clients who have experienced relational trauma originating in families and wider social structures, as well as the impact of systemic events of significance on minoritised communities. She has first-hand experience of straddling the Nigerian and British cultures, and has some understanding of the complexities and nuances of this lived experience.

Charles Brown is a practicing psychoanalytic psychotherapist, an addiction therapist and clinical supervisor in independent practice. He is a member of The Guild of Psychotherapists and an UKCP Honorary Fellow. Charles is chair of The British Association for Psychodynamic and Psychoanalytic Supervisors and of the Race and Culture Committee at the UKCP Council for Psychoanalytic and Jungian Analyst College. He is former chair of the ethics committee. He currently sits as a member of the executive. Charles is an Honorary Associate member of the Association of Individual and Group Psychotherapists (AGIP). He teaches on several psychoanalytic trainings, has published several articles, and contributed to book chapters.

Dilek Güngör is a bi-lingual psychoanalytic psychotherapist, clinical supervisor, and a group analyst. Dilek is member of the United Kingdom Council for Psychotherapy (UKCP) and NAFSIYAT Intercultural Therapy Centre, where she has worked with individuals, couples, and groups since 1993. Dilek's mother tongue is Turkish; she was born in Turkey to a Turk/Mongol mother and a Kurd/Kirmanji father. She holds a PG Diploma in group analytic psychotherapy (Institute of Group Analysis) and an MA in group and intercultural therapy (Goldsmiths University). She has lectured at several London Colleges and universities, including Goldsmiths' University of London. She has many years of experience working within the NHS, social services, Family Action, and the Women's Therapy Centre as a clinician and clinical lead. She is a published writer and an independent artist (E-mail: dilekfridakahlo@hotmail.com, Blog: dilekfridakahlo.wordpress.com).

Eda Avcioglu is a psychodynamic counsellor who completed her training at Manor House Centre for psychotherapy. She did her clinical placements at the Nafsiyat Intercultural Therapy Centre, and Waterloo Community Counselling. She currently works at IMECE Women's Centre with racially minoritised women who have survived domestic abuse. Eda is bilingual and of Turkish and German heritage. She has a private practice in London.

Gita Patel has a BSc in biological sciences, a diploma in counselling, and an MSc in psychoanalytic intercultural psychotherapy from University College London. She is a registered adult and child psychotherapist with UKCP. Gita was born in the United Kingdom to parents who migrated from India in the 1950s giving her a personal perspective on identity and its relationships with race, culture, and racism. Her career has been mainly in the voluntary sector, starting as a community worker then going on to work at Nafsiyat, Womens Therapy Centre, and Open Door as a psychoanalytic psychotherapist with adults, children, adolescents, and families. Gita has published articles and currently works in private practice offering psychotherapy, supervision, training, and consultation. She is also a Trustee at Nafsiyat.

Hady Kamar is a psychotherapist based in London, United Kingdom. He trained at Nafsiyat Intercultural Therapy Centre, where he worked with English- and Arabic-speaking clients. He now works in private practice and as a senior therapist with the NHS, where he provides counselling and culturally adapted specialist consultation within local communities. He focuses on developing co-produced projects around mental health and well-being. Hady also maintains a visual art practice, where he explores themes of language, humour, and the concept of self within Islamic philosophy.

Kiros Hetep was born and raised in South London to Jamaican parents, Kiros first entered the helping profession as a youth mentor in 2010. In 2013, Kiros undertook his clinical placement at the Nafsiyat intercultural therapy centre. Kiros qualified as an intercultural, integrative therapist in 2016 and developed his practice by supporting various organisations within inner London. Kiros currently works as a primary care therapist in forensic settings and continues to provide counselling to students in their secondary school years. Although Kiros's fundamental approach to counselling and psychotherapy is an intercultural one, he has recently integrated an interpersonal neurobiological framework.

Oye Agoro is of Yoruba ancestry, and practices as a BACP Senior Accredited Social Justice Allied trauma informed Integrative Intercultural Therapist and Supervisor, with over 30 years' experience of working as a therapist and supervisor in a range of community, NHS, and social care services. Oye has a BA in Sociology and Social Anthropology and trained at University College London/Nafsiyat Intercultural Therapy Centre. Alongside her clinical role, Oye has managed nine therapy services in London and been the Director of the Lorrimore, a charity based in Southwark, providing therapy and social support to people with mental health difficulties. She was also the Director of The African Family Mediation Service, a charity providing a range of support services to people in Lambeth, including a child contact centre, school and family mediation services, and a therapy service for black men. In addition, Oye has worked as the community services manager of Kush, a black housing association in northeast London that provided a range of housing, community support, and respite therapeutic services for black communities. Oye has published articles, co-founded the Multi Ethnic Counselling Service (MECS) in South London, and has previously worked as a social action psychotherapist at The Forward Project, a black mental health resource in west London.

Peter Cockersell is a UKCP-registered Psychoanalytic Psychotherapist who trained in Intercultural Therapy with Nafsiyat, of which he is a professional member; Peter has since gone on to be awarded a Doctorate in Psychotherapy through Metanoia and Middlesex University. He has been in practice post-qualification for over 20 years and has always practised interculturally; he currently has a small private practice and supervises psychotherapists in the NHS and voluntary sector. He is also CEO of Community Housing and Therapy, a charity providing residential recovery communities for people with diagnoses of personality disorders and psychoses. He has published various articles and chapters and edited a book on psychologically informed environments (PIE) and the psychological processes of homelessness and rough sleeping. He was co-author of the national guidance on PIE and a founding member of the Faculty of Homeless and Inclusion Health, and is on the Board of The Consortium of Therapeutic Communities (TCTC), the International Network of Therapeutic Communities (INDTC), and the Enabling Environments steering group of the Royal College of Psychiatrists. He lives in Hampshire with his partner and children, and various cats, rabbits, and bats.

Ravind Jeawon MIACP is a Dublin-based psychotherapist and founder of Talk Therapy Dublin, a service that aims to provide inclusive counselling support to clients experiencing distress. Born in Dublin, Ravind, the son of an immigrant father and rural Irish mother, comes from a diverse family background. His father, descended from Indian indentured labourers, was forced to emigrate from South Africa during the apartheid era. These experiences ignited an interest in mental health support from a multicultural perspective. Alongside private practice, he mentors students and newly qualified therapists from diverse backgrounds and also provides counselling services to the International Organization for Migration (IOM) in Ireland linked to their voluntary return programme. Prior to psychotherapy, Ravind's career background was in business development. Ravind spent five years as a voluntary youth mentor on behalf of the organisation Foróige, which involved mentoring teenagers who grew up in foster care. His voluntary work also extended to supporting and advocating for individuals affected by the ongoing housing crisis in Ireland. As a therapist, Ravind continues to advocate for more inclusivity within mental health practice, particularly linked to core trainings and an improvement in multicultural responsiveness from caring professions when providing services to minoritised communities.

Waheeda Islam is a psychotherapist, supervisor, and amateur poet. Waheeda passionately believes in working in a compassionate and heart-centred manner, rooted in her training as an Islamic Counsellor with Stephen

Maynard & Associates. She has her own private practice, specialising in trauma and working with survivors of abuse. She currently works with Nour, a charity working with survivors of domestic abuse, sexual violence, and childhood abuse, strategically managing projects and Nour's counselling service. Waheeda also leads in the delivery of the Women's Health & Family Services Healing Conversations Counselling Service, working with FGM survivors. Following her postgraduate certificate in clinical supervision, Waheeda has been providing clinical supervision to counsellors in private practice, at the Women's Health & Family Services and Afghan Association Paiwand, a charity working with refugees and asylum seekers.

Acknowledgements

I am thankful to friends, colleagues, and family members who supported this volume. I am grateful to all the contributors who have generously and courageously put their work to print. I want to acknowledge some names from the community of clinicians and writers who have written extensively in this area, Lennox Thomas, Roland Littlewood, Jafar Kareem, Elaine Arnold, Frank Lowe, Inga-Britt Krause, Isha Mavinga-McKenzie, and Eugene Ellis.

I thank Roland Littlewood, Charles daCosta, Natassia Brenman, Hilly Ababio, Jale Yazar, and Gervist Neale for their editorial comments.

A big thank you to Grace McDonnell at Taylor & Francis for her support, to Sarah Hafeez, and the production team.

My gratitude to my mixed ethnic intercultural Ghanaian heritage, my father, Nana Baffour Owusu Ansah Ababio and my mother, Grace Evelyn Kokui Tamakloe.

Finally, to Hilly, Esinam, and Gzifa for their patience, support, and inspiration.

Introduction

Baffour Ababio

A Black colleague of Antiguan heritage once recounted an experience from the early years of his child psychotherapy placement training in London. I will call him Clive. During therapeutic play, Clive's client, who was about 8 years old, bit his knee. As a trainee therapist, he was not sure what to do, and although it did not feel antagonistic or aggressive, he found it confusing. On presenting this for exploration in supervision, he observed the supervisor's raised eyebrows and the look of disbelief in their widening eyes. The supervisor then offered the following comment: the client was not used to being around Black people. At the moment, Clive scrambled to rationalise or make sense of the comment. Was it the White supervisor's attempt to introduce race into the discussion, albeit quite clumsily? Clive felt activated as he considered the possibility that this comment may well have revealed the supervisor's impression of Black people. It felt unsafe, unsettling, numbing, and silencing. Clive described feeling "othered" and he emotionally withdrew but continued to see this supervisor for the next 11 months.

McKenzie-Mavinga (2019) draws attention to the danger of how such experiences of silencing in supervision in the context of racial difference and disparity could result in a re-enactment of the silencing by the therapist when they work with clients. For the racially minoritised therapist, such silencing reinforces an internalisation of negative tropes about Black people which she has termed "trickster shadow" (ibid). Supervision that mutates into exclusionary zones detracts from its function as a space designated for support and creative exploration in the interest of the client. These occurrences place therapists, particularly those who are racially minoritised therapists, in uncomfortable, unhoused locations and they can feel constricted and withdrawn. These are well-rehearsed stories, familiar in anti-racist corridors, where they are whispered about, argued over, and strongly stated. As a mixed-ethnic Ghanaian, British therapist and supervisor, I too have heard, witnessed, and engaged in these stories. I have been a griot amongst other griots in retelling these experiences and ensuring (through the envisioning of imaginative affirming approaches) that they are heard in a way that it is transformative and enables

DOI: 10.4324/9781003380214-1

change. This, in part, animated the way these chapters have been collected and assembled within this book.

Academic publishing on psychotherapy supervision is on the increase. The content pages of a number of these publications might feature a chapter or two on diversity. These chapters and the occasional rare volume exploring the borders of race and culture in supervision are invariably the works of qualified and experienced clinicians. As important as it is that these senior and experienced voices are recorded and that a corpus is built on their foundational voices and works, it does beg the question: where are the direct voices of the therapists in training? Are the expressions and accounts of their clinical encounters being edited out and left on the cutting room floor? This volume assembles a group of colleagues: comprising therapists in training and qualified therapists (not supervisors) who recount their experiences of being supervised. It also includes supervisors' descriptions on record of what has been helpful and of their errors in learning and application. The contributors are from a range of racial and cultural identities.

Transmission and cross-fertilisation

If conversations about the dearth of explorations of race and culture within supervisory spaces are being had in the proverbial corridors of predomi-nantly racially minoritised psychotherapists, how then can psychotherapy service provision be transformed into something that experientially con-siders a fuller psychic realm of the client, supervisor, and supervisee in these clinical spaces? (Kareem, 2006). One response to this might be the adoption of a mixed race and culture team approach (Thomas, 1998). A mixed supervision team with members from various cultural, racial, and inter-secting identities might present with interesting dynamics and explorations. Some members in such differing groups might process their comments through a Eurocentric, conceptual, particularised modality framework. For example, prioritising the dynamics of defences, transference, and counter-transference in the supervision is important. However, let us engage in a thought experiment that such a group includes an Indian female profes-sional, born and raised in India, who moved to England to complete her analytic training, and has since lived and practised in the United Kingdom. Her spoken English is accented by the tonality of her mother tongue, Urdu. In a supervision discussion, this colleague offers her analytic perceptions, beamed through her cultural and racial experiences and sensibilities, touching on aspects of the case, not of primary consideration in the room. However, her voice adds something of interest to the picture being formed of the client under discussion – something of value emanating from the cultural and racial processes of her personal journey within the wider social, political, and psychotherapeutic institutional structures. She might not wield "culture" from any theoretical framework but offer it through her lived experience and observations. As a consequence, she enables colleagues to pause and consider the missing parts now being tendered by this Indian therapist. Take another hypothetical example involving the same therapist in group discussion about a client of Haitian origin, who seems somewhat restrained and is not getting to the crux of the issues she had initially presented at the consultation and assessment stage. The ensuing supervision discussion might well rightly be framed around defences and trauma. The Indian colleague might, however, wonder whether the client, a recent immigrant, might still be getting used to the new cultural and geographical strains of England – is it the case that the client is taking time to understand how things work here? Or is it in the process of getting to know themselves and gradually getting to a place where they feel they can open up about other things? This does not undercut the ongoing formulations around defences and trauma but adds to it by bringing an observation from somebody whose perspicacity comes from having a different perspective.

The mixed team context (Thomas, 1998) enables the consciously and unconsciously glossed-over parts in discussions to be examined, aired, named, and considered. It, of course, calls for a certain kind of listening: an open attitudinal positioning from the other members to enable a reception of the other perspectives being reflectively offered. It is an ongoing enlightening process of development equally applicable to "seasoned culturally/racially aware practitioners." One such "seasoned" clinician presented a case where she displayed a strong antipathy to her client's abusive parents. The supervisor in the discussion wondered about the strength of the countertransference and whether there might be other elements at play, such as the clinician's unexamined store of historic cultural hostility to the client's culture. We may wonder how and why the supervisor considered possible historic regional conflicts (between the therapist's part of the world and her client's) and offered that up for discussion. In the openness of the supervisory space, the therapist recognised the degree to which her countertransference had been intensified by these pre-existing regional conflicts to which she did not have access prior to the supervisor's intervention. They were at play in the therapy under the cover of the acceptable expression of concern and disapproval of abuse. The supervisor had, perhaps, developed a sense for the alternative, missing parts of the stories that clients and supervisees tell. The "how and why" of the cultivation of this sensibility may well be predicated on the degree to which attention was given to these matters in the supervisor's own training, analyses, personal, cultural, racial journey, and discussions with colleagues.

Context

In 2019, Mckenzie-Mavinga issued a caution about the false notion of a post-racial phase in Britain (Mckenzie-Mavinga, 2019). She was prescient, having observed the gathering storm clouds reflected in the Grenfell Tower tragedy of 2017 and the "Windrush scandal" that broke in the spring of 2018 in the United Kingdom. The years following these events were tumultuous and the effects seismic. Late 2019 saw the global outbreak of the COVID-19 pandemic. Its impact on individuals from racially minoritised communities in the United Kingdom has been widely documented in terms of disproportionate death rates and the unequal economic impact (Nazroo and Becares, 2021). Off the back of this came the public murder of an African American man by a White policeman on 25 May 2020. The final nine minutes of George Floyd's life were captured on a smartphone camera. The widely shared video clip of this barbaric act blew the lid off, resulting in protests and demonstrations across America and ricocheting around the globe, with the singular message that Black lives matter (Ababio, 2020). Mr Floyd's murder and the associated events ushered in active movements and open conversations about race, racism, and whiteness, while allyship gathered pace. Two years prior to Mr Floyd's murder, William Anderson drew attention to the dynamics of the libidinal economy of anti-blackness and the production and reproduction of images and references to violence against racialised people for casual consumption. This reinforces the racially minoritised individual's position being constructed by and sustained within White supremacist thought and structures. For that reason, therapists, supervisors, and writers should avoid the casual consumption of such images of violence. Any reference to or images of such acts ought to be thoughtfully and respectfully processed. According to Anderson, "violence does not need to be constantly repurposed, reproduced, and consumed; it needs to be stopped. We need redistribution of resources not trauma" (Anderson, 2018).

Against the backdrop of these events, the Conservative government of the United Kingdom commissioned a report on race and ethnic minorities' disparities in 2020. On 31 March 2021, the report, dubbed the "Sewell report," was published and caused a huge storm of anger and disbelief in sections of racialised minorities and allies. The report was experienced as a failure to acknowledge the "very real suffering of black and [racially minoritised] communities here in the UK. The suggestion that government evidence confirms that institutional racism does not exist was [disturbing to many]" (The Runnymede Trust, 2021). This was received as structural gaslighting, an anti-Black (baiting) manoeuvre by the UK government.

In a recent podcast interview, Saidiya Hartman (2020) pointed out that images and texts of anti-Black violence presented with a desire to effect change do not necessarily always lead to transformation. History points to the recurrence and reinforcement of White supremacist currents following testaments of anti-Black violence. Hartman suggests persisting with racial justice work whilst also engaging in a radical reimagining of how we do things, of the kind of world we would like to see and live in. This volume echoes Hartman in signposting and inviting its readers to ponder the testimonies recorded by the contributors and then to reimagine ways in which we think about and do supervision. It provokes readers to consider the kind of supervision they would like to see, and the structures, processes, and practices that might tackle and dismantle systems listed by Hartman as representing, "anti-blackness, settler colonialism, hetero-patriarchy and racial capitalism" (ibid).

The intent in returning to the cumulative effect and cost of the previously cited major events is to chronicle and draw attention to the history of adaptive responses of organisations from the affected racialised communities. In the 1980s, the Nafsiyat Intercultural Therapy Centre in their bid to check and mitigate the impact of analogous malign occurrences on mental health outcomes was one of many such organisations established as a response to and amidst concerns regarding poor mental health provision and treatment of racialised individuals (Littlewood and Ababio, 2019). The events of 2020 onwards, again, saw the mobilisation of similar organisations from the affected communities coalescing to provide a response to these enduring mental health issues, stemming from the bereavements wrought by the COVID-19 pandemic, the impact of racism and the disproportionate number of racially minoritised individuals on the front line of the COVID-19 response and the associated increased burn-out rate. One such umbrella organisation was BAMEStream, which brought together an alliance of practitioners, therapists, policy specialists, organisations, activists, and academics who specialise in the areas of mental health and well-being to respond specifically to the fallout from COVID-19 within racially minoritised communities (Murray, 2020: 3).

I propose the cumulative effects of these explosive events can be experienced and described as a shift, a *psychic unfettering* of racially minoritised individuals and some accomplices from their hitherto prescribed enduring locations. The perspectives then afforded by the various unmoored locations can facilitate an agentic view of self, others, and the world through lenses of possibilities, similar to Hartman's "radical reimagining." The exploration of these perspectives is the concern of intercultural psychotherapeutic work, supported by a kind of clinical supervision that concerns itself with focusing on race and culture. By including the narratives of trainees and supervisees alongside supervisor narratives (of all shades and interiorities), this volume endorses the intercultural and decolonial sensibility of enabling stories from the bottom up. If interculturality was to be threaded through this book, then it was imperative from the outset to create a textual environment for the chorus of voices from their varied developmental positions to sing and engage in a call-and-response dynamic.

Part I: Mapping supervisions

Chapters 1, 2, and 3 offer a critique of training and supervision and advance a process framework of supervision which evolves and responds to the range of "racial" and cultural identities present in the supervision. In the first chapter, Charles Brown, a psychoanalytic psychotherapist and clinical supervisor who also sits on the executive board of a psychoanalytic supervision accrediting body, centres on the therapist-in-training's experience. Like the other contributors, he deploys his own terms for racially minoritised individuals. Brown deliberately prefers "global majority" as the term, a choice that repositions and relocates these communities whilst still providing a record of anti-Black ontologies. Brown traces the genealogy of psychoanalytic supervision from Freud's Wednesday Psychological Society to the Eitingon model. By framing his chapter around the lived experiences of the racially minoritised therapist in training and supervision, he illuminates the textual dominance and workings of White supremacy in the supervision at training institutes and by this route, seeks to undo the invisibilising of the "global majority" trainee. His invitation is an open one, for a process of personal and institutional reflection on whiteness and an acknowledgement and recognition of the much-suppressed epistemes and ontologies of racially minoritised therapists in training and supervision.

In Chapter 2, Oye Agoro presents us with a conceptual framework and map to facilitate the navigations of BAME (her chosen term) and White supervisors in a therapeutic world suffused with Eurocentric ideologies. She calls for supervisors to enable a decolonising supervision space through the centring of race and the intersecting identities of the supervisor, supervisee(s) and the client. She demonstrates this by stating and naming her social location at the beginning of her chapter. She is clear that decolonising supervision requires a historical analysis of racism and a mindfulness of the potential re-enactment of the oppressed and oppressor positions in supervision and therapy. In the case example, we see Robert, the White trainee therapist, query the credentials of Darren, the Black supervisor. Darren grasps the nettle and invites Robert to engage in a reflection on their racial locations as a Black supervisor and White therapist. This supports Robert's work with his Black client, T.J. Robert's attitude in his initial contact with T.J. conveyed a micro-aggressive quality which T.J. (who has a capacity for resistance and struggle in this encounter) challenges, to Robert's chagrin. Darren's earlier introduction of race into the supervision made it possible for the dynamics between Robert and T.J. to be aired, resulting in a kind of "racial consciousness awakening" in Robert. Agoro uses this to illustrate an aspect of one of the frameworks she proposes – the "Racial Identity Development model" – where, as a consequence of his encounters with a supervisor operating in a "racially mature" status, and an "assertive" T.J., Robert moves from his colour-blind status of "conformity" to the "conflicted dissonance phase." He begins to connect with a recognition of his biases and the operation of his "White" racialised lens in the therapy.

Chapter 3 offers a partnership by Angie Knorpel and Peter Cockersell. Similarly, to Agoro, and as implied by other contributors, Knorpel and

Cockersell accentuate the value of the supervisor's personal work in introspection and knowledge regarding their own cultural, racial, and intersecting locations. They are both White British, of different genders and divergent class origins. The recognition of their subjective positions, they say, mitigates the dangers of assumptions and the attendant projections in their work as experienced therapists and supervisors. They recommend mixed race and culture teams as instrumental in enabling the intercultural sensibility of the supervisor and therapist. They understand that the experiences in diverse supervision and therapy dyads might evoke discomfort, silences, and avoidance but they say this must be faced. Knorpel and Cockersell differentiate discomfort from the placing of unprepared supervisors and therapists in positions of great responsibility. In one of their personal case examples, in an art therapy institute in a South American country, we see how the dynamics of whiteness are enacted by the course director, who places Knorpel in a role that she is unqualified to occupy. The outcome was the therapist's unease and anxiety which also revealed the supervisor's inexperience in intercultural perspectives, activated by their internalised racial dynamics. Knorpel and Cockersell say this experience raises the ethical issue of working beyond one's professional competence. The development of an intercultural lens is a training matter, one which must be thoughtfully attended to at varied structural levels in the therapeutic world. The writers link the supervisor's position to the responsibility to be cognizant of, and to facilitate, discussions when race and culture emerge in the supervision space. In another case example, the writers illustrate how assumptions relating to difference and choice of therapists might fail the client. In challenging assumptions in the supervision that clients should be "matched" with therapists of the same community or gender, Jamilah, a Black female Muslim client, consequently benefitted from the distance afforded by working with a White male therapist. This therapeutic distance would have been difficult to establish, had she been expected to work with a member of her own community on these particular issues. The authors conclude by highlighting an area for consideration in intercultural supervision work, which is the silence in the literature surrounding the lived experiences of supervisors with mental health problems.

Part II: Supervision and the social

Chapters 4, 5, and 6 are by two intercultural psychoanalytic psychotherapists and an integrative intercultural therapist who describe their supervisory delivery experiences. They demonstrate processes of intercultural psychotherapy supervision application within community settings in the context of refugee and gender-based violence. The first supervision group is a mixed professional group offering support to women who have suffered domestic violence and the other supervision group is designed for therapists engaged in therapeutic work with communities of refugees. In Chapter 4, Dilek Güngör, a group analyst and intercultural psychoanalytic psychotherapist, chronicles the processes in her reflective group, comprised of women from diverse professional backgrounds working with female survivors of male violence. Güngör treads a fine line between supervision and personal therapy. She achieves this through the explorations, dialogues, and understandings of the negative transferences stemming from internalised patriarchal structures expressed as antipathy towards men and women. These workers, in their professional roles, lacked organisational reflective supervision spaces – and therefore struggled to receive Güngör's offering as it conflicted with their "strong sufficient female" internal representations. Their moments of recognition of this organisational neglect were significant as it communicated to them their clients' experience of being neglected.

In Chapter 5, Gita Patel, an intercultural psychoanalytic psychotherapist, uses her case examples of supervising therapists working with refugee communities to enable access to how the tools of psychoanalysis could be deployed to elucidate racial and cultural transferences. Patel states that bringing cultural and racial elements of psychotherapy into consciousness through interpretive work is contingent on a deliberate induction to intercultural training and supervision. She, like other contributors, considers this an important training area – an intercultural sensibility is not arrived at unwittingly but through the experiential and the didactic. In one of her case examples, Patel describes the processes of a client's assimilation to British values: the adoption of a professional identity and the client's glossing over her cultural and ethnic refugee experience through denigration and splitting. The therapist grapples with the invitation to collude and to also gloss over the client's painful early refugee experience which is being expressed through her panic attacks, depression, and anxiety. The supervision supports the therapist's work in working through this impasse and surviving the client's negative transference and anger. With this, the client began to connect with the parts of her narrative to which she had attached shame. The costs of a therapist working within their small, closely knit communities is registered, recognised, supported, and explored. Patel notes instances where therapists in the supervision discuss dilemmas such as foregoing certain community gatherings and rituals to maintain boundaries as the likelihood of meeting a client in other settings is quite high.

Much like Güngör, Waheeda Islam outlines in Chapter 6, supervisions with therapists supporting women affected by gender violence. There are two cases presented and the first involves Islam who is Salma's therapist. From this therapist's perspective, she describes her supervisor's social justice, trauma-informed lens and framework in supporting her work with Salma. She reflects on the strong transferences and countertransferences in the therapy and explications of its parallels in her supervisory relationship. In another case example, Islam supervises the work of Hannah, a therapist of North African and French heritage, with her client Mala, of East African origin. As a supervisor, she utilises intercultural principles and observes amongst other dynamics, the theme of colourism between client and therapist. She clarifies the influence of her Islamic counselling training in enabling her to frame her work in safety and trust with her clients. She cautions us against political agendas that "other" racially minoritised communities and warns against essentialising these communities as production centres of gender violence. She calls for resistance against the reproduction of such tropes in the supervision.

Part III: Developmental perspectives

This section traces developmental trajectories in supervision, of a psychotherapist and then of trainees within a placement organisational setting (portrayed from the perspective of the conducting placement supervisor). In Chapter 7 Ravind Jeawon recounts a personal reflection on his professional psychotherapy journey in the context of being multiracial in the Republic of Ireland. He describes how interlocking social, political, and educational institutions valorise Eurocentric narratives whilst silencing their colonial histories and, thereby, the voices and identities of racialised communities. Jeawon foregrounds his lineage from his South African-born Indian father whose adult identity developed in White Catholic Ireland in the 1950s and 1960s as a student and junior doctor. Jeawon himself deployed the defence of passing and speculated the extent to which his own father had, in his assimilation journey, edited out aspects of his Indian heritage to be "more Irish than the Irish." The silencing of colonial histories, narratives, and the centring of Eurocentric perspectives permeated Jeawon's training experiences, producing and reinforcing his dynamics about passing. He identifies the processes involved in a shift from passing to embracing his biracial heritage in both his thinking and practice – beginning with a change of supervisor, through to the post-qualification experience of developing his private practice, including the aspects of self-disclosure involved in publicising his practice (such as posting his picture). His practice, subsequently, attracted a diverse range of clients who sought him out to discuss issues of race and culture. This phase in his practice was given space in his supervision. Like Brown, he requires and places a duty on psychotherapy training institutes to overhaul their curriculum, enabling other perspectives as a counterweight to the hegemony of Eurocentric narratives. Jeawon positions supervision as a potentially transformative critical space where these institutional silences can be broken, thus facilitating the experiences of racially minoritised supervisees and clients. For him, supervision which accounts for and is receptive to whole stories of racially minoritised communities could counterbalance the Eurocentric narratives baked into psychotherapy training institutes.

Caroline Adewole is a supervisor situated in an organisational setting. In Chapter 8, she deploys an intercultural and attachment-based perspective in conducting group supervisions with trainee therapists. Adewole's vignettes detail the intersecting identities of race, religion, and gender of the trainees reflected in the identities of clients in therapy with the supervisees. She attends to the early stages of the group formation and the anxieties evoked by the new, uncertain placement terrain while facilitating the connecting tissues of the new relationships between supervisees within the group, as well as relationships with Adewole as the conductor and to the organisational setting – an intercultural therapy setting. She treads a helpful line in enabling the group supervision to be a secure site; one in which client material can be discussed but where linking personal countertransferential evocations to client material is only encouraged if the trainee feels safe to do so – there is no compulsion. The chapter follows Adewole's maternal-like processes as she attends to clients and trainees – ensuring there is openness within a safe, secure space. She hovers in and out of client material and, next to, trainees as individuals and as a group with finesse, attention and care. Of note, is her observation of the rhythms of growth, individually and as a group. In one example, Adewole describes a disruption with Marisha, a trainee whose increasing challenges to the supervisor were interpreted as a communication about her growth. Adewole had initially misconstrued them as she had been responding to her as if she was still at an earlier developmental stage. Once she realised the real meaning, her insight, as a conductor, translated to recognition and acknowledgement in the group. Marisha's challenges became less heated from that moment on.

Part IV: Supervision as intercultural training (potentialities and pitfalls)

Chapters 9–13 are offered from the useful critical perspective of therapists who had experienced their supervision as trainees within an intercultural organisational setting. Three chapters are from therapists who have completed their training and continued work in the intercultural organisation, the other two chapters are written from an external lens of no longer being within the organisation.

Eda Avcioglu opens Chapter 9 by describing an experience in a placement centre with a Black client. Avcioglu self-identifies as a White woman of Turkish and German heritage. The Black client (her heritage is not disclosed) did not return after the first session and offered no explanation for this. Following this, Avcioglu reflected on feelings of insecurity, of failure and a lack of confidence – her interest in working with race and culture after this encounter was piqued and led her to take up a placement at an intercultural therapy centre. She suggests her mixed heritage played an important part in the decision she made to understand and work with race and culture in therapy. Avcioglu's supervision provided her with a space to explore and process the work she did with a British Arab woman – the supervision process seemed revelatory and moved the therapy work on. Her peers in the supervision were all from racially minoritised communities and she was in the minority. Her relationship with her supervision peers raised questions which she felt could have been responded to, facilitated and further explored, in the supervision. Avcioglu concludes by underlining the exploration of peer differences in group supervision as an area she would encourage analysis of, were she to take up the role of supervisor in the future.

In Chapter 10, Ali Donat, a psychotherapist of Turkish origin, considers his therapeutic work with Omar early on in his psychotherapy placement as significant and formative. In the chapter, he brings together the threads of class, ethnicity, historical conflict, and trauma. Donat felt that during their time together, Omar was assessing his efficacy as a therapist by the standards of his own lived experience of suffering and pain. Could Donat understand, empathise and assist if their worlds seemed that far apart? In the account, Omar tests Donat through probing questions which require self-disclosure, evoking increasing levels of anxiety, frustration, and anger in Donat. He feels Omar is not playing by the rules and resents what he experiences as incursions that are goading and humiliating. Donat recollects his supervisor encouraging him to raise and explore the differences present in his relationship with Omar, who was Kurdish. The invasion of the Kurdish population by Turkish troops in the northern part of the region during the period of the therapy significantly impacted the work. Omar directly asks what he, a Turkish therapist, thinks of this invasion and he feels Donat's response to his question is evasive and unsatisfactory. The work stalls halfway through when Omar delivers a devastating assessment of the therapy, saying that it is not working. Omar terminates the treatment. This is a vulnerable time in the early life of a trainee therapist. For Donat, the exploration of these dynamics in the group supervision with peers from diverse cultural, gender, and racial groups was containing, holding, and illuminating. Donat experienced and privileged the exploration of differences among his peers in the supervision. He rated this as pivotal in his intercultural developmental process in the placement.

Hady Kamar approaches his formulation from a post-placement and post-qualification perspective. In Chapter 11, Kamar queries the dominant narratives operating in training institutes, placement organisations, dynamically present in the interiorities of trainees and reaching into the intercultural therapy supervision space. He argues that the Campbellian European hero and adventure narrative propels the therapist on a trajectory of the *story*; to encounter the challenge, conquer, culminating in a declaration of victory. Kamar details the pernicious impact of these internalisations – akin to internalised oppression and racism. If unexamined, the trainee, as in Kamar's example, co-opts the client, whose goal in therapy is mutated in service to the therapist's hero narrative. This narrative Kamar observes acts on the trainee who edits his supervisee style, proffers a proxy self and "others" the intercultural organisation, the supervision, client (and supervisor). As with the other contributors, he sees this as an important training issue but contends the supervisor has a duty in facilitating and bringing the trainee's "narrative structure" into his or her consciousness. The treading of the line between supervision and therapy as suggested by Adewole, is amplified here by Kamar as it pertains to the trainee's deco-lonial positioning in their supervision. For Kamar, it extends beyond the trainee. It is, he says, for these therapy organisations to examine their epistemes of internalised "embedded story structures."

Kiros Hetep exhibited an equivocal, cautious attitude in the initial stages of his relationship with counselling. In his personal account in Chapter 12, he locates himself as a Black British man of Caribbean heritage and a working-class South Londoner. His cautiousness extended to the psychodynamic approach, perhaps due to the perspective of depth it espoused and its Eurocentric origins. It did not do much for Hetep and his lived experience as a Black man in a majority-White Britain. He, like Kamar, considered adopting a proxy self in the initial stages of his placement supervision. His position moved as he experienced matters which concerned him, such as inequalities, culture, and racism being explored and facilitated by his super-visor, a Black man conducting a mixed-racial group of supervisees. Hetep felt seen and recognised in the supervision and his curiosity was, apparently, stimulated by how psychodynamics in the supervision were deployed (deco-lonised) in service to explications around themes of race, culture, inequalities, and poverty. He describes the processes involved in the education and evo-lution of the intercultural trainee. Following his placement at the inter-cultural therapy centre, Hetep took up a counselling position in another organisation. He uses these experiences to present supervised cases from each organisation. His work with Kwame was supervised at the intercultural centre where dynamics of power, refugee experience, poverty, race, and the nuances of being Black men from different cultural locations had an airing. Hetep concludes that whilst his work with his client Kingsley was adequately supervised within the non-intercultural agency, it was enriched by his inter-cultural placement and experience. Hetep recognised the pressures Kingsley was under as a young Black British Londoner and Kingsley's awareness of his mother's fears about his future and his exposure to the dangers inherent in London for a young Black man. Hetep adds to what was offered in the Kingsley case supervision by referencing his understanding and experience of working with clients of Jamaican heritages and his observation of the impact on their attachment styles due to separation and reunion. Hetep contends that an intercultural supervisory space enables representation, visibility, recognition, and authentic encounters for the supervisee and peers, supervisor and client. It democratises and expands the entry points into the therapy world for racially minoritised individuals from different class positions.

Anna Chait calls for an integration of the psychosocial world into the work of psychoanalysis. She argues that de-emphasising the psychosocial serves to reinforce a certain White Western hierarchical framework. In Chapter 13, she puts forward mitigations such as discussing the patient's material within a diverse supervision setting and a theory that takes account of the full realm of the cultural and racial realities in the lives of patients, therapists, and supervisor. Chait undertook her training placement within an intercultural therapy organisation and presents her insights from a post-qualification perspective. She alludes to the danger inherent in the maintenance of unanalysed cultural and racial interiorities by patient, therapist, and supervisor, inviting us to consider the consequences of such unanalysed positions functioning under the sway of a dominant Eurocentric discourse. In the case study, Nadia, a White therapist who describes her complexion as light brown, sees a client called Zahra, a Lebanese Muslim woman. Chait outlines how Zahra's problems revolve round race, misogyny, and Islamophobia. Her thesis on the value of considering the psychosocial world in the analytic work is reflected in this case. Nadia's positioning as a White woman who is in the minority in the supervision group appears to provide useful grist for the intercultural therapy and supervision mill. Nadia reflects on powerful countertransferences in the supervision, providing her with useful speculative insights into Zahra's minoritised location. A rupture occurs in the supervision where Nadia sustains a denigrating attack from a White male peer, and she feels alone and abandoned by the other participants (and supervisor). The subsequent processing and repair work explicated the hidden dynamics of power around gender, race, and religion germane to her work with Zahra. It also enabled Nadia to connect with aspects of her own racism as well as anger towards men, deepening her understanding and engagement with her patient. Chait pinpoints the operation of the parallel processes of race and intersecting identities in the therapy and supervision, where their identification and ensuing analysis facilitates safety and competence in the supervision and therapy.

In Chapter 14, I offer the Anansesem wisdom pot folktale of the Akan people as illustrative of the possibilities of reimagining the locations of supervisor and supervisee(s) in the supervision space. In the tale, Ananse, the spider, assumes power and wisdom in his role as a parent vis à vis his young child. I contend the positions of senior, experienced, junior, and inexperienced as occupied in the supervision often undergo fluid dynamic movements where these positions switch, enabling learning opportunities for supervisor and supervisee. These switches in the supervision, I argue with case examples, have implications and provide possibilities to recast the hierarchies embedded and constructed in racial and colonial narratives and their enactment in the supervision and therapy. Like Chait, I invite readers to consider the effect of the external realities (psychosocial world) as well as engaging a "not knowing" stance alongside the experienced supervisory role to engage with themes which are expressed from differing cultural locations.

The contributors to this volume, through their differing personalities, racial, cultural identities, and locations, have all committed to documenting their clinical experiences as supervisees and supervisors, focusing on their experience of race and culture in the clinical supervisory space. The reader, in contemplating these accounts, is also invited to reflect on the devaluing impact of racism on the transgressor; as averred by Kovel, "all are losers" (Kovel, 1998). This is a point highlighted by Wynter (2022). In her review of Lady Nugent's journal, Wynter comments on the brutal relationships on Jamaican sugar plantations (ca. 19th century), she says "these slaves are kept at their cauldron by the practise and threat of violence. The Whites who must practise this violence must brutalise their [own] souls, and they do" (Wynter, 2022: 61). To this, I posit a dystopian reimagining, that racialised structural construction and positioning are sustained by the figments of racialised White negative projections. Closer inspection unveils problematic, hollowed-out marionettes whose animators project misshapen perceptions. The obvious limitations of the marionettes exposed. The "racialised" black, gone. Slipped out. Now, negotiating and navigating life in invisibility, with askance occasional glances at those engrossed in the manipulation of husks. The horizon might with increasing intensity assume this nightmarish hue if the racial morphing malignant "othering" dynamic is not mitigated. Encountering realism and the emergent *intentionality* in the intercultural supervision position reflected by the contributions in this book, could not be more opportune. I have a view of potential energies as infused in fragmented pockets, kept separate in part by colonial internalisations. Emboldened intercultural supervisors, researchers, theorists, and practitioners could, by creating interconnecting portals, reach into existing vibrant dynamic resources and forms from the Global South, including but not limited to, visual arts, fashion, dance, history, literature, sociology, philosophy, and science (current, historical, and pre-colonial) to integrate and inform their practice (a countermeasure to the despondency every so often engendered by the intercultural work). *Intentionality* acknowledges that the struggle, sadness and overwhelming encounters in the intercultural supervisory work can result in practitioner disequilibrium, disenchantment, and suffering. A despondency, nevertheless, can be attenuated through decolonised relationships and engagements with the dynamic resources of the Global South. *Intentionality*, inhabits this space (structurally) and enables the practitioner to safely continue their work in realistic hope.

In connection to *intentionality*, I am reminded of Jared Sexton's comments regarding the taxing contradictions faced by practitioners in the field of Black studies. Sexton draws from studies where the "commodification of emotional life" and caregiving inaugurate burnout and a disconnect from the capacity to emote (Sexton, 2021). Is there a particular toll in undertaking this kind of work in the pervasive contested spaces of race (and its frustrations, failures, triumphs, struggles, rollbacks), and culture on supervisors and therapists of all hues? In the chapters that follow, contributors respond to this question by highlighting their style and approach: that of supervision treading a line between foregrounding client material and engaging the supervisee in racial, cultural countertransferential exploration. The kind of support and care being advanced suggests an intervention of a different order (drawing on the energies of *intentionality*) to be thoughtfully attended to by (and for) the supervisee and the supervisor.

In the chapters, the writers tell their stories as honestly and as far as the reach of their insights allow. They are all in accord regarding the urgency of addressing race and culture in training and especially in supervision – they acknowledge that the beginnings of these adaptations seem to be occurring in therapy consulting rooms. A related question also being asked in this volume, is whether clinical supervision is keeping in step with these shifts, or might a split be developing?

The writers, in their various theses, propose an option; that of advancing progress through intercultural, mixed-race supervisee and supervisor dyads and groups interacting in supervision clinical discussions. This was the vision that inspired the Nafsiyat Intercultural Therapy Centre in the 1990s in their collaboration with University College London. The founders of Nafsiyat embarked on an imaginative project by implementing the intercultural psychoanalytic psychotherapy training programme, placing race and culture at the heart of its curriculum and praxis. The supervisors of training therapists on the programme followed through and facilitated these themes in the clinical supervision. Germinal conversations about cultures, racism, whiteness, and Global South therapeutic approaches were being routinely had by all with the course leaders taking the lead in initiating these conversations in their role as lecturers; a model which was taken up by racially minoritised and "White" racialised students. The communities represented on the training had opportunities to rehearse and embody these important interactional conversations; relationships and dialogues, described by a colleague then as the process of building therapeutic anti-racist, social justice emotional muscles. I am stating here that the supervision approaches under discussion in this book have previously, in part, been trialled with some success.

Finally, the Nafsiyat intercultural model (touching on Black fugitivity and marronage) and the themes of *intentionality* and *psychic unfettering*, are echoed, added to and further developed in the following chapters and are foundationally encapsulated by Kareem's (2006: 14) definition of intercultural (supervision) therapy. He described it as:

A form of dynamic psychotherapy [supervision] that takes into account the whole being of the patient [supervisor and supervisee] – not only the individual concepts and constructs as presented to the therapist [and supervisor], but also the patient's [and supervisees and supervisor's] communal life experience in the world – both past and present. The very fact of being from another culture involves both conscious and unconscious assumptions, both in the patient and the therapist [and supervisor]. I believe that for the successful outcome of therapy [and supervision] it is essential to address these conscious and unconscious assumptions from the beginning.

Kareem's characterisation, however, requires an ongoing focus on the integration of disruptive anti-racist social justice perspectives into the intercultural supervisory approach. Without this, it would be nothing more than a general, placatory sentiment lacking any real force for change. Intercultural supervision should avoid the lure of "the politics of representation, [presenting] a sort of picture of what reconstruction might look like without any of the material benefits of reconstruction at all" (Hartman, 2020). The voices in this volume, rise to this challenge, going beyond description and representation – to imagine and even create a different kind of supervisory approach.

Note

Patients' clients and some therapist names in the book are all pseudonyms. In addition, details of their personal biographies which could identify them have been altered. We are grateful to all of them for allowing us to share their personal and professional stories. Thank you all.

References

Ababio, B. (2020). Nafsiyat intercultural therapy centre black lives matter statement, 8 June 2020. Available at: https://www.nafsiyat.org.uk/index.php/2020/06/08/nafsiyat-intercultural-therapy-centre-statement-black-lives-matter/ (Accessed 26 June 2022).

Anderson, W.C. (2018). Against consuming images of the brutalized, dead, and dying. *Hyperallergic*. Available at: https://hyperallergic.com/445105/against-consuming-images-of-the-brutalized-dead-and-dying/ (Accessed 26 June 2022).

Kareem, J. (2006). The Nafsiyat intercultural therapy centre: Ideas and experience in intercultural therapy. In: Kareem, J., Littlewood, R. (eds) *Intercultural Therapy* (2nd ed.). Oxford: Blackwell.

Kovel, J. (1998). *White Racism. A Psychohistory*. London: Free Association Books.

Littlewood, R., Ababio, B. (eds). (2019). Process and Development in Intercultural Therapy. In: *Intercultural Therapy: Challenges, Insights and Developments*. London: Routledge.

Mckenzie-Mavinga, I. (2019). The challenge of racism in clinical supervision. In: Ababio, B., Littlewood, R. (eds) *Intercultural Therapy: Challenges, Insights and Developments* (1st ed.). Abingdon: Routledge.

Murray, K. (2020), *National Mapping of BAME Mental Health Service*. London: published by BAMEStream. http://www.bamestream.org.uk/ (Accessed 26 June 2022).

Nazroo, J., Becares, L. (2021). Ethnic inequalities in COVID-19 mortality: A consequence of persistent racism (Runnymede/CoDE Covid Briefings). Runnymede Trust.

Pod Save The People with Deray. (2020). Imagine more radically (Saidiya Hartman) 14th January 2020. Available at: https://podcasts.apple.com/gb/podcast/imagine-more-radically-with-saidiya-hartman/id1230148653?i=1000462445584   (Accessed 17 June 2022).

Sexton, J. (2021). Antidoting. *The Black Scholar*, *51*(3), 5–24. 10.1080/00064246.2021. 1932383.

The Runnymede Trust. Statement regarding the report from the Commission on Race and Ethnic Disparities. Available at: https://www.runnymedetrust.org/news/statement-regarding-the-cred-report-2021 (Accessed 19 July 2022).

Thomas, L. (1998). Psychotherapy in the context of race and culture: An intercultural therapeutic approach. In: Fernando, S. (ed.) *Mental Health in a Multi-Ethnic Society: A Multi-Disciplinary Handbook*. London: Routledge.

Wynter, S. (2022). Lady nugent's journal. In: Eudell, D. (ed.) *We Must Learn to Sit Down Together and Talk about a Little Culture*. Leeds: Peepal Trees Press Ltd.

Part 1

Mapping Supervisions

Chapter 1

Beyond Recognition

Rac(ing) in Supervision: In Relation to
Global Majority Therapists-in-Training and
Its Relevance to Professional Identity

Charles Brown

This chapter examines psychoanalytic and psychodynamic supervision as it relates to cultural literacy, cultural humility, and its relevance to professional identity.

I present a brief review of the history of psychoanalytic supervision before exploring how power, privilege, and position play out in the supervision matrix. The supervision matrix refers to all those unconscious and conscious dynamics which influence the supervision pair or group and becomes relevant with an intrusion into the supervision by extraneous elements. This opens up material that not only attends to the material of the client and the supervisee but also illuminates the relationship between supervisor and supervisee. The neglect of culture and recognition of cultural issues in theory and practice impedes engagement and learning.

I discuss some of the problems that many Black therapists-in-training often experience. I argue that the failure of recognition has its origins in psychoanalytic theorising and is constituted and performed in psychodynamic and psychoanalytic psychotherapy institutions.

Introduction

Supervision is a significant aspect of clinical development, professional status, and accountability, but in the literature, there is little written about the experience of the development of a professional identity concerning the therapist-in-training. By taking a perspective that spans the racial and cultural divide and paying close attention to internal processes and the transference–countertransference relationship, the supervisor is able to help the supervisee develop professionally and enhance innate abilities that will form their future professional selves.

Race has important implications for clinical supervision and service provision for the racialised other. Supervisors from the dominant culture who may have been exposed to different cultural identities and who have not sufficiently explored their own identity are probably not sufficiently articulate to address such issues and are rarely questioned on this. In this way,

DOI: 10.4324/9781003380214-3

Whiteness impinges upon the learning experience of the supervision enterprise with respect to the racialised supervisee.

Where there is difference, transference and countertransference dynamics produced by the complex matrix of the relational field can be problematic if unrecognised or left unacknowledged.

A lack of diversity within the psychoanalytic profession has inhibited the White supervisor's attention to the particulars of the cultural aspects of therapists-in-training. One reason for failing to integrate cultural identity and competencies in supervision is that psychoanalysis has traditionally viewed racialised minorities as unsophisticated and resisted recognising the ways social reality impinges on the psychic life of the global majority.

Although cultural competency has been recognised as important in supervision (Sue, 1998; Tummala-Narra, 2004), scant attention has been given to cultural formulation or the cultural identity of the psychotherapy profession. From the normative performance of Whiteness emerges a lack of understanding of bias and the intersecting identities of supervisor, therapist, and client.

Multiple social identities and culturalities are recognised as dimensions of lived experience and of clinical work and supervision (Brown, 2010; Watkins, 2016). The kind of learning in supervision for Black global majority therapists-in-training that provides a repertoire of cultural responses that help supervisees become culturally responsive needs articulating. In other words, culturally sensitive supervision understands dominant pedagogical concepts and cultural values are not normative or universal and may help to ensure that these concepts/values are not transmitted to supervisees.

Historical origins

To date, three distinct interpellations of the supervision enterprise can be identified.

The first was an informal one beginning in 1902 when Freud began holding meetings with a number of young doctors with the intention of learning, practising, and disseminating the knowledge of psychoanalysis. They called the group "The Wednesday Psychological Society." Discussions centred on the patient's psychopathology and the analyst's interest in the ways the patient's psychology manifested. In 1908, the name of the group was changed to the "Vienna Psychoanalytical Society." Guests were allowed to attend the meetings, and some became important for psychoanalysis such as Max Eitingon, who was a member of the "secret society," which functioned as a sort of old guard around Freud (Coburn, 1997; Fink, 2007; Frawley-O'Dea and Sarnat, 2001; Watkins, 2013).

The second phase of supervision came about when Eitingon institutionalised supervision at the Berlin Institute (Eitingon, 1926), where it was known as the Eitingon model and became the most common training model in psychoanalysis. Eittington established the tripartite essentials of psychoanalytic training that are in place today: training analysis, theoretical instruction, and treatment of analysands under supervision (Fleming and Benedek, 1966). Although Eitingon may have formalised supervision, Freud is credited with the first supervisory practice through three events: firstly, consultation/peer supervision with Breuer where they talked about their patients' hysterical symptomatology (Hess, 2008), secondly, instigating the discussion of cases at the Wednesday meetings, and thirdly, the supervising of Little Hans' father in the treatment of his son's phobia (Freud, 1909).

The 21st century has seen a third iteration where the focus of supervision functions as gatekeeping for the protection of the public. The variations that institutions apply would be the prerogative of the local training organisation and the projection of the organisational super ego. Eitingon's model required clinical cases of both genders. Recently, questions about the efficacy of internet platforms such as Skype/Zoom for supervision persist.

The early history of psychoanalysis shows Ferenczi was committed to integrating cultural structures. In a 1910 letter, he attempted to dissuade Freud from his belief in the inherent destructiveness of human beings by arguing for the role of social factors in human suffering. Ferenczi drew parallels between anti-Semitic and anti-Black racism, writing to Freud that "[t]he persecutions of [B]lacks in America [is because] [B]lacks represent the unconscious of [White] Americans. Thus, the hate ... against one's own vices ... could also be the basis for anti-Semitism" (Meyer, 2005). Ferenczi posited that psychoanalysts "investigate[d] the real conditions in the various levels of society, cleansed of all hypocrisy and conventionalism, just as they are mirrored in the individual" (Aron and Harris, 2010). When Anton von Freund, a friend and training analysand of both Freud and Ferenczi (Danto, 2005), considered donating part of his fortune to help create a psychoanalytic clinic for the poor, Freud wrote that von Freund's vision would "sharpen in all directions the sense of social justice" within psychoanalysis (Freud, 1920).

Winnicott's attention to the psychological and socio-cultural dimensions in his work revealed a failure to take into account the nature of the object, not as a projection, but as a thing in itself (Winnicott, 1969). Winnicott proposed that research be conducted on how the idea of Black and Blackness came into the material of analysis (Winnicott, 1965). He raised issues about skin colour, cultural associations, personal meanings, issues around recognition, and the dimensions of the social relations that were disregarded.

Benjamin (1990) clarified the development of the capacity for mutual recognition by emphasising the difference between the experience of the other perceived as external and the subjectively conceived object. For Winnicott, the withdrawal of the mother created a space that the baby attempts to fill with his own objects or tries to destroy the space through bed-wetting and oral sadistic attacks. Winnicott called this space the place of fulfilment and cultural representation. Winnicott also described the place where the baby can meet the other in creative activity and mutual learning. He points out how the subject comes to know and remember the other as separate through the capacity for attunement and tolerance of difference. It is this process that culminates in separation and the establishment of shared reality. Winnicott (1971) and others (e.g., Benjamin, 1990; Eigen, 1981; Ghent, 1989; Stern, 1985) outlined the process of recognition and attunement arising from co-construction of the other.

Benjamin says that "the intrapsychic ego has reality imposed from the outside; the intersubjective ego discovers reality." Relational psychoanalysis has elaborated on realities which has resulted in shifts that have affected how supervision is conceived and practiced (Berman, 2000; Sarnat, 2012). Attending not only to the internal world of our patients but also to the social realities for the patient, the global majority therapist-in-training, as well as the supervisor's own culture, allows each participant in the supervisory matrix to become the subject in their own existence enabling development and growth.

Culture is context

The task of supervision, what constitutes supervision, and the function of supervision has been extensively written about. Supervision might be described as enhancing the supervisee's skillset and patient outcomes (Jacobs et al., 1995; Wallerstein, 1981).

Supervision is anachronistic because it takes place in the tradition of orality. This is an important marker of class and privilege, highlighting the relationship between orality and knowledge. Narrative and storytelling are universal features in all cultures as they are the means by which wisdom and social norms are passed down through generations. The psychoanalytic supervision process is affected by the absence of the Black therapist-in-training's own lived experience and existence because of systemic anti-Black thinking.

The supervisor recognises that the patient is the source of that which has meaning. However, if the supervisor is the perceived holder of knowledge, the Black-supervisee-in-training in the process of becoming will act, formulate, and intervene like the supervisor. For the Black supervisee-in training, such a situation can ultimately lead to a preference for White values, interpreted as White being better. This would be reproduced in the analytic hour, resulting in a psychoanalysis of obedience.

Supervision with a suitably qualified supervisor ensures the safety of the patient through mutual reflection on the clinical process and in the case of training candidates, evaluation of the clinical work whilst ensuring ethical standards are upheld (Kernberg, 2010; Szecsody, 2003). The reporting of cases by the therapist serves three functions. The presentation of clinical material is the foundation on which the relationship between the therapist and supervisor depends since this is the source of the information necessary for understanding the patient and the analyst as they interact with each other in their analytic work (Fleming and Benedek, 1983).

Szecsody (1997) makes an important distinction between teaching and learning when she says that "teaching can be studied in *statu nascendi* [but] learning is more subtle: it is difficult to determine if it has occurred, if it is functional and if it is illusory." In other words, the supervisor supervises the technique. It is a career-long enterprise, a significant element in education and a requirement for qualification. It models effective relationship building, the sensitive giving and receiving of feedback and the management of power and difference. Supervision and its hierarchical nature means that an aspect of the supervisor's role is the exploration of how dominant ideologies, including race and culture, may be mandated and hierarchical identity prescriptives lived in the supervisory setting.

Discussions about racial issues in supervision are elaborated when racialised psychic and social historicity of the Black body can be explored (Leary, 2000) in order to avoid re-enacting the privilege and oppressive dynamics that exist in wider Western society. The psychoanalytic culture will have a bearing on the supervision, and these dynamics will influence the nature and quality of the supervisory relationship and the task (Constantine and Sue, 2007; Jernigan et al., 2010).

Kareem and Littlewood (2000) highlighted the drawbacks of the monadic view of the psychoanalytic concept of "self" even though it is viewed as emerging in relationship and, once established, exists and operates independently. One of the problems for the Black therapist-in-training in organisations is that of not being recognised as individuals (in social relationships), and thus their self-image is at risk of dissociative processes, being subjugated or split off giving rise to macro and micro-aggressions.

Each participant in the supervision has to be aware of and sensitive to the differences between themselves and between them and the patient. The supervisor who is from the dominant culture will, consciously or unconsciously, further the racist discourse in the supervisory relationship. These reactions and re-enactments can be openly explored in the supervisory space. The influence and performance of Whiteness on the patient/therapist interaction in the supervisory relationship may hamper the Black therapist-in-training who is effectively subjected to forces that contradict the reality of the global majority therapists-in-training.

White privilege, through invisible and subtle operations, fosters Whiteness and privileges, racism is, therefore, not only enacted through physical violence but is also achieved through symbolic power relations.

The importance of discussing race in supervision cannot be overstated and contributes significantly to mitigating the situation that places Black and racialised others at risk of mental health misdiagnosis. If the supervisor and therapist-in-training are unable to recognise or understand each other it will lead to an inevitable rupture. Narratives of identities and being-in-the-world experiences are multiple; thus, identity can be conceived as having a dynamic narrative core sustained through a historical and mythical agency.

Ethnic and racial identities are complex, multidimensional constructs that share similarities with the concept of self-hood and culture. Within the construction, deconstruction, and reconstruction of a coherent identity resides the importance of culture. Since individuals are defined within the particularity of their circumstances, located in time and space and determined partly by dominant groupings and institutions. Thus, identity is a dynamic interpersonal process in a cultural space which is transformative and con-stitutes the stage on which ethnic dramas are performed.

Harrell (2014) wrote, "If the relationship of racism [in supervision] is to be illuminated, the multiple ways that racism is experienced must be uncovered and identified."

She identified six examples of "racism-related stressors" and saw racial self-awareness as the most important starting point for equity. She noted how racism can exert its influence vicariously through racist micro-stressors/micro-incivilities and that vicarious experiences are critical in understanding the nature of racism's effect on individuals, members of one's family, close friends and in society as well as those involving strangers (e.g., the 2020 lynching of George Floyd in Minneapolis, USA).

Hook et al. (2017) shifted the focus from cultural competence to cultural humility. Discussing practical strategies for cultural awareness included repairing ruptures through hands-on exercises. The authors demonstrated ways in which therapists can become "ally's of justice"; or co-conspirators who seek and create meaningful relationships with the people they actively support. Cultural humility acknowledges individual limitations and views them as opportunities to connect with their patients (and the global majority therapists-in-training) at a deeper level.

Supervisors have the task of helping global majority therapists-in-training access spaces in which transformative learning can take place in the experi-ence between the internal and the social that is mutually contributed to by each of the participants in the supervisory matrix.

This space is where primary illusion can develop or "dreaming the patient" takes place and presents an opportunity to bridge the social intersections of differences. Dream images, reveries, and symbols can open the psyche to the linguistics of human imagination, fantasies, myths, and symbols (Ogden, 2005; Vassilopoulou and Layiou-Lignos, 2019).

Supervision in the United Kingdom has been hesitant in bringing into sharp relief the transference, countertransference, and unconscious reactive elements concerning race and the negative connotations associated with blackness in both Britain and within psychoanalytic therapies. This has lent itself to an absence of the sort of discussions in supervision that demonstrate an aspiration to serve racialised communities and calls into being an inconvenient truth and a site for rupture. Some examples of these sort of ruptures in the supervision are invalidating racial-cultural issues, making stereotypic assumptions about supervisees, dismissing racial/cultural dynamics between supervisor and supervisee, and offering supervisees culturally insensitive treatment recommendations (e.g., Brooks, 2014; Pieterse, 2018).

The British Association for Psychodynamic and Psychoanalytic Supervisors (BAPPS, 2019) is a member organisation of the Council for Psychoanalytic and Jungian Analysts (CPJA) and maintains adherence to the highest standards of supervisor competency stipulating that psychodynamic psychoanalytic supervisor training follows a presentation of detailed, in-depth clinical material as evidence of the standard of work and includes theoretical teaching and supervised supervision as required components (see BAPPS Criteria for membership 2019). Supervisors are required to undergo supervision of supervision as a part of their training yet can remain unaware of when privilege and related factors are present in the supervisory setting. An unawareness which lies dormant and unarticulated in the supervision of supervision. The continued extrusion of these factors, given the widespread acknowledgement of the negative psychological outcomes associated with power and oppression on the members of Black and racialised communities (Pieterse and Powell, 2016) can be understood as a type of violence.

UKCP 2019 published guidelines and standards for the education, training, and practice of supervisors and supervision which includes addressing cultural, racial, and equality issues in the curriculum and practice that demonstrate "adherence and positive intent to diversity and equality" (see UKCP Supervision Standards of Education and Training 2018). UKCP, at the time of writing, does not have a process to deal with complaints against its own supervisors.

Supervision's evaluative component for the therapist-in-training encompasses professional identity, competencies, and ethical practice. These sit at the heart of professional practice and are significant elements in analytic education. One question that has often arisen is whether the Black therapist should raise the issue of race in the clinical setting from the outset. The relevant question is *where* this should be raised. The supervisor ought to raise this issue in the supervision. It should not be left to the therapist-in-training. This has relevance for the effectiveness of the supervision relationship, in the giving and receiving of feedback, discussion of complex conscious and unconscious forces around issues of power, privilege, and difference, and areas often insufficiently addressed. Any sidestepping of these discussions could leave the therapist-in-training problematising their own bBlackness and subjective thoughts.

Rac(ing) in supervision

A Black male therapist who I had been consulting with over some years had been working once weekly for almost a year with a 37-year-old Ghanaian female, whom I shall call Gayle. She was a compulsive hoarder who was also diagnosed with bipolar II disorder. The therapy had been interrupted three times as she was admitted to hospital for periods ranging from a few days to several weeks. The therapist had been struggling to acknowledge and name the underlying tensions in the therapeutic relationship but also crucially within the supervision space.

Gayle was the second of three children. Her mother had died in a car crash whilst driving to pick up the older sister from a school sports event. The father suffered from long-term chronic health problems. The patient was living with her teenage son who had enduring emotional and mental health difficulties that included suicide attempts. He would run away from home and would go missing for days. Gayle had been separated from her husband after what had become a sexless marriage following her son's birth. Whenever the father, who was White, visited his son, Gayle felt that he was trying to move back into the house, as it seemed that he did not want to leave. She also felt that whenever she was assertive, he, the husband, responded by questioning her mental health and asking "Are you alright? Do I need to call social services?"

In the last session, Gayle had been particularly distressed and disclosed that she had sent 200 text messages in the previous two weeks to her ex-husband. A few days after her session, Gayle called the therapist asking for an emergency appointment to which the therapist agreed. However, Gayle did not attend the session.

Whilst discussing the case in supervision, the supervisee said he had felt the husband was re-enacting something to do with his own early maternal conflict and that this might have evoked something which was experienced as upsetting for Gayle, given her history. The supervisee ventured that perhaps the presence of aggressive and envious elements located with the husband resonated with Gayle's own unconscious feelings about her own self-image and her mother's death. In addition, I wondered about the therapist's feelings about Gayle's missed session. My feeling was one of irritability and some degree of resentment. Acknowledging these feelings allowed the supervisee access to his own experience of exclusion.

"The ex-husband did not allow his son or Gayle to enter into his flat and moreover, his family did not allow them to come to their home" the supervisor informed me. He recalled that Gayle had said she experienced her mother-in-law as "antagonistic" and someone who she would get into "racially charged situations" with. Gayle's own family were unsupportive, and she felt they sided with her ex-husband.

Raising the matter of race in the supervision space triggered a "lightbulb moment" for the supervisee allowing us to talk in a more open way about his countertransference feelings in his relationship with the patient which we were then able to understand in a more useful way.

Discussion in supervision explored how the therapist had become, in the transference, the "superhero" to whom Gayle clung "like a woman who was drowning." This was understood as the patient's hope for a powerful wished-for father figure. The patient's ex-husband was also an embedded part of the supervision transference matrix and appeared to be a representation of a frustrating and withholding object. The supervisee's interest in the husband had taken up much space in the discussion. The countertransference dynamics relating to this were not explored. Perhaps, for this reason, some issues had not been opened up in the therapy relationship and in the supervision but had been projected into the "crazy Black woman."

The racial tensions in the therapy, in the social environment and the patient's internal object relationships captured in this snapshot illuminated the supervision space. To put it another way, the clinical encounter, as well as the supervision space, was imbued with racialised thoughts/feelings which were disowned and projected into elements of the therapeutic and the supervision space. Skin colour in the dynamic supervision field increases the likelihood that racial issues will arise or be illuminated. Defences against thinking about race can be seen as racial enactments in the form of failures in recognition.

It is not easy to decide and prioritise which problems are essential as and when they emerge in the supervision process. However, any account of the lived experience of racism is incomplete without recognising that racism and racial oppression is felt and expressed through the living body.

Race and culture are controversial terms because precise definitions are complicated, complex, and evolve over time. It can be said that they are potent forces that underlie and shape the ways in which we think, feel, behave, and interact with others. The inescapable and inevitable importance of race in every analysis has relevance, whether there are obvious differences in the race or culture of the participants. The failure of analytic therapists to address the issue of race in the therapeutic situation is paralleled in the supervision space.

The challenge that the global majority therapists-in-training face in talking about their lived experience of oppression and privilege is a problem that has important implications for self-awareness, patient outcomes and the authenticity and recognition of Black bodies. As far as cultural and economic development for Blacks is concerned, the intergenerational impact can be seen in shifts in migratory trends and economic privation. Discussion of these problematic and uncomfortable dialogues forms a critical lens for reflection in supervision and has implications for learning, enhancing, and broadening effective clinical practice and developing professional identities.

Holmes demonstrated the power of race in organising defences against awareness and showed how "race and countertransference operate similarly and synergistically ... racial reactions are more potent and potentially more destructive [of therapy] than countertransference reactions ... since responses to race are determined and reinforced externally, that is, in the culture at large *and* intrapsychically" (Holmes, 1990).

Observing the ego-distorting effects stemming from the defensive use of race, Holmes argued that neither didactic approaches nor self-analysis were *sufficient* [not my italics] to give the supervisor or therapist-in-training mastery over racial blind spots. The process by which meaning is attributed to particular signifiers such as portraiture, biological features, space, or (sur) names is known as racialisation, a result of which individuals may be assigned as belonging to general categories (Miles, 2004). Fanon used the term "racialisation of thought" to highlight the failure of Europeans to recognise that Black people had a distinct culture that was unique to them (Fanon, 1961). Garner (2010) elaborated on this with his argument that racialisation is a set of ideas and actions that result in the introduction of racism into the social system allocating particular persons to races that are projected as accurate and thereby become the basis for analysing all social relations. Racialisation, therefore, can be understood as involving, among other things, power and hierarchy, dehumanisation, stereotypes, colour blindness, violence, and aggression (Dalal, 2002). Hall (2001) described this language construction as the "grammar of difference" which constantly has to be remade and imagined. It serves as the point of reference for measuring others, thus informing and shaping racial ideology and manifests as a shifting, formless, empty, valorised space.

For the racialised therapist-in-training, experiences can be negated through senior members interpreting their lived experiences as pathological aspects of self and their own projections. Once therapists have fulfilled the requirements of registration, they move to a different relationship with a supervisor. This new relationship is more consultatory and is reflected in the CPJA statement

> After the first year of post qualification practice a member is viewed as being able to determine their own supervisory needs including using the resources of peer supervision or group supervision. The member remains responsible for assessing the adequacy of their supervision needs and their own professional and personal development. (CPJA statement on supervision, 2018)

The impact of systemic processes in psychoanalytic training organisations is often overlooked and the experience of Black candidates which are fuelled by racisms has "reached a level of acceptance such that in presentations of clinical work race for the most part is mentioned only when the patient is not White." Stoute (2017) and others (e.g., Leary, 1997; Powell, 2018) have highlighted psychological assaults and challenges for Blacks who pursue an analytic training which include using interpretations to locate problems in the therapist-to-be, such as innate aggressivity, or a lack of mental capacity. A familiar one (for me) is being told that I am not understood, as though my speech is impaired or that I am speaking in another language. These projective mechanisms and/or micro/macro aggressions are too often traumatising experiences for many candidates of colour.

The cultural and institutional values will determine the systemic performativity of professionalism. How White supervisors manage their ideas and unconscious impulses about the therapist-in-training may be the same way that the therapist-in-training does – keep your head down, remember who "they" are, do not question what must not be questioned and focus on qualifying. in the supervisory space, overt or covert racism may influence the quality of patient care and the therapist's-in-training ability to talk about certain things as they sense the supervisor's hostility. To relate effectively, supervisors need to be aware of their own identity and the meaning of Whiteness as a racial position. White people generally do not see themselves as having a racial identity. Without sufficient attention to identity and racial dynamics in therapeutic interactions, there is a possibility for the therapist-in-training to have a racist experience, to feel stymied, silenced, pathologised, or perceived as "difficult."

Racialised global majority therapists-in-training in reshaping and reconstructing themselves psychically on both a personal and social level, form a stable and enduring constellation of attributes, values, and motives that will define themselves in a professional role and become an integral part of their nuclear self. Identity formation can be an internal compass to regulate clinical work, and a strong identity can mitigate "burnout" and alienation.

Silencing the race dialogue can be viewed as a form of violence denying a central aspect of Black identity. A Black heritage organises how that person navigates the social world and their professional membership organisations as part of their lived experience.

Similarly, professional identity may come at the risk of perpetuating harm to racialised patients because of the profession's adherence to specific models of the mind. There is an added expectation that the Black therapist-in-training develop the capacity to work with oppressive structures that reinforce inequalities at the individual, interpersonal, and institutional levels. The White professional identity and self-esteem acquired through their community of colleagues, formally and informally, functions in creating, maintaining, and supporting the supervisor's authority and the performance of Whiteness.

One of the outcomes of Black therapists only hearing, seeing, and practising what can be learned through acculturation means that Black supervisees are more likely to fail to recognise those who are most like themselves, identifying and allying themselves with the supervisor's performative role, where unconscious identifications are a central part of the institutional processes involved in the induction and identity of a professional. In this way, Whiteness impinges upon the learning experience of the Black therapist-in-training, resulting in the perpetuation of "vanilla therapy" (Pitcan et al., 2018) and robbing the Black supervisee of speaking without fear of intimidation.

A parallel fragmentation between the inner world and socio-cultural dimensions of the self and others can be seen in the notion of the proxy self (Thomas, 1996). He named the proxy self as the mask that some Black and brown people put on in a society that might be hostile or threatening to them. This proxy self is a protection against the racist attack and a way of avoiding the need for explanation. Thomas outlines that a bifurcation develops in the context of the failure of a prejudiced environment and the child's awareness and interaction requiring the adoption of a proxy or mask for survival.

Conclusion

Race as a negative factor can be diminished by didactic means; for example, maintaining an intercultural focus on discovering more about the culture of the racially different patient. Thus, race-based reactions of patient and therapist-in-training may be diminished.

Valuable points of access to a patient's transferences and references to race may provide additional points of entry to transference enactments. This particular vehicle is available in varying degrees in same-race and cross-racial therapist-patient dyads and along the treatment continuum of psychotherapy to psychoanalysis (Holmes, 1992). White supervisors continue to practice in a manner that seeks to replicate themselves. This perspective allows for dominant ideologies of Whiteness to centre themselves at the core of White hegemony and ethics whilst pathologising racial experiences. Privileging White interests, values, experiences, and beliefs limit conversations about race and racism.

It is essential that cultural competencies, racial identity awareness and discussion of these uncomfortable and unsettling topics become core aspects of exploration of the self, self in relation to others and learning in psychoanalytic supervision. Achieving this requires addressing the foundations of the training curriculum, the training standards, trainee and student demographics, and organisational and institutional systems.

Increasing the presence of Black psychotherapists involves recruitment and engagement with racialised others in teaching and training. Low retention rates often complicate this process because racialised others are placed in situations that are particularly challenging with limited support. The inclusion of more senior Black therapists can mitigate this problem and heighten intercultural understanding, disseminate culturally relevant teaching, and facilitate connectedness to the broader community. Finally, increasing the use of contemporary literature on training courses that are written by Black analysts highlights the importance of critiquing foundational texts and theoretical advances.

References

Aron, L., Harris, A. (2010). A new (2010) introduction to Aron and Harris (1993) Sándor Ferenczi: Discovery and rediscovery: An introduction to: The legacy of Sándor Ferenczi. *Psychoanalytic Perspectives, 7*(1), 1–4.

Benjamin, J. (1990). An outline of intersubjectivity: The development of recognition. *Psychoanalytic Psychology, 7* (Suppl), 33–46.

Berman, E. (2000). Psychoanalytic supervision: The intersubjective development. *International Journal of Psychoanalysis, 81*(2), 273–290.

Brooks, O. (2014). Race and our evasions of invitations to think: How identifications and idealizations may prevent us from thinking. In: Lowe, F. (ed.) *Thinking Space: Promoting Thinking about Race, Colour, and Diversity in Psychotherapy and Beyond.* London: Karnac.

Brown, C. (2010). Perspectives on difference in psychoanalytic supervision. Attachment: New directions in relational. *Psychoanalysis and Psychotherapy, 4,* 275–287.

Coburn, W. J. (1997). The vision in supervision: Transference-countertransference dynamics and disclosure in supervision relationships. *Bulletin of the Menninger Clinic, 61,* 481–494.

Constantine, M. G., Sue, D. W. (2007). Perceptions of racial microaggressions among black supervisees in cross-racial dyads. *Journal of Counseling Psychology, 54*(2), 142–153.

Dalal, F. (2002). *Race, Colour and the Processes of Racialization: New Perspectives from Group Analysis, Psychoanalysis and Sociology.* London: Routledge.

Danto, E. A. (2005). *Freud's Free Clinics: Psychoanalysis & Social Justice, 1918-1938.* Columbia University Press.

Eigen, M. (1981). The area of faith in Winnicott, Lacan and Bion. *International Journal of Psychoanalysis, 62,* 413–433.

Eitingon, M. (1926). An address to the international training commission. *International Journal of Psychoanalysis, 7,* 130–134.

Fanon, F. (1961/2001). *The Wretched of the Earth.* p. 171. London: Penguin.

Fink, K. (2007). Supervision, transference, and countertransference. *International Journal of Psychoanalysis, 88,* 1263–1273.

Fleming, J., Benedek, T. F. (1966). *Psychoanalytic Supervision: A Method of Clinical Teaching.* Australia: Grune & Stratton.

Fleming, J., Benedek, T. F. (1983). *Psychoanalytic Supervision: A Method of Clinical Teaching.* New York: International Universities Press.

Frawley-O'Dea, M. G., Sarnat, J. E. (2001). *The Supervisory Relationship: A Contemporary Psychodynamic Approach.* New York: Guilford.

Freud, S. (1909). Analysis of a phobia in a five-year-old boy. In: *Standard Edition X.* pp. 3–149.London: Hogarth Press.

Freud, S. (1920). Letter from Sigmund Freud to Rozsi Von Freund, May 14, 1920. *Letters of Sigmund Freud 1873-1939*, p. 330.

Garner, S. (2010). *Racisms: An Introduction.* Ch 2. London: SAGE Publications.

Ghent, E. (1989). Credo—the dialectics of one-person and two-person psychologies. *Contemporary Psychoanalysis, 25*, 169–211.

Hall, C. (2001). The lords of humankind re-visited. *Bulletin of the School of Oriental and African Studies, University of London* (Vol. 66, No. 3, pp. 472–485). Cambridge: Cambridge University Press.

Harrell, S. P. (2014). Compassionate confrontation and empathic exploration: The integration of race-related narratives in clinical supervision. In: Falender, C. A., Shafranske, E. P., Falicov, C. J. (eds) *Multiculturalism and Diversity in Clinical Supervision: A Competency-Based Approach* (pp. 83–110). Washington, D.C.: American Psychological Association.

Hess, A. K. (2008). Psychotherapy supervision: A conceptual review. In: Hess, A. K., Hess, K. D., Hess, T. H. (eds) *Psychotherapy Supervision: Theory, Research, and Practice* (pp. 3–22). Oxford: John Wiley & Sons, Inc.

Holmes, D. E. (1990). Race and countertransference: Two "blind spots" in psycho-analytic perception. *International Journal of Applied Psychoanalytic Studies, 1*(4), 319–332.

Holmes, D. E. (1992). Race and transference in psychoanalysis and psychotherapy. *International Journal of Psychoanalysis, 73*, 1–11.

Hook, J. N., Davis, D. D., Owen, J., DeBlare, C. (2017). *Cultural Humility: Engaging Diverse Identities in Therapy.* Washington, DC: American Psychological Association.

Jacobs, D., David, P., Meyer, D. J. (1995). *The Supervisory Encounter: A Guide for Teachers of Psychodynamic Psychotherapy and Psychoanalysis.* USA: Yale University Press.

Jernigan, M. M., Green, C. E., Helms, J. E., Perez-Gualdron, L., Henze, K. (2010). An examination of people of color supervision dyads: Racial identity matters as much as race. *Training and Education in Professional Psychology, 4*(1), 62–73.

Kareem, J., Littlewood, R. (2000). *Intercultural Therapy.* London: Blackwell Science Ltd. [First edition 1992]

Kernberg, O. (2010). Psychoanalytic supervision: The supervisor's tasks. *Psychoanalytic Quarterly, 79*, 603–627.

Leary, K. (1997). Race, self-disclosure, and "forbidden talk": Race and ethnicity in contemporary clinical practice. *The Psychoanalytic Quarterly, 66*(2), 163–189.

Leary, K. (2000). Racial enactments in dynamic treatment. *Psychoanalytic Dialogues, 10*(4), 639–653.

Meyer, W. S. (2005). The 'mother' returns to psychoanalysis. *Smith College Studies in Social Work, 75*(3), 15–31.

Miles, R., Torres, R. (2004). Does "race" matter? Transatlantic perspectives on racism after "race relations." In: Amit-Talai, V., Knowles, C. (eds) *Re-Situating*

Identities: The Politics of Race, Ethnicity, and Culture. Toronto: University of Toronto Press.

Ogden, T. H. (2005). On psychoanalytic supervision. *International Journal of Psychoanalysis, 86*(5), 1265–1280.

Pieterse, A., Powell, S. (2016). A theoretical overview of the impact of racism on people of color. In: Alvarez, A. N., Liang, C. T. H., Neville, H. A. (eds) *The Cost of Racism for People of Color: Contextualizing Experiences of Discrimination.* Washington, DC: American Psychological Association.

Pieterse, A. L. (2018). Attending to racial trauma in clinical supervision: Enhancing client and supervisee outcomes, *The Clinical Supervisor, 37*, 1.

Pitcan, M., Marwick, A. E., Boyd, D. (2018). Performing a vanilla self: Respectability politics, social class and the digital world. *Journal of Computer-Mediated Communication, 23*(3), 163–179.

Powell, D. R. (2018). African Americans, and psychoanalysis: Collective silence in the therapeutic situation. *Journal of the American Psychoanalytic Association, 66*(6), 1021–1049. *Psychoanalysis, 4*, 275–287.

Sarnat, J. E. (2012). Supervising psychoanalytic psychotherapy: Present knowledge, pressing needs, future possibilities. *Journal of Contemporary Psychotherapy, 42*, 151–160.

Stern, D. (1985). *The Interpersonal World of the Infant.* New York: Basic Books.

Stoute, B. J. (2017). Race and racism in psychoanalytic thought: The ghosts in our nursery. *The American Psychoanalytic Association, 51*(1), 10–29 Winter/Spring.

Sue, S. (1998). In search of cultural competence in psychotherapy and counseling. *American Psychologist, 53*(4), 440–448.

Szecsody, I. (1997). How is learning possible in supervision? Chapter in supervision and its vicissitudes. In: Martin, B., Morner, M., Cid Rodriguez, M. E., Vidit, J.-P. (eds). *Supervision and Its Vicissitudes.* London: Karnac.

Szecsody, I. (2003). To become or be made a psychoanalyst. *Scandinavian Psychoanalytic Review, 26*, 141–150.

The British Association for Psychodynamic and Psychoanalytic Supervisors (2019). Criteria for membership. www.supervision.org.uk

Thomas, L. (1996). Psychotherapy in the context of race and culture: An inter-cultural therapeutic approach. In: Fernando, S. (ed.) *Mental Health in a Multi-Ethnic Society: A Multi-Disciplinary Handbook.* London: Routledge.

Tummala-Narra, P. (2004). Dynamics of race and culture in the supervisory encounter. *Psychoanalytic Psychology, 21*, 300–331.

UK Council for Psychotherapy (UKCP) (2019). CPJA statement on supervision. www.psychotherapy.org.uk

Vassilopoulou, V., Layiou-Lignos, E. (2019). Dreaming up the patient in supervision: From the concrete to the symbolic. *Journal of Child Psychotherapy, 45*(2), 176–190.

Wallerstein, R. S. (ed.) (1981). *Becoming a Psychoanalyst: A Study of Psychoanalytic Supervision.* New York: International Universities Press.

Watkins, C. E. (2013). The beginnings of psychoanalytic supervision: The crucial role of Max Eitingon. *The American Journal of Psychoanalysis 2013, 73*, 254–270. Association for the Advancement of Psychoanalysis 0002-9548/13.

Watkins, C. E., Jr., Hook, J.N. (2016). On a culturally humble psychoanalytic supervision perspective: Creating the cultural third. *Psychoanalytic Psychology*, *33*(3), 487–517.

Winnicott, D. W. (1965). The price of disregarding psychoanalytic research, p. 174; in CW 1986, vol. 7).

Winnicott, D. W. (1969). The use of an object. *International Journal of Psychoanalysis*, *50*, 711–716.

Winnicott, D. W. (1971). *Playing and Reality*. London: Taylor & Francis Ltd.

Chapter 2

Supervision within the Context of Decolonisation and Intersectionality

Oye Agoro

Yoruba proverb:

> If one throws a stone in the market, it may hit a relative.
> Meaning: avoid doing things that will have serious repercussions or effect.

In thinking about supervision within the context of decolonisation and intersectionality, an important starting point for me has been an understanding and awareness of my social location. Central to my social location is my Yoruba ancestry and being born in London in the 1960s as a consequence of the complex colonial history of Nigeria and Britain. Our personal and family histories and our ever-changing identities affect what we see, what we are unable to see, how we hear the narratives of the therapists we supervise, and the way we hear and interpret the narratives of clients we listen to.

In attempting to provide supervision from a "decolonised" position, I am going to outline the elements that I have brought together during my 30 years of experience of delivering therapy and supervision in London.

Arguably, the intention of most supervision and therapeutic work starts from the ethical position of doing no harm to clients or the therapists that we supervise. This ethical position is clearly outlined in the British Association for Counselling and Psychotherapy (BACP) Ethical Framework (2018) which can be seen as drawing from the classical Western traditions of medicine, outlined in the Hippocratic Oath and the importance placed on doing no harm to patients.

The BACP Ethical Framework for Counselling professions commits all members to "Respect our clients as people by providing services that endeavour to demonstrate equality, value diversity and ensure the inclusion for all clients and avoid unfairly discriminating against clients or colleagues."

The COVID-19 pandemic has drawn increasing attention to healthcare inequities in the United Kingdom.

Data released by the Office for National Statistics indicated that black people were four times more likely to die from COVID-19 than white people.

DOI: 10.4324/9781003380214-4

Concerns about healthcare disparities in the United Kingdom have raised critical questions about racism and the role it plays in health inequalities in the Global North, with racism being described as a public health issue (McKenzie, 2003).

The case for racism being treated as a public health issue is illustrated by the following health disparities amongst Black, Asian, and Minority Ethnic (BAME) communities in the United Kingdom:

- Higher rates of hypertension
- Higher rates of General Practitioner diagnosed diabetes
- Higher rates of cardiovascular disease
- Higher rates of kidney transplantation
- Black women being five times more likely to die in childbirth

The increasing focus on the role that racism plays in healthcare inequalities is adding to a disturbing volume of data available on the ways that racism impacts BAME communities in panoptic ways that include the following:

- Black men being six times more likely to be forcibly detained under the Mental Health Act.
- BAME communities being two times more likely to be over-medicated and less likely to be offered talk therapies.
- BAME communities are 24–45% more likely to experience economic poverty.
- One in six more BAME families experience housing hazards with significant health and safety concerns as outlined by the residents of Grenfell before the Fire in 2017.
- Black men being 40 times more likely to be stopped by the police.
- BAME communities are 50% more likely to be unemployed.
- Black and mixed-race pupils of Caribbean heritage being two times more likely to experience temporary exclusion from school.

The impact of racism on the lives of individuals and communities is being described as not only a public health issue in the Global North but a second pandemic alongside COVID-19 (Ajamu et al., 2010; Nobles, 2006).

Racism

Racism has been defined as: "An ideology which identifies a social group according to a particular biological characteristic and uses this to draw negative assumptions regarding that group's nature or capabilities" (Karlsen and Nazroo, 2007).

Essentially, skin colour has been the rationale and justification for racialised social hierarchies. White racism, rooted in ideas of white supremacy, has become historically enmeshed and fused with the development and expansion of capitalism and neoliberalism. Ruth Wilson Gilmore, the well-known geographer, describes this as racial capitalism (2020).

It is being increasingly understood that any analysis of racism needs to be historic and recognise that the histories of the Global North include the emergence of capitalism from trans-Atlantic trade in enslaved peoples and the colonisation of North America, along with the economic plunder, exploitation, and genocides of peoples from Australasia, Asia, and the Americas.

Skin colour hierarchies have been and still are an integral part of the histories of the Global North and South. With racialised capitalism and racialised neoliberalism still observable today in the exploitation of people and the environment, especially in the Global South. This is seen through the destruction of rainforests in South America; the widespread pollution and effects of the oil industry in the delta regions in Nigeria; the detrimental effects of the extraction and mining of Coltan for electronic devices in the Democratic Republic of Congo; the deforestation and destruction of communities caused by palm oil plantations in Indonesia.

To this day, white/lighter and darker skin tones are coded based on ideas of white supremacy where lighter skin tones are widely still admired and coveted – consciously or unconsciously – because they symbolise the colour of colonial rulers. Within white supremacist ideology, white skin tones are seen as more beautiful and embodying superior traits such as: purity, intelligence, civilisation, etc. In comparison, darker skin tones are seen as being negative, inferior, a marker of being primitive, dirty, uncivilised, and sexually provocative.

Historically, Western psychotherapy, psychology, and psychiatry have had little to say about racism. At best, there has been an absence of an analysis of racism. At worse, racism and colonisation practices of the Global North have been actively supported through the influence of some aspects of European science, namely eugenics, which has been closely associated with white supremacy.

Decolonising therapy and supervision practices begin with a moral and ethical responsibility to accept, acknowledge, and have a historical analysis of racism and how it affects the well-being of individuals, communities, clients, and the therapists we supervise. Without this analysis, we run the risk of denying or ignoring racism which can cause additional psychological and emotional damage to BAME clients and therapists, which means that we are doing harm despite our best intentions.

Intersectionality

Understanding racism within an intersectional framework provides a more sophisticated and nuanced way of understanding racism and oppression and how they impact clients, therapists, communities, and ourselves.

Intersectionality definition

Ways of understanding how aspects of a person's social and political identity combine to create different modes of discrimination and privilege.

The term was first introduced by Kimberlee Crenshaw, drawing on the work of Audrey Lorde (1984, 2017) and Collins (2000). It encourages an understanding and analysis of oppression that recognises that racism, gender, class, religion, and other forms of discrimination are not stand-alone inequalities but are often intertwined, interconnected, and fused together in complex ways. For example, in thinking intersectionally about COVID-19 infections and deaths, we can hypothesise that the higher death dates in BAME communities may be a combination of race/racism, class, gender, housing, occupation, and working patterns.

Using an intersectional framework as supervisors can help us to be more self-aware in understanding our own social location in relation to privilege, discrimination, inequalities, and oppressions related to class, race/racism, gender, ethnicity, education, ability, sexuality, age, immigration status, religion, and whether somebody's first, second, or third language is English (see Figure 2.1).

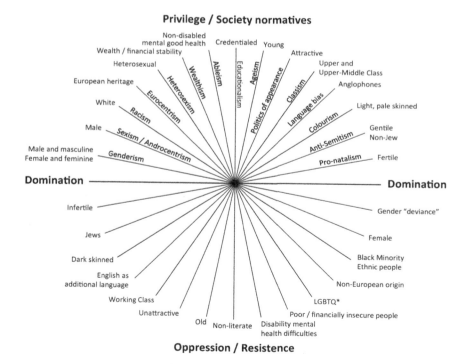

Figure 2.1 Intersectional vectors. Adapted from Natalya D (2014).

Most of us experience positions of privilege and discrimination. Being aware of this can help us to be mindful of power dynamics with therapists in our supervisory roles and how the social location of therapists and clients may impact the therapeutic process. Our visible markers of privilege and discrimination such as our gender, skin colour, the way we present ourselves in our bodies, our names, and how we use language are all likely to impact the supervisory relationships we have with therapists and the relationships that therapists have with clients. Having conscious awareness of this enables us to make conscious choices as supervisors, which might mean that we just hold this awareness in mind, or this awareness may be an important area of exploration in our supervisory role with therapists and the therapeutic work that therapists do with clients.

As highlighted earlier, when working as a supervisor within an intersectional framework, a critical starting place is having an understanding and awareness of our social location and lived experiences. They affect the way we see the world and how we hear therapist and client narratives. Our social locations and identities will also impact the things that we are unable to hear or acknowledge in therapist and client narratives. I think this point is well illustrated in a video entitled Carl Rogers Counsels an Individual on Anger (1974). In the video, Rogers, the white therapist despite his pioneering work in developing person-centred therapies, struggles to hear and attend to the black male client's experience of racism and the pain it generates and the power dynamics operating in the space between them.

Racial trauma

Racism, discrimination, and other forms of intersectional violence are increasingly being seen as a trauma. Racism is now being understood as producing a chronic stress response resulting in trauma and in some cases, intergenerational trauma (McKenzie-Mavinga, 2009).

Oppression trauma is a social trauma that deeply impacts the psyche of the individual and affects the well-being of whole communities. Recent developments in the field of epigenetics have established that trauma can be transmitted through parental genes over generations (Menakem, 2017).

Eduardo Duran has developed innovative therapeutic practices around identifying culturally appropriate ways of working with first nations and indigenous communities, and the effects of social traumas such as genocide, land loss, and devaluation of culture. Indigenous/first nation communities themselves recognise these issues to be historical traumas going back over several generations. From their ancestral knowledge, they see these past traumas as alive in current generations. Eduardo Duran's therapeutic work provides a powerful and inspiring way of working therapeutically within the value and belief systems of ingenious and first nations peoples. Eduardo Duran chooses to describe his work as Healing Cultural Soul Wounds (2021).

Essentially, the current understanding of oppression and intersectional violence indicates that many people are continuously living in a high-stress response state, which for many individuals moves into post-traumatic stress disorder (PTSD) and complex post-traumatic stress disorder (CPTSD) that can be transmitted over generations and effects whole communities over generations.

As a supervisor, when we identify and become aware that a therapist or a client may have experienced social trauma it opens the possibility to name and explore the therapist's or client's experience and narrative around the experience. Promoting the possibility of this exploration allows for the naming of historical and current survival strategies and resilience. It also allows for the opportunity to collaboratively explore the strengths and disadvantages of different strategies and resilience practices and identifying different ones. These interventions are likely to promote safety, resilience, and well-being, which are important protective factors in coping with and resisting oppression and structural inequalities, and central to working within a decolonising and intersectional framework. Without conscious awareness of social trauma, the opportunity for consideration and exploration of this area in supervision or the therapeutic alliance can be easily missed.

Internalised racism

From my experience of working as a therapist and supervisor, I have concluded that no understanding of inequalities and oppression from a therapeutic perspective can be complete without an understanding of internalised oppression.

Internalised oppression is the process where we internalise and act out the negative stereotypes and myths about social groups which are often promoted by dominant cultural groups, which Gramsci (1999) has described as ruling class hegemony. Frantz Fanon clearly describes the effects of internalised racism in his book: Black Skin, White Masks (1967).

This internalisation process can result in feelings of self-hatred, shame, low self-esteem, conscious, and subconscious feelings of not being good enough and can lead to false, negative stereotypes becoming self-fulfilling prophecy.

The ways we consciously and subconsciously act out dominant discourses around ableism, ageism, class, gender, heteronormality, patriarchy, and racism are complex and diverse. Examples of this include the following.

Colourism

The acceptance and acting out of white-racial-skin colour hierarchies in BAME communities, where lighter skin tones are admired and desired because they consciously or unconsciously symbolise the colour of white colonial rulers.

One of the manifestations of shadism and colourism throughout the world can be seen in the use of skin whitening products. Seventy-seven per cent of Nigerian women, 59% in Togo, 50% in the Philippines, and 45% in Hong Kong use skin-whitening products (Mercury Policy Project, 2010). The World Health Organisation has linked skin-whitening products to skin scarring, skin rashes, kidney failure, anxiety, and depression (David, 2013). Skin bleaching products are on sale in many London black beauty shops.

Uncritical acceptance of capitalism

Being enslaved to consumerism, the accumulation of money and material goods is seen as the primary marker of self-worth. The internalisation and glorification of capitalist/Western values can be seen in the embracement of rugged individualism, objectification, and commodification. Although the material wealth of the capitalist economies of the Global North is directly related to the profits obtained from the historic trans-Atlantic trade in enslaved peoples, colonisation, and appropriation of natural resources. Those mechanisms of exploitation of black and brown peoples from the global south are entrenched and ongoing.

Overworking

This is where marginalised/oppressed group members overwork to gain acceptance from the dominant group. Overworking is the major driving force in one's life due to conscious or subconscious feelings of not being good enough and needing white approval to feel validated, which can be seen as the internalisation of historical colonial and plantation-type dynamics.

Hypersexualisation of Black women and men

The internalisation of white supremacist stereotypes of black sexuality, with black men and women typically being portrayed as sexually uninhibited and provocative, is often reflected in the number of portrayals of Black women on screen as "whore" or "prostitutes." The sexualisation of black women within white supremacy can be seen as justifying the systemic perpetration of sexual violence against black women during colonisation and the trans-Atlantic trade in enslaved peoples. Alongside this was the portrayal of black men as a threat to white femininity (hooks, 1996).

Passive acquiescence

Being passive in response to inequality, living lives of unrealised potential (Watermeyer and Gorgens, 2014). Reflecting the subjugation and disempowerment that can occur under oppression. A form of learned helplessness.

"Strong black women" trope

Promotes the stereotype of black women as caregivers, servicing others with a smile, being there for everybody, creating the expectation that black women can cope with everything (Wallace, 1979). The strong black woman trope can be seen as a form of dehumanisation that assumes that black women do not have emotions and have a superhuman ability to deal with everything. Internalisation of this stereotype can lead to self-sacrificing behaviours and difficulties in showing vulnerability or seeking help, along with an extreme drive to succeed despite limited resources. The internalisation and acting out of this stereotype can have significant consequences for black women's physical, emotional, and spiritual health Woods-Giscombe, 2019; Ira, 2020).

Internalisation and acting out of violence

In the United Kingdom, black men are twice as likely to be the victims of inner-city violent crime, with police identifying that most inner-city crime is committed by black men. The high death rates of young black men from homicide in the United Kingdom and the United States have been linked to the internalisation and glorification of black male stereotypes, often characterised as criminal, violent, aggressive, and masculinist. As a result of peer group members being seen as inferior, anger and rage are directed horizontally at other group members rather than upwards at the dominant group.

As practitioners, there are critical issues around how rage and anger associated with intersectional violence and oppression can be expressed which can have enormous ramifications. Traditionally and currently, there are significant sanctions around some individuals/groups showing anger, for example, black men and women (hooks, 1996).

If, as supervisors, we choose to position ourselves within a decolonising and anti-oppressive framework, the supervision that we offer will have at its root a moral commitment to eradicating racism and delivering interventions that actively promote anti-racism. Consequentially, an important function of supervision and therapy is to provide a space where patterns of internalised racism can be explored and dismantled in a safe, non-judgemental, and compassionate environment. I believe that a safe and compassionate environment can be created by supervisors being aware of the ways that we are all in positions of privilege and discrimination. We all, at some point, act out internalised oppression dynamics as a way of surviving in environments which are hostile to the bodies that we inhabit.

Bringing an understanding of oppression and internalised oppression into supervision and therapeutic work with clients can have a significant impact on the way we conceptualise a client's narrative and experiences of distress.

Many presentations of distress, such as depression and self-harming within marginalised populations, can be viewed as an unambiguous expression of oppression.

Internalised oppression and domination

Internalised dominance survival strategies

Vanissar Tarakali (2011) outlines how there are identifiable strategies adopted by those in privileged positions and those experiencing oppression. Internalised dominance strategies include denial, dissociation, numbness, being unaware of oppression, defensiveness, attacking and blaming marginalised groups, refusal to take responsibility for oppression, self-absorption, and avoidance of marginalised groups.

Internalised domination describes how members of dominant privileged groups adapt and accept the denigration, subjugation, marginalisation, and discrimination of a group as natural and inevitable.

Internalised oppression survival strategies

Internalised oppression survival strategies can often include the following: appeasing, caretaking of dominant members, staying silent or attempting invisibility, withdrawal, and isolation from dominant group members, spacing out, disassociating, numbing, hyper-vigilant scanning, interpreting everything in the social environment as a threat.

Microaggressions, a term now well-known and used in popular culture, can be seen as an internalised dominance strategy, in that it describes the subtle ways dominant group members affirm negative stereotypes without meaning to cause offence (Pierce, 1974; Sue, 2010). I am aware that some people find the idea of microaggressions to be challenging. Microaggressions for me are a very good description of the many challenging statements that have been said to me over the years. I have listed two examples below, which I think are classic examples of microaggressions:

"You don't act like a normal black person."

This always leaves me to wonder what assumptions the person making the statement has about the way that black people act.

While I was part of a hosting team as a therapy manager of a therapy service for a clinical event/conference, I was asked by an eminent white psychoanalyst ...

"How long have you been working here as the cleaner?"

I reckon that their assumption was that a dark-skinned African woman could not be therapist, or manager of therapy service, and therefore concluded that I must be a cleaner.

When people make statements, like these, I can see that the intention generally may not be to offend or be disrespectful, and perhaps some of the comments are meant as compliments. However, generally, if I express feelings of upset, irritation, annoyance, or anger about these comments, I am often told that I am being hostile or oversensitive.

Racism and other oppressions are often seen as only impacting and affecting the group directly experiencing racism – members of BAME communities. But racism and other oppressions can also be seen as affecting those in positions of power and dominance. By being complicit in oppression within our positions of privilege we not only dehumanise those being oppressed but also dehumanise ourselves as perpetuators of oppression/intersectional violence. Diminishing our humanity has emotional, psychological, and spiritual consequences.

As mentioned previously the interconnected nature of oppression, discrimination and intersectional violence can result in most of us unconsciously or consciously moving in and out of re-enacting positions of internalised domination and oppression in dynamic and complex ways.

As supervisors being aware of internalised racism survival strategies and internalised dominance strategies provides an important lens for considering and analysing relationship dynamics within supervision and the therapeutic alliances formed between therapists and clients. A compassionate and non-judgemental awareness of these dynamics can enable us to provide emotionally safe spaces for therapists to think through and unpack client narratives. This may help to ensure that clients are more likely to bring more of themselves into the therapeutic space, rather than feeling the need to self-censor to avoid further social trauma from the supervisory or therapeutic relationship.

Supervision scenario – Robert, Darren, and TJ

Supervision: Robert (therapist) and Darren (supervisor) dialogue

Robert is a 40-year-old white British trainee therapist in the second year of his talking therapy placement and training, who had previously established a good working alliance with his white female supervisor. Darren has recently taken over as Robert's placement supervisor after the retirement of Roberts's previous supervisor. Robert has repeatedly asked Darren about his experience and qualifications as a supervisor and appeared irritated and non-communicative in supervision. In a supervision session together, Darren asked Robert about how he felt about having a new supervisor and more specifically Robert's feelings and thoughts about having a younger black male supervisor. Robert chooses not to verbally respond to Darren's query but shrugged his shoulders and seemed to shift uncomfortably in his seat. Darren consequently asked Robert to think about this and let him know about his reflections in the next supervision session.

In the next supervision session, Robert needs to present his new client allocation as part of the requirements of his course and placement. With visible reluctance, Robert outlines his first meeting with TJ. Robert starts by saying that he does not think that therapy is the appropriate treatment option for the client. Stating that he found the client to be aggressive, confrontational, and not psychologically minded. Darren encourages Robert to present TJ and to outline what happened in the first meeting.

Client: TJ

Thomas James, who likes to be called TJ, is a 35-year-old tall well-built, dark-skinned black British man of Caribbean descent. TJ cares for his older brother with Downs syndrome and his mother who has Parkinson's and type 1 diabetes. TJ has been the main carer for his mother and brother since the sudden death of his father from COVID-19 at the start of the pandemic, shortly after being admitted to the hospital. TJ is currently unemployed but aspires to be a professional photographer.

TJ has been referred to talking therapy for "anger management issues" because of a recent incident at the local GP practice, where TJ is alleged to have been verbally abusive to a GP receptionist. TJ however had been trying to access talking therapy for over a year, to come to terms with the death of his father and caring responsibilities and has regularly requested additional support to care for his mother and brother but has been unsuccessful. TJ has been offered a prescription for anti-depressants which he has declined, repeatedly requesting to be referred for talking therapy.

TJ is the youngest of three children. His father was a schoolteacher, and his mother a homemaker and tailor, who came to the United Kingdom in the late 1970s from Grenada. TJ's brother and sister were born in the Caribbean, and TJ was born in London. TJ has a close relationship with his mother and brother but often feels overwhelmed by his caring responsibilities and the lack of support from his sister. TJ has a strained relationship with his sister who works as an insurance broker in the city.

Robert admits that he arrived ten minutes late for his session with TJ, meeting TJ in the reception area by calling Thomas James, after reading TJ's name from a clipboard without making eye contact or talking, putting on a face mask and leading TJ to the therapy room without comment. Robert describes how he started the session by informing TJ that he would need to complete the registration and therapy outcome forms before the session could begin. Robert then continues telling Darren with an indignant attitude that TJ looked him directly in the eye and said:

"What's the matter with you people? You have no heart man."

Darren asks Robert what he thinks happened in the reception area at the start of the session and to reflect on why he thinks that talking therapy is not the right option for TJ.

A long silence ensues. Robert finally says:

"I messed up, didn't I?"

Darren nods his head and suggests that they explore together what could have been done differently and what might help to repair the therapeutic rupture with TJ.

Like many families and BAME families in particular, TJ's family have been dramatically impacted by COVID-19 and the traumatic death of TJ's father, early in the pandemic. Along with the necessity of TJ's mother to continually shelter at home due to her vulnerability to COVID from type 1 diabetes.

From an intersectional positioning, we could hypothesise that TJ's inability to access support services for his family or talking therapy for himself despite many requests, may be a result of institutional racism and the assumptions and stereotypes that white professionals hold about him. It is also possible that TJ's articulate assertion of his rights and the calling out of unprofessional behaviour are being seen as confrontational and aggressive due to white internalised dominance strategies.

We could also interpret Robert's inability to hear or understand TJ's situation and distress as a consequence of his social location as a white British man. A location probably mobilising a denial about black people's experiences of racism.

Looking at the dynamics between Robert and Darren, we could speculate that a significant factor in Robert's unease with Darren as a supervisor may be due to his discomfort around showing his emotional vulnerability to a black male supervisor because of his internal perceptions about masculinity and race.

We could also postulate that Darren's ability as a supervisor to observe names and hold a space for Robert to reflect on his unease in the supervisory relationship helped Robert to become more self-aware and take responsibility for his own lack of engagement with TJ. Opening the space for Robert to reflect more on his white identity and its potential impact on interpersonal relationships.

Cultural humility

Cultural humility or competence has been identified as a key issue in anti-racist and anti-oppressive practice and an essential skill when working cross-culturally, interculturally, or transculturally (Duran, 2021; Nichols, 1997).

The major areas of cultural humility are generally understood to be

- Self-awareness
- An understanding of other cultures
- A conceptualisation of identity formation under structural inequalities

Our values beliefs and identities as practitioners can have a significant impact on how we understand client narratives. An awareness of dominant Western cultural values within psychotherapy and wider society can be seen as essential to ensure that these values are not imposed on our clients without a conscious awareness, negotiation, or agreement with our clients. Otherwise, we will be in danger of practicing cultural imperialism, which has been referenced as a critical issue when working interculturally, cross-culturally, or transculturally.

The values of Western culture and science are often obscured by the myth that Western philosophy, culture, and science are described as being natural, value-free, objective, and without bias. With the unspoken and implicit assumption that other belief systems are deficient, an outlook is described by Sebene Selassie as epistemicide (2020).

To think about the issues that cultural differences raise and how these differences can be played out in supervisory and therapeutic relationships, I will draw on the pioneering work of Edwin Nichols in his Axiology Paradigm (see Figure 2.2) which highlights the importance of recognising the axiology or values of differing world views.

Edwin Nichols suggests that there are four main axiologies or world views, with each worldview seen as having a "cultural essence":

- European, Euro-American
- African Arab and Latinx
- Asian/Polynesian
- Native American/Indigenous

However, given the ideological influence of white supremacist stereotypes, I believe it is important to be mindful about not reinforcing negative stereotypes or making generalisation about whole communities.

Member (relating/relationships)

Nichols identifies that Western – European, Euro-American culture – relationships and relating have a focus on the object or the acquisition of the object. I would suggest this can be linked to the values and belief systems underlying capitalism and neoliberalism. People are seen as production units, where individualism, commodification, and materialism are actively valued and pursued. In comparison, in Asian cultures, the highest value in

EPIDEMOLOGY

	AXIOLOGY	Applied	Pedagogy	Methodology	LOGIC
European Euro American	Member-Object *The Highest Value Lies in the Object and Acquisition of Said Objects*	One Knows Through Counting & Measuring	Parts to Whole Atomistic – Inductive Thinking	Linear and Sequential *Step 1 Leads to Step 2 Leads Step 3, etc.*	Dichotomous *Either/Or and No In Between*
African African American Latino/a* Arab*	Member-Member *The Highest Value Lies in the Relationship Between Persons*	*One Knows Through Symbolic Imagery and Rhythm*	Whole Holistic – Deductive Thinking *The Big Picture*	Critical Path Analysis *Cut to the Chase*	Diunital *Union of Opposites*
Asian Asian American Polynesian*	Member-Group *The Highest Value Lies in the Cohesiveness of the Group*	One Knows Through Transcendental Striving	Whole and Parts are Seen Simultaneously	Cyclical and Repetitive	Nyaya The Objective World is Conceived Independent of Thought and Mind
Native American	Member-Great Spirit *The Highest Value Lies in Oneness with the Great Spirit*	One Knows Through Reception and Spiritual Receptivity	Whole is Seen in Cyclic Movement Seasons Medicine Wheel	Environmentally Experiential Reflection *Rite of Passage*	Great Mysteries Disrasismo – Union of Opposites *A Set of 4 and a Set of 3 Form the Whole*

Nichols, 2008

Figure 2.2 Cultural competency paradigm – the philosophical aspects of cultural difference developed by Nichols PH. D, 1974, 1987, 2004 Nichols and associates.

relationships and relating is seen as being in the cohesion of the group. In African cultures, the highest value in relationships and relating is recognised in the relationship between people. In Indigenous cultures, the highest value is seen as being in the relationship with a great spirit and togetherness with the great spirit.

Epistemology – applied (knowing)

In terms of understanding the world, Nichols suggests that Indigenous peoples/Native Americans know through reflection and spiritual receptivity, for example, purification rites. African cultures know through symbolic imagery, rhythm, and intuition, or the ability to understand something immediately without the need for conscious reasoning, whereas in European/Euro-American culture, knowing is achieved through counting and measuring with a focus on cognition. In certain Asian cultures (Chinese), knowing is seen as emerging from transcendental striving – conation.

Epistemology – pedagogy (knowledge)

Knowledge systems in Asian cultural beliefs are characterised by the whole and parts being seen simultaneously. I feel this is expressed in Daoist knowledge systems and the idea of yin and yang and the emphasis on balance between the two. In comparison, in Indigenous knowledge systems, the whole is seen in cyclic movement and seasons – the Medicine Wheel. African knowledge systems are viewed as having more holistic knowledge systems, with a focus on the whole big picture. Whereas European/Euro-American knowledge systems go from parts to the whole, taking an atomistic view. In Western medicine, psychiatry, and talking therapies, this can be seen in the focus on symptoms to make a diagnosis.

Epistemology – methodology (thinking process)

In Indigenous/Native American culture, the methodology or thinking process is seen as environmentally experiential reflection, for example, rites of passage. In European/Euro-American culture, the thinking process is linear and sequential, perhaps best illustrated by the assembly line. In Asian cultures, the methodology can be seen as cyclical and repetitive, whereas in African, Latinx, and Arab cultures Nichols describes the thinking process as critical path analysis – cutting to the chase.

Logic

In African, Latinx, and Arab cultures logic can be seen as Diunital, a unison of opposites, a kind of duality which Nichols compares to Quantum theory.

On the other hand, in Asian cultures, the objective world is independent of mind and thought – Nyaya – comparable to Chaos Theory. Within Native American cultures, Nichols describes logic as being the Great Mystery, with a set of four and a set of three forming the whole – like Super String Theory. Lastly, western European Euro/American logic is characterised as being dicrotous or binary – comparable to Newtonian Theory.

In thinking about these essences within cultures, it becomes easier to identify the Western values that are present in Western therapy practice:

- Emphasis on the mind and cognition of the individual.
- Importance of counting and measuring, which can be seen in the importance placed on randomised trials to identify the effectiveness of therapies/ interventions.
- Seeing individuals as separate units – rather than the individual being seen as primarily, part of a wider community.
- Emphasis on time and deadlines. Nichols, in his works, outlines how the focus and preoccupation with time and deadlines in the Global North is related to historical geographical conditions and the importance of growing seasons in the northern hemisphere.
- Importance being placed on doing and action orientation, with a tendency to pathologise being.
- A progress and future orientation, which can negate the value of being in the moment.

White cultural values

Having a conscious awareness of dominant white, cultural values as supervisors can help us to ensure these values are not automatically being transmitted in our supervision practices or through the therapeutic practices of therapists. White Western culture has been identified by Katz (1985) as having the following markers:

- Rugged individualism – independence and autonomy are seen as desirable states and the individual is seen as being in control of their own lives and environment.
- Competition – winning is everything: a win/loose dichotomy.
- Action orientation – emphasis on the being master and in control of nature, and the expectation that something can always be done in a situation.
- Communication – standard English, the importance of the written word, direct eye contact, limited physical contact and control of emotions.
- Time – adherence to rigid time; time being viewed as a commodity.
- Holidays – based on Christian religion, white history, and male leaders.
- Protestant work ethic – working hard to bring success.

- Progress and future orientation – planning for the future and delayed gratification. Value placed on continual improvement and progress.
- Emphasis on the scientific method – objective rational linear thinking, cause and effect relationships, quantitative emphasis.
- Status and power – measured by economic possessions, credentials, titles, and positions. The importance of owning goods, space, and property.
- Family structure – the nuclear family is seen as the ideal unit. The male is the breadwinner and head of the household. The female is the homemaker and subordinate to the husband – a patriarchal structure.
- Aesthetics – music and arts based on European cultures. Women's beauty is based on the blonde, blue-eyed, thin, and young archetype. Men's attractiveness is based on athletic ability, power, and economic status.
- Religion – belief in Christianity, no tolerance for deviation from a single God.

Deconstructing cultural imperialism

From a decolonisation and intersectional framework having clarity about one's own social location in terms of culture, class, gender, sexuality, and race is critical to think about the shared world views that we might have with clients and the world views that we might not share. Cultural differences can have ramifications for how power dynamics connected to positions of social privilege and dominance can be played out in supervisory and therapist–client relationships. Fakhry Davids, in his book *Internal Racism: A Psychoanalytic Approach to Race and Difference* (2011), describes the type of dynamic that can occur as a brown-skinned male therapist working with a white male client in his clinical study of a racist attack that occurred in the therapeutic space.

Identity models

Another important consideration in anti-racist supervision and therapy is an understanding of identity formation under white supremacy.

The racial identity models developed in America (Adler, 1986; Atkinson and Thompson, 1993; Bennett, 1986; Cross, 1991; Helms, 1995; Rowe et al., 1994; Sue, 2003) provide a useful tool for thinking about racial identity in the United Kingdom and understanding the complex and multifaceted nature of identity within an anti-oppressive intersectional framework.

Sue et al. (2002) have developed a five-stage white identity model influenced by the work of Hardiman (1982), Helms (1995), and Carter (1998), which outlines a model for white identity formation under white supremacy. I use the model as a therapeutic aid to develop awareness and self-reflective capabilities around identity and values. The model can also be used as a matrix or entrance into understanding and thinking about identity issues in supervisory relationships and for collaboratively reflecting on and exploring the therapeutic work that therapists are undertaking with clients.

White identity model

Sue and Sue have written extensively on this. I have adapted Sue and Sue's model to ensure greater relevance to the United Kingdom. The white identity model has various phases which are dynamic and not always linear, as we can go in and out of identity phases in fluid ways depending on what's happening in our lives externally and internally.

Conformity phase

This phase is characterised as colour blindness. At this phase supervisors, counsellors, and clients are unlikely to see themselves in a racial or cultural way but hold a belief that white British culture is superior and that other cultures are inferior. Typically, there is little awareness of their own beliefs and an assumption that their values are normal and universal. A common philosophy is that people are people, and that difference is not important – "colour blindness." Supervisors and therapists generally deny BAME clients' experiences of racism, and consciously or unconsciously act out racial dynamics based on white supremacy. Clients are likely to hold a preference for white counsellors. Therapists are likely to prefer working with white supervisors and supervisors are likely to feel more comfortable supervising white therapists.

Dissonance – conflict phase

In this phase, there is an increasing realisation of one's own cultural biases and recognition that white cultural values play an important part in oppressing minorities. Rationalisation is often used to exonerate personal inactivity in combating racism and discrimination. Supervisors, therapists and clients are likely to experience conflict between appreciation for white British culture, and awareness of discrimination. White supervisors and counsellors may have difficulty in responding consistently to BAME therapists' and clients' experiences of discrimination and may be vulnerable to using the supervisory and therapeutic process with therapists and clients to work through feelings about their own white identity.

Reflecting on the dynamics between Robert, TJ, and Darren in the earlier supervision scenario. We could hypothesise that Robert may have been at a place of conformity in his identity initially. Which we can see moving to a more conflicted white identity phase, because of a combination of Darren naming the racial difference in the supervisory relationship, Robert's encounter with TJ, and the indication of some cultural and racial awareness emerging.

This phase is identifiable by a questioning of one's own racism and an increasing awareness of how racism operates and its pervasiveness in white British culture, along with a growing socio-political consciousness, and acknowledgement of past personal collusion with racism. There is likely to be a tendency towards racial and cultural self-hatred and feeling ashamed of whiteness. Supervisors and therapists at this phase are prone to over identifying with BAME therapists and clients and be preoccupied with issues relating to race and culture at the expense of everything else. The counselling relationship is likely to be paternalistic; supervisors and therapists may experience difficulties in setting appropriate boundaries because of anxieties about their own identity.

Introspection phase

There is a rethinking of what it means to be white and an acknowledgement of past participation in racism and the benefits gained from white privilege. Supervisors and therapists will have an awareness that racism is an integral part of British society, along with an acceptance of whiteness and a desire to combat oppression. Supervisors and therapists at this phase, can create a supervisory and therapeutic environment where BAME therapists' and clients' experiences of racism are heard and acknowledged. They are also likely to have a high level of self-awareness about their own cultural identity but experience a high level of anxiety and loss: "existential anxiety."

Integrative awareness "freedom"

Supervisors, therapists, and clients understand the "self" as a cultural and racial being, along with an awareness of the political and social nature of racism. Supervisors and therapists at this phase are likely to have an appreciation of racial and cultural diversity and commitment to the eradication of racism within therapy and wider society. During this stage, a non-racist, white, British identity, and an ease around members of different groups, emerges.

I have learned – through my lived experiences of being a client, practicing as a therapist and receiving supervision, and through my own practice as a supervisor – that those white supervisors and therapists who are at a place of introspection or integrative awareness are more able to have the capacity to listen to BAME clients' and therapists' experiences of racism and to work with cultural competence.

BAME identity model

I have adapted the Minority Identity Model described by Adler (1986), Cross et al. (1991), and Atkinson et al. (1993) to outline a model of BAME identity formation in Britain.

Conformity phase

Supervisors, therapists, and clients are unlikely to see themselves in a cultural or racial way but are likely to prefer white British values. This phase is characterised by down-playing one's own cultural and racial heritage, combined with a strong desire to emulate and assimilate white British culture and institutions, along with depreciation of self and others in the same cultural and racial group. Supervisors and therapists may prefer to work with white therapists and clients and can be punitive to BAME therapists and clients. Clients at this phase are likely to hold a preference to work with white therapists.

Dissonance – conflict phase

During this phase, there is increasing acknowledgement of one's own racial and cultural ancestry and an awakening of socio-political consciousness. There is a questioning of previous white identifications and the beginnings of viewing one's own cultural racial group positively. BAME supervisors, therapists, and clients may experience conflict between appreciation for their own cultural and racial heritage and a desire to conform to white norms. Supervisors and therapists may be vulnerable to using the supervisory and therapeutic process with therapists and clients in a voyeuristic way, to explore and work through their own feelings about cultural and racial identity.

Realisation and immersion phase

There is a complete surrender to the values of one's own cultural and racial group and a rejection of all values from the dominant group. Supervisors, therapists, and clients are likely to have negative attitudes towards white culture and be inclined to romanticise their own cultural group. Typically, there may be a discomfort with cultural and racial differences and a difficulty in seeing or understanding other oppressions. At this phase, shadism may be expressed consciously by a preference or attraction to dark skin tones. BAME supervisors and therapists may have trouble in forming therapeutic alliances with white therapists and clients. Clients are likely to prefer to see a BAME therapist.

Introjection phase

During this phase, there is comfort and security in one's own cultural and racial identity and the emergence of an assured BAME identity. There is a questioning of previous hostility to white culture, white British culture being increasingly understood within the context of a historical past and present. There is likely to be an appreciation and acceptance of some aspects of white culture. Supervisors, therapists, and clients are likely to use their anger about racial and cultural discrimination positively within their own social group.

Synergetic articulation and awareness – "freedom" phase

Supervisors, therapists, and clients have a sense of fulfilment with their own cultural and racial identity and have a positive regard towards themselves and their own cultural and racial group. Cultural and racial identity are likely to be just one of many important aspects of one's life. There is likely to be a high level of personal autonomy, along with an appreciation and respect for other cultural/racial groups. Characteristically, supervisors, counsellors, and clients will have a desire to eliminate all forms of oppression and be inclined to make alliances with members of dominant cultures who are committed to ending oppression.

White and BAME identity models can be useful in providing a starting place to facilitate an understanding of identity and thinking about the varied and complex dynamics related to race/culture that may occur between practitioners and clients. These models can also be adapted to think about differences around ages sets, classes, differing abilities, genders, sexualities.

Supervising BAME therapists

During my career, I have worked as a therapist, supervisor, and manager of several therapy and mental health services. I have felt privileged to have the opportunity to hold these positions – accompanying, witnessing, and supporting BAME and white clients in their healing journeys. Along with seeing BAME and white therapists develop their therapeutic skills and establish their careers. My lived experience has shown me that the emotional, psychological, physical, and spiritual challenges that BAME therapists, supervisors, and managers encounter are significant, especially when working in predominantly white environments, given the endemic nature of white supremacy, racism, and other forms of oppression and intersectional violence.

Many BAME therapists find themselves experiencing oppression and intersectional violence in the workplace whilst working with clients who are having similar life experiences. This situation frequently occurs within a context of supervisors, senior management teams, and organisations not having a historical analysis of racism and its legacy or an understating of the social trauma and the complex trauma caused by intersectional violence. This can leave BAME therapists vulnerable to experiencing vicarious trauma: indirect trauma caused by exposure to trauma stories. In some cases, this may trigger a therapist's memories of oppression and interactional violence. These multiple social trauma narratives can create a perfect storm. I have seen many BAME therapists manage these cyclonic conditions with amazing resilience and creativity, despite few resources and often in extreme isolation in their work setting

As supervisors, we are in a unique position to create safe spaces for BAME therapists, where these cyclonic conditions can be unpacked, allowing therapists to identify the resources they need to navigate these extreme conditions. The provision of appropriate emotional and psychological support for BAME therapists who are experiencing these conditions is critical to support their capacity to hold, attend to and respond compassionately to client trauma narratives. In doing so, helping to minimise the potential risks of therapists being overwhelmed by multiple layers of intersectional violence and trauma. As supervisors, we are situated in a unique place to be able to support therapists to navigate these stormy waters.

To conclude, when providing supervision within a context of decolonisation and intersectionality, I have outlined how this positioning is multifaceted and complex. I believe that the following are important elements that need to be incorporated into the supervision frame:

- An understanding of intersectionality and the violence of intersecting oppressions.
- A historical analysis of racism and awareness of the racialisation of capitalism and neo-liberalism.
- A high level of self-awareness and ability to understand our own social location, and the social locations of therapists/clients. Along with an awareness of how these social locations may impact the supervisory relationships and therapeutic alliances.
- An understanding of social trauma and oppression trauma legacies, for clients within a context of communities and intergeneration trauma.
- A critical awareness of Western cultural values and the fact they are not universal, and a sensitivity to not promoting epistemicide.
- Cultural humility and an ability to think about interventions that take into consideration a client's beliefs and value systems.
- An understanding of white and BAME identity formation within dominant white cultures.
- Externalisation of social inequalities – mindfully and proactively moving away from supervisory and therapeutic interventions that blame clients for their experiences of racism and other oppressions and intersectional violence.
- Respect for and awareness of, cultural diversity, a personal commitment to move towards synergetic articulation and awareness – emotional and psychological liberation.

It could be said that much of Yoruba philosophy and cultural values are held within the meaning of proverbs which are passed from generation to generation. As a cis woman of the Yoruba diaspora, the following proverb aptly reflects my challenges around attempting to offer supervision and therapy within the context of decolonisation and intersectionality:

Yoruba proverb:

When a king's palace burns down, the rebuilt palace is more beautiful (Owomoyela, 2005).
Meaning: necessity is the mother of invention; creativity is often achieved after overcoming many difficulties.

References

Adler, N. J. (1986). Cultural synergy: Managing the impact of cultural diversity. *The 1986 Annual: Developing Human Resources*. San Diego, CA: University Associates.

Ajamu, A., Parkham, T. A., White. J. L. (2010). *The Psychology of Blacks: Centering Our Perspectives in the African Consciousness*. Hove, East Sussex: Psychology Press.

Atkinson, D. R., Thompson, C. E., Grant, S. K. (1993). A three-dimensional model for counselling racial/ethnic minorities. *The Counselling Psychologist, 21*, 257–277.

BACP. (2018). Ethical Framework for the counselling Professions; Respect 22,a,b. Available at: https://www.bacp.co.uk/events-and-resources/ethics-and-standards (Accessed:13th March 2023).

Bennett, M. J. (1986). A development approach to training for intercultural sensitivity. *International Journal of Intercultural Relations, 10*, 179–196.

Carter, R. T. (1998). *The Influence of Race and Racial Identity in Psychotherapy : Toward a Racially Inclusive Model*. New York' Chichester: Wiley.

Collins, P. H. (2000). *Black Feminist Thought: Knowledge, Consciousness, and the Politics of Empowerment*. 2nd ed. New York: Routledge.

Cross, W. E. (1991). *Shades of Black; Diversity in African American Identity*. Philadelphia: Temple University Press.

David, E. (2013). *Internalized Oppression: The Psychology of Marginalized Groups*. United States: Springer Publishing.

Davids, F. (2011). *Internal Racism: A psychoanalytic Approach to Race and Difference*. London: Palgrave.

Duran, E. (2021). Decolonizing therapy and healing the soul wound [video]. Available at: https://www.compassionintherapy.com/stream/eduardo-duran/

Fanon, F. (1967). *Black Skin, White Masks*. New York: Grove Press.

Gilmore, R. W. (2020). A moment of true decolonization #31 [podcast]. The Funambulist Podcast. Available at: https://thefunambulist.net/podcast/daily-podcast-31-ruth-wilson-gilmore-the-beginning-of-a-perfect-decolonial-moment

Gramsci, A. (1999). *Prison Notebooks*Edited and translated by Quentin Hoare and Geoffrey Nowell Smith. London: Elecbook.

Hardiman, R. (1982). White identity development: A process orientated model for describing the racial consciousness of White Americans. Dissertation Abstracts International, 43 104A Models. In: Ponterotto, J. G., Casas, J. M., Suzuki, L. A., Alexander, C. M. (eds).

Helms, J. E. (1995). An update of Helms's White and people of colour racial identity models. In: Ponterotto, J. G., Casas, J. M., Suzuki, L. A., Alexander, C. M. (eds) *Handbook of Multicultural Counselling.* (pp. 181–191). Thousand Oaks, CA: SAGE Publications.

Hill Collins, P. (2000). *Black Feminist Thought: Knowledge, Consciousness, and the Politics of Empowerment.* New York: Taylor & Francis.

hooks, b. (1996). *Killing Rage: Ending Racism.* United Kingdom: Penguin.

Ira, P. (2020) Why we need to stop the "Strong Black Woman" trope, it is not a compliment. Available at: https://medium.com/equality-includes-you/why-we-need-to-stop-the-strong-black-woman-trope-it-is-not-a-compliment-c0b57a052c05

Karlsen, S. & Nazroo, J. Y. (2007). Better Health Briefing 3 - Ethnic– ethnic inequalities in health: the impact of racism. [online] Race Equality Foundation. Available at: http://raceequalityfoundation.org.uk/wp-content/uploads/2018/03/health-brief3.pdf

Katz, J. (1985). The socio-political nature of counselling. *Counselling Psychologist, 13,* 615–624.

Lorde, A. (2017). *Your Silence Will Not Protect You.* United Kingdom: Silver Press.

Lorde, P. A. (1984). *Sister Outsider: Essays and Speeches.* United Kingdom: Crossing Press.

McKenzie, K. (2003). Racism and health: Antiracism is an important health issue. *BMJ (Clinical research ed.), 326*(7380), 65–66. 10.1136/bmj.326.7380.65

McKenzie-Mavinga, I. (2009). *Black Issues in the Therapeutic Process.* Basingstoke England: Palgrave Macmillan.

Menakem, R. (2017). *My Grandmother's Hands: Racialized Trauma and the Pathway to Mending Our Hearts and Bodies.* Las Vegas: Central Recovery Press.

Mercury Project. (2010). *Factsheet: Mercury in Skin Lightening Cosmetics.* Montpelier, VT: Author. Available at: http://mercurypolicy.org/wp.content/uploads/2010/06skincreamfactsheet_may31_final.pdf

Nichols, E. (1997). The philosophical aspects of cultural difference [video]. Available at: https://www.youtube.com/watch?v=n1L86lAaFng

Nobles, W. (2006). *Seeking the Sakhu: Foundation Writings for an African Psychology.* US: Third World Press.

Owomoyela, O. (2005). *Yoruba Proverbs.* United States: University of Nebraska Press.

Pierce, C. (1974). Psychiatric problems of the black minority.*American Handbook of Psychiatry, 2,* 5–36. Available at: https://www.freepsychotherapybooks.org/download/psychiatric-problems-of-the-black-minority/?v=5991 [Accessed 14AD]

Rogers, C. (1974). Carl Rogers counsels an individual on anger [video]. Available at: https://youtu.be/uRCD3anKsa0

Rowe, W., Bennett, S., Atkinson, D. R. (1994). White racial identity models: Critique and alternative proposal. *The Counselling Psychologist, 22,* 120–146.

Selassie, S. (2020). *You Belong a Call for Connection.* New York: HarperOne.

Sue, D., Sue, D. W. (2013). *Counseling the Culturally Diverse.* United Kingdom: Wiley.

Sue, D. W. (2010). *Microaggression in Everyday Life. Race, Gender and Sexual Orientation.* Hoboken, N.J.: John Wiley & Sons.

Tarakali, V. (2011). Exploring the places where body & spirit, healing & social justice intersect. Vanissar Tarakali Blog June 2010.

Wallace, M. (1979). *Black Macho and the Myth of Superwomen*. New York: Dial.

Watermeyer, B., Görgens, T. (2014). Disability and internalized oppression. In: David, E. J. R. (ed.) *Internalized Oppression: The Psychology of Marginalized Groups* (pp. 253–280). New York: Springer Publishing Company.

Woods-Giscombe, C. L., Allen, A. M., Black, A. R., Steed, T. C., Li, Y., Lackey, C. (2019). The Giscombe Superwoman Schema Questionnaire: Psychometric properties and associations with mental health and health behaviours in African American Women,. *Issues in Mental Health Nursing, 40*(8), 672–681. 10.1080/01612840. 2019.1584654

Drawing Attention to What Is and Isn't Said, Seen, Heard, Felt, and Communicated in the Intercultural Supervisory Space

Angie Knorpel and Peter Cockersell

Introduction

Counselling and therapy can be thought about as a formal process of helping people individually or collectively to make sense of what they are experiencing and how and why they experience it that way, through a psychodynamic and somatopsychic process involving at least two minds in at least two bodies, the client's and the therapist's. Therapy works, and therapists practise, at many levels and it is used for different purposes including self-exploration, relieving distress, working through and coping with a wide variety of mental, emotional, and physical health problems, loss, trauma, crises, transitions, and other difficult times in life. It can be life-changing and life-saving.

Clinical supervision can be thought about as a formal process of helping therapist/s[1] make sense of the stories they are told and of what they experience in their therapeutic work, and how they respond to and work with it and their clients, also through a dynamic process involving two or more minds and bodies, the supervisor's and the supervisee's or supervision groups. The role of supervision is to support the therapist/s in containing and working through their clients' presentations and to help keep the clients safe.

Both therapy and supervision involve the meeting and interaction between two or more minds. "Mind" is "the totality of conscious and unconscious activities in an emergent, self-organising process of the extended nervous system and its relationships that collectively deliver the regulatory function" (Siegel, 2015). The regulatory function is intersubjective: "... infants, from the beginning, are social beings who constantly seek other persons in order to engage in reciprocal imitation and mutual emotional regulation ..." (Ammaniti and Gallese, 2014). Intersubjectivity is the natural process by which we regulate each other and ourselves, and through which relationships – and ultimately social structures, and then cultures – are created and maintained. Intersubjectivity and interpersonal regulation happen between people and in groups.

DOI: 10.4324/9781003380214-5

Therapy and supervision are both intersubjective processes and our infantile selves are *re*-present-*ed* in our work, at the core of the self we bring to it, which hopefully we regulate and keep from engaging too actively in the process. We learn to regulate ourselves as therapists and as supervisors through our training and hopefully our own therapy, and through our upbringing and life experience, all of which involve acculturation. Throughout our upbringing, we are fed the perspectives of our primary carers, parents and families, their beliefs, religions, politics, and their experiences of life, and those of the people around us – neighbours, schools, social groups of all sorts, and their cultures – much of which we internalise, mostly unconsciously. Our own individual life experience adds more to our acculturation: experiences of inclusion or exclusion, of privilege or disadvantage, of being welcome/d or unwelcome, rejection, acceptance, belonging, racism, or "othering."[2] Our professional trainings as therapist add another layer of acculturation, of exposure to particular ways of thinking and of working – for example, concepts of the mind and body and what mental health, well-being or mental distress actually mean and how they function. So, the "mind" we bring to therapy, and then to supervision, is not only, as Siegel says, "the totality of conscious and unconscious activities in an emergent, self-organising process of the extended nervous system and its relationships" but also an *acculturated* set of self-organising conscious and unconscious activities or dynamic processes: and it is with this acculturated mind that in supervision, in intersubjective interaction with the acculturated mind/s of our supervisors and supervisee/s, we attempt to find meaning and understanding in and through the therapeutic process together.

> It is critical to recognise that what we deem to be appropriate or inappropriate is culturally conditioned and constructed. Working competently in supervision with difference and diversity therefore means routinely deconstructing in the counselling relationship, in supervision, in the work setting, and in society at large, how we as social beings continually participate in the construction of meaning. This automatically leads us to an examination of political ideologies ... historically cemented and institutionally ingrained '-isms' of all kinds, and the systematic, purposive or inadvertent oppression, suppression, marginalisation and exclusion of people on grounds of politicised differences. (Rapp, 2001, pp. 149–150)

In short, whether supervisor or supervisee, we bring our total acculturated self consciously or unconsciously to the process of supervision which itself takes place within an acculturated setting. Indeed, having supervision at all is a process of culture: it's normal in psychology, psychotherapy, and counselling and quite common in other therapeutic settings. Additionally, each setting will have its own culture whether in private practice, third sector, the National Health Service (NHS), or other public health settings, and each clinic, service, sector, or modality, will also project elements of its culture into the supervisory process.

Most of the "difficulties" or "problems" that therapists bring to supervision, or supervisors bring to supervision of supervision, are presented as difficulties or problems in understanding the minds of client/s and/or the interpersonal or intrapersonal dynamics in the therapeutic dyad or group, and sometimes of the organisation. However, we suggest that many of these difficulties or problems are actually difficulties of understanding between cultures: cultures of race, class, skin colour, origin, language, location, education, mental and/or physical health and ill-health, ability and/or disability, gender, sexual orientation, religion, etc. Issues of culture, therefore, need considering not only in counselling/therapy and therapeutic work (Ababio and Littlewood, 2019; Kareem and Littlewood, 1992) but also in their supervision and in supervision of supervision (Fong, 1994; Tummala-Narra, 2004).

Consequentially, in order to be effective, a supervisor must be thoughtful of and sensitive to the importance of cultural, intercultural, and intracultural influences, values, norms, and differences. It is – or should be – the supervisor's responsibility to ensure they are attended to and because they are crucial it should not be left to supervisees to raise it. As Fong says,

> A consistent theme in the literature is the critical role of the supervisor: in promoting cultural awareness; in identifying cultural influences on client behaviour, on counsellor-client interactions, and on the supervisory relationship; and in providing culture-sensitive support and challenge to the supervisee. (Fong, 1994)

The supervisor and supervisee or supervision group bring their own intercultural and intracultural dimensions to the supervisory process and by raising the subject of culture it becomes open for discussion, analysis, reflection, and insight. There is therefore inherent value and meaning in examining both the intercultural/intracultural matrix of supervisor–therapist–client dyad/triad/group and the intercultural and intracultural experiences of the client/s in the supervisory process.

We both came to be supervisors unintentionally, because of work roles that required us to take clinical responsibility. Now, over many years in which we have each established a secure professional base, we work to continuously develop and maintain the kind of intercultural supervisory space we wish to practice in. However, to keep our practice up to date and fit for purpose – a safe, open, and welcoming space for our supervisees to bring their authentic selves and their work with their clients – requires a certain amount of house-keeping: clearing out of accumulated, redundant, and outmoded concepts and ideas and updating and upgrading of those that stand the test of time. Cultures change over time and generations and, as well as maintaining core concepts and values, it is essential to keep open to current cultural shifts and norms from and through our supervisees and their work with their clients, and ours and our supervisors, as well as through continuous professional development, study, and training. Culture is not static, and, as do the cultural and social worlds from which we and our supervisees and their clients come, it also evolves within psychotherapeutic traditions, counselling, therapy, and related organisations.

> Another critical dimension of the multicultural supervisory relationship is the management of power. The supervisor is viewed as having expertise and has the responsibility of evaluating the supervisee, both contributing to an unavoidable power differential in the relationship. In situations of a minority supervisee and a white supervisor or a white supervisee and a minority supervisor, both participants may attribute power to majority group membership. This additional perceived power differential and past experiences with power abuses by whites may make trust formation difficult and result in cautious, guarded communication. This, in turn, may result in the opposite of the personal self-disclosure and openness to feedback required in supervision. (Fong, 1994, p. 4)

Supervisors have in most cases been in the profession longer than their supervisees, and as we become more established – and almost inevitably more part of the *establishment* of the particular psychotherapeutic territory we reside in – there is an inevitable increase in the position/s of power and privilege, actual and/or perceived, that we occupy. This is certainly often seen to be so from the vantage points of supervisees and especially supervisees in training. This, we have found in ourselves and experienced in others, is all too easy to forget – and equally vital not to – if we are to be able to be, and carry on being, good-enough supervisors. It is important that we strive to retain the position described by Watkins and Hook as "culturally humble":

> … cultural humility can be considered to be both intrapersonal and interpersonal in nature. Intrapersonally, cultural humility involves a willingness and openness to reflect on one's own self as an embedded cultural being, being aware of personal limitations in understanding the cultural other and guarding against forming culturally unfounded, automatic assumptions; interpersonally, cultural humility involves being open to hearing and striving to understand aspects of the other's cultural background and identity. (Watkins and Hook, 2016, p. 490)

We believe that it is essential to work interculturally to enable the creation of a mutually constructed and co-inhabited, safe-enough space in supervision, as in therapy, with a sense of shared ownership, in which issues of power and privilege, and their historic preconception/s and current dynamic/s, can be explored and made sense of. This includes the cultural differences between and among the supervisor and supervisee(s) and between the supervisees and their clients, and *all* cultural differences and assumptions need to be open to question and exploration, as well as those of the setting itself; whether supervision is private or based in a training institution, or the NHS, or a private or public organisation, each will have their own cultural heritage, traditions, strengths, and flaws.

Something about us

We are both supervisors and of course supervisees, with experience/s in supervision, of being supervised and of supervising, through and in multiple trainings, roles, and positions in the NHS, training, and third sector organisations. We are both white-skinned and apparently mono-cultural: English is our first language, and at this stage in our work and lives we are well on our way to appearing to be senior residents of middle-class England.

However, we originate from quite different cultural backgrounds: one of us comes from generations of British families and grew up in middle-class suburban London; the other comes from second- and third-generation immigrants (who moved from affluence to poverty on one side and poverty to affluence on the other), and a childhood on the welfare state in a small country town. One of us was born in the United Kingdom, the other in Southeast Asia. We each had very disrupted educations for different reasons and one of us left school at 13 and had no further academic education; the other left school at 15 but eventually went on to university and several degrees. We have both had varied life experiences and been shaped, formed and re-formed by our experiences, including significant trauma and loss. Both of us have spent time in and worked in various residential institutions, including children's homes, therapeutic communities, psychiatric institutions, and prisons. Each of us has lived and worked in other countries on other continents in other languages as well as in Europe. We have both done many professional trainings, though different ones. Looking at us now you wouldn't know and probably wouldn't guess much, if any, of that.

This point is pertinent in itself: as supervisees, we do not usually know much about our supervisors beyond what we see and hear, and (probably) something about their professional qualifications and status, and (perhaps) also position and experience – plus, of course, what we think, sense, feel, and project – much of which will be generated by initial external information and perception as well as our own internalised transferences. As supervisors too, we generally do not know very much about our supervisees' and their personal lives and circumstances, cultural histories, and lived experience – though more so as training supervisors – or how it interacts with that of their clients. However, what we do come to know of their clients will be drawn and coloured, tinted and/or tainted, through the lenses of the therapist's own perspectives of the world or part(s) of it they inhabit. The same is usually true within the therapist–client dyad, with the client not knowing much about the therapist other than the information they get from the referral source or in their professional blurb and from any personal–professional disclosures such as in initial contact/s, session/s, etc., but conscious or unconscious assumptions will be made in seeing a "professional" in whatever the setting and likely carried through into the therapy. The same applies to supervision. Unless cultural differences and congruences are specifically mentioned or deliberately raised – and explored – they are likely to remain clouded and obscured by assumptions, prejudices, and ignorance. We do not know unless we explore people's cultures how diverse, or convergent, they may be: assumptions could perhaps be said to be the antithesis of intercultural working (Cockersell, 2019).

Thinking we know and being afraid of not knowing, or being seen to not know, are perhaps among the most insidious polarisations that impact the supervisor role. We have to be comfortable about not knowing (Green, 1973; Petrucelli, 2018) and at the same time able to hold in mind what we do know. This "not knowing" is a crucial part of supervision – as it is of counselling and therapy – allowing us access to our supervisees' and their clients' ideas, impressions, fantasies, feelings, and transferences. It perhaps becomes harder as we get older and more experienced, in part because we do indeed know more and also because there is often a pressure from, and temptation to succumb to, being cast in the role of "expert" by our supervisees, our organisations, and us ourselves, as we all struggle with the insecurity and fear of not knowing and getting it wrong. This is perhaps increasingly so in the current ever more politically correct and divided culture/s we inhabit, with prescribed ways of practising, manualised therapies, and the institutional fantasy of psychotherapy being about "treatments" that "work" rather than individuals who work through difficult life situations in treatment. We are both unwilling occupants of this world whilst also not wanting to lose the privileges it affords us.

Keeping our minds open, being curious, able to say when we do not understand; to ask, "what does this mean?" – and not to feel we must, should, or ought to have the answers whilst also being able to imagine and consider many possible ones – is essential to the art and craft of culturally sensitive supervision. As Watkins and Hook (2016) put it: "A culturally responsive, culturally humble psychoanalytic supervision recognizes and privileges the cultural in the patient, the supervisee, and supervisor and strives to understand how culture impacts the treatment and supervision experience" (p. 494).

Examples from supervision

There is perhaps a tendency to think of intercultural perspectives on pre-senting issues in supervision when there are evident differences such as skin colour and/or ethnicity, or religion, or country or language of origin, between supervisee/therapist and client and/or between supervisor and supervisee. Less often thought of as benefitting from intercultural approaches are sex, gender identity, and/or sexuality differences, or differences in geographical regions (e.g., north–south, etc.), or socio-economic positions (e.g., class background).

We think it is an abdication of, or gap in, our supervisory responsibility and functionality if we are not aware of or do not consider the cultural picture and intercultural perspective/s within which the therapeutic en-deavour is framed and we will give an example where institutional culture is an intercultural issue needing attention in supervision, as well as the cultural differences/similarities of the therapeutic dyad and supervision group, and cite some examples of institutional cultures on intercultural work in general. We will look more closely at some examples where supervisor and supervisee have different ethnicities and where the client and supervisor seem to have the same cultural background, and others where the client is evidently culturally different from their therapist (our supervisee/s) in which supervisor and su-pervisee/s seem to have the same cultural background and the supervision group appears mono-cultural.

Whether there is really such a thing as a mono-cultural supervision group – or even dyad or triad – is perhaps questionable; "… in fact every working alliance is multi-cultural. What is noticed and worked with is the degree of supervisor, counsellor, and client similarity or dissimilarity in terms of race, ethnicity, sexual orientation, gender and cultural back-ground" (Igwe, 2003, p. 215).

However, there are many groups that are more culturally uniform rather than more culturally diverse and it is really important that this is recognised, acknowledged, understood, and worked with, so that parallel processes in the therapy, counselling, and therapeutic work, and crucial intercultural issues and experiences, and notably the impacts of racism, can be identified and attended to.

How often do we assume that we are alike because we come from the same place, speak or use the same language, have the same/similar skin colour, live in the same or similar locations, work in the same or similar environments, look alike, dress alike, sound alike, behave alike? Identify with each other? Have shared or similar histories? How often do we presume that (because) we come from and/or inhabit the same culture, we share attitudes to, perceptions and understandings of our similarities and our differences?

We propose that shining light on the cultural differences and assumptions in a therapeutic dyad/triad or group may throw into relief otherwise unseen –

but nonetheless felt – facets of clients' experience and bring hidden or buried details of their/her/his stories into view; "... the integration of racial and cultural diversity related issues in clinical supervision ... has important implications for the provision of services to ethnic minorities and, more broadly, to better addressing the full realms of clients' intrapsychic and interpersonal worlds" (Tummala-Narra, 2004). This can be transformative, within supervision and in the therapy itself, as it enables and illuminates the occupation and exploration of a different and important emotional and psychological dimension.

Taking time to think and work through the intercultural aspects of the situation or dynamic brings benefits to supervisory spaces and the organisations within which they happen and enables more positive therapeutic encounters to take place at the interpersonal level within which therapy itself happens. It could be argued that unexplored aspects of culture – whether cultural similarities or differences – get in the way of the intersubjective dynamic processes of therapy which need to engage with the deeply personal and individual experience of the client.

We hope our examples may illustrate this point, and the broader importance of making explicit and working through intercultural issues in supervision. The first examples begin to say something about intercultural competence itself or lack of it, and the ability, capacity and confidence of therapists to work across and with cultural differences, and the role supervisors can play in that. We suggest that anxiety about openly, overtly, and directly, addressing issues of otherness may often be a greater obstacle to working interculturally than not having any specialist competence and/or training in intercultural work, whether as a therapist or supervisor.

Example 1

In my early years of exploring therapeutic work, I volunteered at an art therapy workshop, then started a training in Art Therapy and did a training placement in a psychiatric hospital. Having completed the foundation course, I took an opportunity to go and live and work in South America and whilst there completed a short post-graduate art therapy course. The South American Course Leader/Director invited me to work for the Institute where I had done the course and, trusting her judgement, as well as being flattered, I accepted her offer. I later discovered she was inexperienced in supervising from an intercultural perspective and unqualified as well as outside her competence as a supervisor. We both perhaps made the same assumptions about each other from our different cultural perspectives: i.e., that we were qualified to do the work. I quite quickly became aware that I was out of my depth, culturally, linguistically, and professionally. I found it very difficult to say no to her exhortations as both my employer and supervisor to continue the work but I knew that "no" was what I needed to say: I felt very anxious, ill at ease and inauthentic in the room with clients and it felt wrong to continue. In retrospect and with more training I have come to see that it was also an ethical issue and that the work was beyond my professional competence (BACP, 2018; UKCP, 2019) not just beyond my cultural comfort zone. My supervisor/director did not recognise this and perhaps had lost sight of the "primary task" (Rice, 1963) of the service – to provide effective therapy for the clients – in her keenness to increase the standing of the organisation. There was cultural kudos in having a white British art therapist on the staff (though I wasn't qualified by British standards) and she did not consider the cultural and linguistic gulf between me and the clients to be an issue or thought it was compensated for by the "added value" of my ethnic origin, privileged skin colour, and English accent; this was compounded by the gulf in my professional experience and ability to do the work adequately, which she also did not recognise because of her biased belief that the partial training I had done in Britain was as good or better than the full training that was available there.

Example 2

In another situation, working back in Britain, the supervisor (also of a different ethnicity to me) suggested that I could work with a family who had been referred: recently arrived in Britain, two young children and their very young mother who spoke little English, who had experienced a devastating and life-threatening attack here in the place they had come in order to find a better life and opportunities for the children. We had been unable to find anywhere we could refer them on to where they could be seen quickly. I demurred, saying that I was not trained or qualified to see them; she reminded me that I had worked with people from many cultures, and in different settings with women and children, as well as having experience of working therapeutically without a fluently spoken language in common (Zarbafi and Wilson, 2021). Her faith in me and in her own judgement as a supervisor enabled me to work with the family in what was a profoundly affecting therapeutic encounter. They left me with their pictures which they did not want to take with them, and with my impression of their vivacity, warmth, humour, courage, and resilience, as well as their trauma, etched into my memory which I still have to this day. In this situation, the supervisor was aware of and alert to the intercultural challenges of the situation: she could think about what could be good enough to meet the needs of the clients, assess my capability to provide it, and had the awareness and experience to be able to help me work through the material they came with. The intercultural challenges were overtly stated and explored and therefore could be worked with and I was by then well-enough qualified and had enough psychotherapeutic and life experience to be able to work with the clients' experience.

As supervisors, we have both had experiences of supervisees, especially trainees, being allocated clients who they are not equipped or experienced enough to work with safely or in a therapeutically adequate sense. We also have experience of supervisees who feel doubtful about taking on clients who are either culturally foreign or culturally akin to them and of supporting our supervisees to challenge themselves and to stretch and extend their professional competence and self-development, as well as to challenge and disagree with us and assert their own opinion/s when they differ, and ultimately make up their own minds. In these situations, the supervisor either has to feel confident enough to say "no" when they disagree with the allocation[3] even if the supervisee feels obliged to or actually wants to accept it or to encourage and support the supervisee in working outside their comfort (but not their competence[4]) zone. This requires judgement, knowledge, trust, and understanding between supervisor and supervisee – a working alliance that is often intercultural – which can only be achieved with an explicit discussion of the intercultural dynamics involved, the culture of the organisation they work in or the training they are coming from, and each participants' own capacity for open questioning of themselves and if necessary each other. As Igwe puts it "real awareness is a process of examining and being open to the possibility of changing principles and beliefs where and when necessary" (2003, p. 213).

Example 3

This example may illustrate the effect on the viability of the therapy/therapeutic relationship of examining in supervision both the intercultural dynamics within the therapist/client dyad *and* the intercultural dynamics of the group and/or organisation on the supervisee/therapist and their work:

In a supervision group of four trainees, three were women: one was Portuguese who spoke very good English, one was black British, and one was white British; the man, Joon, was of Korean origin, and his English was quite limited; in fact, one of the stipulations for his acceptance onto the training course was that he also study English. This, in conjunction with being the only male trainee, meant he felt very self-conscious and anxious about the training. Joon was also afraid that he would not be accepted by clients because of his Korean accent, difficulties with English language construction and limitations, as well as his ethnicity.

All the trainees were allocated therapists by the training organisation from a preferred list of approved therapists. The therapist allocated to Joon was one of the two most expensive on the list – the other was allocated to Martha, the black British trainee. The therapist allocated to Joon was based a long and complicated journey from where he lived; she too was of a different ethnicity and language and her English was heavily accented and influenced by a different grammatical structure. In supervision, we explored the intercultural and language challenges that these factors created which clearly exacerbated both Joon's anxiety about his linguistic competency and ability to be a counsellor counselling in English in Britain and also compounded his difficulty in learning English. He took it on as a by-product or result of his difference, rather than of the situation per se and/or the possibly unconscious and institutional racism, or at least "otherism," of the training organisation in "matching" the "foreign" student to the "foreign" therapist without considering the linguistic differences between them – especially since the organisation had mandated that Joon significantly improve his English, which of course was made a much harder task with a therapist whose own English was not only more difficult for Joon to understand but also different from the English he was trying to learn – yet more so as he was also trying to learn the language of therapy, with his training therapist being a major role-model of that. We explored these issues in the group and encouraged Joon to talk to his therapist – a significant cultural challenge for him. The response he described receiving sounded defensive: apparently putting it all back to him and his internal experience and not acknowledging the external realities or intercultural differences or similarities between them, or the very real additional difficulties these presented Joon with. With the group's support, Joon found the agency to end that therapy and ask for a change of therapist.

When Joon was allocated his first client for therapy, the client was a 49-year-old white British woman. Joon was very anxious and anticipated that she would find him an inadequate counsellor because of his limited English and strong accent, despite it being much improved, and because of his foreignness.

Sarah's presenting problem was that she had started having panic attacks at work; she had recently got a job at a large nursery school and was finding it difficult in the staff group: she felt unaccepted and not good enough; many of the staff were qualified and she wasn't, though she had been a childminder for many years. She was also experiencing difficulties in her fairly new relationship with a man 16 years younger than her, the same age as her daughter (and co-incidentally Joon) and who her 14-year-old twins from her second marriage resented; she was feeling very anxious that it was "going wrong" as well as really upset that her family were all very against the relationship. Her daughter had "done well for herself – unlike me" and had a prestigious role in a global company; she had two young children that Sarah had "minded" for her until her recent relationship when she had decided she wanted to "have some fun and stop looking after kids at all hours" as she had done since she was 12, she said. The intake form described a complex family history: Sarah's mother became pregnant at 15 and she did not know her father. She had been brought up by her grandparents until she was 12 when they had "sent her back" to live with her mother who had married a man 20 years her senior and had two children together. Sarah had had a troubled adolescence and, in her assessment, described "feeling an outsider" in her mother's home. Her mother had died from cancer five years previously.

Dialogue – Session 1

S: I always feel a bit different.

J: You say you are not in work for a while?

S: Yes, I think ... I was having panic attacks, and feeling a bit depressed – started to think something wasn't right in my head ... my GP said (hesitates) women's problems ... but obviously he thinks it's more than that to ask me to come here ...

J: What do you think about coming here?

S: I've always managed on my own.

J: That is different now?

S: Yes (long pause) If I'm honest, I don't believe this is going to help me – I was feeling a bit desperate – something wrong with me mentally – but now ... I'm not sure ... I said I was ok with a trainee because ... my job isn't very well paid ...

J: I can understand how you feel; I am glad you feel safe to say it.

S: I don't want you to think I'm complaining; I don't want to be difficult.

J: What does it mean to you to be difficult?

S: That's the way I am.

J: The way you are?

S: I don't want anyone to see me ... as an annoying person; I don't want people to be angry; I try and cope myself ... handle myself.

J: Handle yourself?

S: ... even if I'm upset, keep it to myself ... if I show my feelings people might react in an unpleasant way.

J: You afraid they react in a way that might be difficult – not ok to show you upset?

S: I would rather not risk it ... I haven't ever done it since I was a child; I lived with my grandparents ... I didn't want to annoy them; I liked it when my Grandad said "You're a good girl"; I felt good when I was good for them. But I don't want to be like them ... looking after my grandchildren till I'm old. I look at old people now and I think, in 10, 15 years time, I'll be one of them ... I'm running out of time and I do want to have a life before then ... but I love my children – my daughter, my sons, my grandsons ...

J: You put yourself behind ... at the same time one voice says you love your children, the other ...

S: You got it. I can't let my children down ... my daughter is saying she really needs me to take care of her boys ... they're lovely boys but ... (long pause).

J: You feel worn out with work and family ... lot of pressure on your time ... conflict?

S: (tearfully) You see I've let my family use up many years of my life ... I just want to live my own life ... I think what's on my mind ... it's hard being alone with all these things – I mean I do have my boyfriend but it's not like having a partner to support me ... like my daughter has ... I see her and I realise I never had that and how long I've been doing all these things on my own ... since my ex ... such a jerk ... I wish it had been different ... someone with me during those times ...

In the first few sessions, their sense of "otherness" to each other seemed like a big obstacle to therapeutic engagement, and there was no engagement with the otherness itself because of Joon's anxiety about being inadequate and feeling sure the client must find him inadequate, which seemed to overshadow not just the work but to render his mind unable to think about anything else. However, the trust and confidence that had been established in the group and his successful negotiation of the end of his first training therapy, and his work with his new therapist, enabled Joon to be open about how he felt and the group could think together about his transference and countertransference feelings and the intercultural dimensions and challenges in his encounters with Sarah, and they were able to explore these and the parallel processes within the group with curiosity, some trepidation, and also excitement. There were the client's and therapist's obvious ethnic, racial, cultural, and language differences; there was the sex difference and there was Joon's almost over-whelming and palpable sense of anxiety and inadequacy that pervaded his presentations of their interactions in the supervision group: there was also the group dynamics: who was favourite or least favoured not only in supervision but also the wider group; who was other and might be ousted, whose position was secure and who wasn't, and was this based on skin colour, ethnicity, heritage, familiarity, prowess, gender, and so on? Joon's sense of belonging felt tenuous and conditional and he couldn't really trust that he was wanted – just as Sarah couldn't in her family of origin or in those she had found and established for herself.

The group thought that there was an impasse – Joon was afraid to ask Sarah how she felt about his English and whether she thought he could understand her and she him, or if any other differences bothered her; Sarah couldn't say anything to him because of her fear of annoying or angering people, especially those she needed or wanted care and support from. The group reflected that Sarah's material also suggested that her experience of men was that they were unreliable, not really there for her but for themselves and left/abandoned her when they got fed up with her or she became too demanding or needy; at best their love and support was conditional on her being "good" and suppressing her "negative," difficult, and angry feelings. Did she have to be a good client for Joon and not express her doubts, sus-picion, or hostility about his cultural difference, his being younger than her and a similar age to her partner, and whether he was well enough equipped as a trainee and a "foreigner" to understand and help her? Similarly, to Joon, Sarah's panic attacks demonstrated that she too felt (almost) overwhelmed by anxiety in a group – and perhaps Joon's sense of this in the group denoted the cumulative feeling of his own experience of extreme otherness in the training group and organisation, and his countertransference to Sarah's feelings of strangeness and estrangement in her work group and family, and his own transferences and countertransferential feelings about being an inadequate man.

Joon shared with the group that he too had been brought up by his grandparents in a culture where he was expected to be good and dutiful and not to talk about his feelings especially angry or difficult ones. He too felt like a burden and a disappointment and he felt other and different within his own family and culture: he also felt other as a gay man who had only been able to come out when he had come to England and had then experienced homophobic and racist attacks.

The group thought that what Joon needed to be able to talk to and ask Sarah about was how she felt about their differences and whether she thought he could possibly understand, and whether she could possibly say how she felt about him to him, and to be able to link those feelings with her sense of otherness, of feeling she didn't belong and wasn't welcome, and was a stranger in and estranged from her own life and the people in it. The group also suggested that Joon took to his own therapy his difficulty talking and listening to a woman old enough to be his mother about personal and intimate things and asking about things that in his culture were taboo, such as menopause and sex, and expressing emotions such as anger and resentment towards parental figures. Joon found the courage to do this and in the coming sessions with Sarah he was able to ask her and they were able to talk about their cultural, linguistic, and gender differences and what they meant to her. Sarah and Joon began to engage with each other and a sense of togetherness in their shared endeavour in the room grew and flourished in the months ahead. Over the course of the therapy, Joon became able to ask questions and introduce subjects that had previously felt impossible for him to voice when they arose in and out of Sarah's material.

The questions that we feel most afraid to ask our clients are inevitably the ones that are most important to explore in supervision (and those we feel least able to ask our supervisees, the ones most needing to be explored in supervision of supervision). Igwe proposes that

> A good supervisor welcomes the opportunity to work on both the conscious and unconscious understandings and misunderstandings in his or her group – a kind of shifting from an unconscious incompetent state (I do not know what I do not know) to a conscious incompetent state (I know what I do not know). (2003, p. 217)

Then – having worked out what our difficulty is in asking or even thinking about them – depending on where they come from and where they belong (our stuff, the clients', the supervisory dyad, triad or group, or some combination of these), we also have to decide whether they should be taken out of the supervisory space, back into the client's therapy, or our own, or some combination of these.

In this example of overt cultural differences, Joon's Korean origin and his limited English was felt as a concrete problem, indeed as "the problem." However, in reality, it was a complex dynamic between Joon's ethnic and linguistic status, his own sense of whether he could be good enough or not, the organisation's lack of thought/ignorance (its "unconscious incompetence" [Broadwell, 1969]) and unconscious racism/otherism – and fear of working with cultural difference openly and questioningly not as a "problem" but as a useful dynamic. Once intercultural aspects and dynamics were brought out into the open in supervision and talked and thought about, "the problem" was resolvable, and both Joon and his client – and the group, and the course – could progress.

Example 4

A client of an overtly different culture and a supervisor and supervision group of cultural proximity, and how the dynamics of intercultural sameness and difference played out in this situation:

The supervision group comprised a Polish man, a Danish man, and a British woman; all were white and fluent in English, all trained and qualified in Britain. The service worked with a significant proportion of refugees and all the counsellors were experienced in working therapeutically with people from different cultures and culture was often a part of the supervisory conversation. In this case, the Polish therapist, Artur, was referred to a black Somalian woman. Jamilah was a refugee and spoke very little English; she was traumatised from her experiences during the civil war in her country and very isolated, even from the Somali community in London. The service had the benefit of being able to access interpreters and when Artur met Jamilah for an initial session it became apparent that she struggled to express herself in English. After the first session Artur wrote, translated into Arabic, and asked whether she would like an interpreter and whether as a Muslim woman, she would prefer to see a female counsellor; Jamilah responded that she would not, she wanted to continue to see Artur.

Artur took his work with Jamilah to supervision frequently and soon admitted he felt stuck and confused and every session felt like an immense struggle: she was not just very different from him in being a black Muslim woman who dressed traditionally, made little eye contact, and spoke very little English. He told the group she spoke very little at all and, despite his experience working with people from many different backgrounds and places in the world, the sessions felt very different than with other clients he had worked with. It seemed so hard to connect with Jamilah or to feel she was connecting with him and he wondered if it were simply that the cultural differences between them were too great and whether it was right to continue. Artur mused that he often felt lost for words and found himself struggling to communicate with Jamilah as much as she seemed to with him. She, however, appeared to continue to want the sessions with him very much even though they were mostly silent: she came every week, arriving early and sitting in the waiting room, and attended the whole session; and she had already said no to an interpreter and a female counsellor and had expressed her desire to continue with Artur.

After a lot of ruminating, Artur was able to express an anxiety that he would unintentionally say something terribly invasive and behave in a completely insensitive way, which surprised the group as he is a very gentle, softly-spoken care-full therapist. He described this as "paralysing" and was able to realise how fragile he felt Jamilah to be and feared that he might cause her to shatter. The group realised they too had felt rendered speechless, neither knowing what to say nor how to support or advise Artur and that they shared his fear of intruding upon Jamilah's sensitivities and his doubt that a white man was the right person to offer therapy to her. The supervisor wondered whether there might be alternative perspectives on the differences between Artur and Jamilah and the way she was using therapy: what might she value in what Artur was providing? The group then wondered if it was the very thing that he/we were concerned about: difference. Perhaps the fact that he was not of her culture, that he was nothing to do with her culture, was valuable to her? Coming from a background of civil war, and of rape, murder, and torture committed by and on people of her own culture and people close to her, did being with Artur's difference feel safer? And that they had limited common language perhaps bothered us more than Jamilah: was she communicating that she didn't actually want to say much at the moment? Perhaps she didn't want to confront the traumatic memories, or the shame that might accompany them, or questions about her identity and sense of self which had been so brutally challenged.

Once we looked at it from the perspective of what Artur's cultural differences might mean to Jamilah, rather than what her cultural difference meant to us, then an "answer" to what had appeared as a "problem" in the therapy became clear: because he was so different, and because he could accompany Jamilah in her silence and say little in the sessions too, co-creating a mutually accepted quiet space, she continued to come to see him. The group speculated that he might provide a safe-enough haven – somewhere really other – where she could risk just being and could begin to feel a little distance from the trauma of her experiences in the civil war and in fleeing her homeland. Over time, Jamilah confirmed this: she confided in Artur that she hadn't wanted an interpreter because she didn't want anyone from her culture to hear her story, and she didn't want to talk about it in her own language: talking about it in a foreign tongue made it as distant and other as it could possibly be (Zarbafi and Wilson, 2021); she wanted to say as little and no more than she felt able, very slowly, to say. She used her limited English to help protect herself. Jamilah had originally been referred for short-term counselling but Artur was able to get agreement to change this to a longer-term intervention, and they went slowly, at her pace, over several years. Eventually, she talked about some very painful things (without going into details) and thought about whether she would ever disclose what had happened to her and her family within the Somali community, with which she had over time started to connect, and decided she would not. Towards the end of her therapy Jamilah was eventually able to express to Artur that she had realised that part of the reason she had clung on to her counselling with him as a man was because she had held an infinitesimal unconscious hope that one day she would be able to trust and relate to a man again, as she had her beloved father and brothers all of whom she had lost in the war, and that she continued to now consciously hope that she might also one day have her own family.

In this case, the high visibility, directness, and degree of cultural difference was initially seen as a "problem": potentially culturally inappropriate and insensitive (which of course it could have been), and a barrier to delivering effective therapy. Even in a service experienced in intercultural work and with a supervisor accustomed to working with intercultural dimensions and perspectives in the supervisory space, there was a huge anxiety about not "getting it right" (and "getting it horribly wrong"): could Jamilah not speak to Artur because he was a man? because he was white? because he was so culturally different? not Muslim? did not speak her language? and so on ... All these were important issues to explore but ultimately what proved enabling for the therapy was the realisation that it was their differences which made the space a place of safety for Jamilah (as well as time, and Artur's ability to be quiet and patient, still and "there" for her). His very differentness gave her the distance and space within which she could slowly work through some of her thoughts, feelings and experiences, enough for her to be able to find a new place in her own cultural community here. The crucial turning point in our understanding was trying to comprehend the meaning of the limited language and the cultural differences from Jamilah's perspective: that these were helpful to her rather than the "problem" we had construed from our own rather anxious position. This perhaps fits with Zarbafi's idea that "the second language offers a life raft to the psyche as it involves a form of distancing from the mother tongue which can be creative as it affords perspective and recovery" (Zarbafi and Wilson, 2021, Introduction).

How often do supervisors' and supervisees'/therapists' own cultural sensitivities and inhibitions, or PCness, or judgemental and hyper-critical attitudes, or fears of them, preclude thinking about and asking questions in relation to aspects of culture and intercultural work? However, when we do look at intercultural aspects in all their breadth and depth – gender/identity, sex, ethnic origins, culture, faith, demographics, and other differences – it opens up and enriches therapeutic interactions, encounters, and engagement that are otherwise blocked off. It is both sad and concerning that sometimes the potential and possibility of openness, interest, and curiosity about intercultural matters, their discussion in supervision, and raising them in the therapy itself are repressed and inhibited by anxieties, ignorance, and/or awareness of our own and/or of others' prejudices and privileges. Rapp notes that "However experienced supervisors might be, they are not exempt from becoming disabled by their own lack of relevant experience, the sudden opening up of old vulnerabilities, and the unexpected re-emergence of prejudices long thought to have been worked through" (2001, p. 151).

Having lived and worked in other countries and having trained and worked interculturally for many years with people of all sorts of backgrounds, ethnicities, and skin colours, we work hard to ensure our practice is interculturally accessible and open. As supervisors, we bring culture into the supervisory process, especially when and if it is not raised by our supervisee/s, and, as we have said earlier, we consider intercultural considerations to be as crucial to effective supervision as they are to effective therapy. Though we have given some examples of intercultural exploration in our work, we have not specifically talked about racism. Mckenzie-Mavinga states that

> it is not enough to assume that multicultural awareness or intercultural experiences can offer an active response to the challenge of racism. This may pathologise clients, as though the problem of racism does not really exist and therefore it does not need attending to. (2019, pp. 173–174)

Awareness of racism, its prevalence and impact, and the impact of internalised racism and unconscious racism are part of intercultural awareness and intercultural supervision; as is awareness of our own white privilege. We are not, as white people, the objects of racist abuse in Britain or many other places, or rarely. The following example highlights the risk that white supervisors with white supervisees may not immediately think of racism when looking for meanings, even within interculturally-informed work, because of the immunity afforded by white privilege; there is a risk for white therapists and supervisors of not immediately thinking of racism in the way that someone experiencing it on a daily or frequent basis does. "The supervisee and the supervisor … need to validate their levels of tacit knowledge about racism as this process will assist their ability to work with the challenges of racism in therapy" (Mckenzie-Mavinga, 2019, p. 173).

Example 5

This group is of white supervisees, two British and one Italian, with a white supervisor in an inner-city practice working with people referred because of "mental health problems." One of the British therapists, Michael, had a client called Jacob; Jacob was a young British black man referred with a diagnosis of obsessive-compulsive disorder (OCD) and relationship difficulties. Jacob had difficulty going out because of the many rituals he had to perform before he could leave his flat in order to feel safe to go out, and he wouldn't let people into his flat unless they also performed a number of purification rituals, took off their shoes, were sprayed with a disinfectant and washed their hands (this was pre-COVID!); he had few friends, and those he had were not very close. He and Michael, who was only a year or two older than him, seemed to form a reasonably good relationship and Jacob attended regularly despite his difficulties with getting to the therapy site (he wouldn't use public transport so walked) and he had to perform his rituals sometimes five or six times before leaving home to feel safe enough to make the journey there and back. Jacob had a history of abuse within his family, including sexual abuse, being bullied at school, and being the victim of racist abuse, including an attack when he was a teenager by some drunk young white men in the street. Michael was sensitive to this and in therapy, they had discussed their relationship, Michael's whiteness, what transferences there might be, and how Jacob's experiences of life might have affected him and led him to feel that he needed to do so much to "purify" himself of contaminants outside and inside and to keep himself safe. Progress was slow because Jacob often wanted to repeat the same story or part of a story over and over, as if the repetition would take out some of the intensity or trauma and make it better or safer or clearer, and there seemed to be a good therapeutic relationship and some progress in the therapy. Jacob was becoming able to go out more often and had begun to go to a church sometimes, something he wanted to do but had felt too intimidated to actually do till now.

Jacob attended therapy fairly regularly, but not every session: he would occasionally miss sessions because going out was proving too much and on these occasions he would ring and talk to Michael on the phone, sometimes briefly and sometimes for the duration of the session. One day he called and said that he couldn't come because he was having breathing difficulties: "I can't get there, I can't breathe" he explained. Jacob said he was going to call his GP and hung up. Michael brought this to supervision, worried about Jacob. The group wondered whether it was a panic attack, or if it was some disorder of his lungs or throat, or if it could be linked to Jacob's OCD diagnosis, or his paranoia? Jacob didn't come the following week either, but rang, again complaining that he couldn't breathe. The following week, again on the phone, he said he had seen the GP and they had done some tests but they hadn't found anything wrong. He was clearly distressed and insisted he couldn't come to therapy and couldn't talk on the phone as he had done previously: "I can't breathe" he said. Michael brought the situation to supervision again: what was going on, some new symptom of mental distress, or something physical that the GP's tests had failed to identify? Michael was struggling to understand; this felt different to Jacob's usual anxious and rather repetitive interactions. The supervisor asked for Michael to present some of his and Jacob's phone conversations to the group so we might be able to think about meanings within it. Michael said, "Well he didn't say much really, which is unusual for him; he explained a bit about going to the GP and about the tests, which he struggled to do because he was obviously having trouble breathing; mainly he just kept saying "I can't breathe." When Michael said it out loud like that, the group realised that these were the words George Floyd had used some months previously when he was being murdered by the police. The following week, Michael was able to raise this with Jacob when he called, and they discussed George Floyd's murder, police racism, and Jacob's experience of it, and Jacob began to find his voice again. He started coming back to therapy, and he and Michael explored Jacob's experience of racist abuse, at the hands of the police, mental health, and other services, and Jacob's experience of multiple minor aggressions interspersed with overtly racist events in more depth than they previously had. Although Jacob continued to experience breathing difficulties for several months, they gradually subsided.

In this example, because racism was not part of the day-to-day or lived experience and vocabulary of the therapist, supervisor or supervision group, the connotations of Jacob's experience and how he expressed it were not picked up as instantly or quickly as they could/should have been. Racism is sadly part of the intercultural experience in racist societies, and it is a pervasive and frequent experience for many people, especially those whose skin colour is not "white." Racism is a special category of intercultural work and has a particular impact:

> Emotional content attached to facilitation of racial issues must therefore be acknowledged and supported in clinical supervision. To facilitate this supervisors and therapists must be aware of and able to conduct a dialogue about racism in supervision and the therapeutic setting. (Mckenzie-Mavinga, 2019, p. 169)

Supervisors, and especially white supervisors, need to hold this in mind alongside but separate from – mentally highlighted if you like – the other categories of intercultural awareness of language, religion, sex, gender, sexuality, ethnicity, etc. to avoid a "misinterpretation of racism or a dilution of key issues by generalising concerns" (Mckenzie-Mavinga, 2019, p. 168).

Example 6

We thought this chapter would be incomplete without any mention of COVID-19 and how it has affected intercultural work which we have supervised through the pandemic. This is just one small snippet of an example and illustrates something of what may be unseen and can be missed in online therapy and its supervision.

A white female therapist was working via Skype on issues around anxiety and lack of self-confidence with a young British woman who had lived all her life in northern Britain until moving to London quite recently. She came from a single-parent extended family with an intergenerational history of poverty and deprivation and multiple mental and physical health issues. She was the first of her family to go to university and had wanted to move south with her boyfriend and have a different life. She had originally contacted the therapist while self-isolating due to her health vulnerabilities and had not returned to her work in a GP surgery having become extremely depressed following the break-up of her relationship. Thought was given in supervision to possible intercultural aspects of her anxiety and lack of social confidence, and the sense of difference that the move from her northern town to the capital had induced or exacerbated, and the sense of difference the middle-class London-born therapist sensed from her client: she was very self-conscious, and frequently apologised for "being in such a state." When after a couple of months, she began to feel better and was able to meet her therapist and have sessions in person, the therapist was really taken aback to see that her client was mixed race. It simply had not been obvious in Skype sessions and the client hadn't mentioned it. What she was completely preoccupied with were her current difficulties at that stage, including her fear that she was becoming like her mother who had had a succession of failed relationships and had been depressed most of her life. Her family background and history and her confusion around her mixed heritage and the conflict between the different sides of her family and within her, came into the therapy once they were working "in the flesh" and she could be fully seen.

One of the issues this raises is that we see an image of someone on video rather than an embodied someone, and we mostly see only see a part or parts of them. Of course, the same situation could happen when we meet a new client and make assumptions about their ethnicity but it is perhaps less likely, though, as Mckenzie-Mavinga notes, "hidden aspects of identity, for example, hidden disabilities and sexuality, and mixed-heritage individuals who appear white" (2019, p. 172) may get overlooked without cultural curiosity. Either way, it reaffirms the need to raise questions of culture in therapy and its supervision.

One of the curious things during the pandemic has been the terminology – "face to face" is often used to mean "in person," yet few things are more face-to-face than therapy on online platforms, which means therapists and clients are (mostly) literally "face to face" and eye to eye too. Group therapy and supervision online are very different again, especially in larger groups where there is no face-to-face and it is difficult if not impossible to tell who is looking at whom. Some supervision provision is returning to in person and/or in group, but much is not, and this is perhaps one of, if not the biggest, cultural shift in the profession.

"In person" when therapist's and client's, supervisee's and supervisor's bodies and minds meet in the same space together, gives much fuller, multi-dimensional whole person experience in each other's presence – the intersubjectivity of the mind–body–brain in relationship that we talked about at the beginning of this chapter. Many services during the first 18+ months of COVID were either closed or restricted to telephone work only – which is not face to face or even ear to ear – and perhaps raises the question of what "in person" really means. There can be a very powerful connection, aurally and orally, and of course some people were working on the phone and/or online before the pandemic.

These all mark substantial cultural shifts in the provision of therapy and supervision – one that has been, and continues to be, difficult for some therapists and supervisors used to working in-person together in a room, who find it more challenging to relate to and embrace the cultural shifts towards video technology and social media as a way of communicating rather than being together, not just professionally but in wider society. These changes pre-date COVID but have been accelerated by the pandemic. For some people, newer ways of doing therapy – and supervision – are more accessible, for others less so. However, if we can maintain the variety of ways in which therapeutic services are now provided, it could mean *real* choice in accessing therapy is available, which will be beneficial for therapy overall, and intercultural work in particular. For different individuals in different cultures, for different reasons, any one of the different ways of engaging with therapy may be more fitting or accessible.

Conclusion

Space in a chapter only allows us to sketch a few stories and permission to use material from them, or lack of it,[5] limits the scenarios and examples which we can use to illustrate them. Out of the countless number of personal histories we have been privileged to hear, bear witness to, and work with as supervisors – and supervisees/therapists – we hope that the themes from them that we have gathered and amalgamated and condensed here, with all of the enlightened and illuminating perspectives of our supervisors, supervisees, and clients from whom we have learned so much, will evoke thoughts, feelings, and ideas that will help to foster and promote reflective practice and creative thinking about how essential intercultural supervision is to good-enough and better psychotherapeutic relationships and practice.

We have looked at the proposition that supervision cannot be satisfactory or adequate without adequate and satisfactory consideration and exploration of the intercultural dynamics in the work, in the light of our experience as supervisors and supervisees, through the prism of group and individual supervision and some supervisees' work with some of their clients and some of our work with some of our supervisees.

If supervisees can have confidence in their supervisor's intercultural sense, sensitivity, and sensibilities, and can trust them with their own material, they can work together to identify and make sense of pre-transferences, projections, identifications, and prejudices, and enable the supervisee to come to their own conclusion/s as to whether taking on a client who challenges their sense of difference would be a valid therapeutic endeavour or beyond their current competence and cultural capacity.

We propose that to become and continue to be as effective, sensitive, and aware practitioners as it is possible to be, supervisees working interculturally and supervisors supervising intercultural work, should, if possible, have supervision, and/or supervision of supervision, with a supervisor of a different culture and/or in a multicultural group. As Fong (1994) remarks:

> All supervisors-in-training should work with supervisees from racial-ethnic groups other than their own and receive supervision of multicultural supervision. Likewise, experienced supervisors will need to seek continuing education, consultation, and focused supervision of supervision with a multicultural emphasis to meet gaps in experience and education.

As therapists, we sometimes learn at our clients' expense, though hopefully, the return on their investment is fruitful overall. As supervisors too we may learn at our supervisees' expense though again hopefully the cost does not outweigh the benefit.

> 'It would not be possible to know something about every different ethnic group, but it is good practice to ask about the things you do not know. Here, you are looking especially to understand what is normal in anyone's culture', as Igwe puts it. (2003, p. 229)

Nowhere is this more important than in the field of mental health. There is a crisis in the provision of good quality therapy for people with mental health problems, and one of the remaining great discriminations in society and in the provision of therapy is against people with lived experience of mental health problems. What has this got to do with a chapter on intercultural supervision? People from minority and minoritised groups are overly represented in facing mental health difficulties because oppression, discrimination, inequality, and racism all take their toll on people's mental health. So do questions of identity and culture for people who are displaced, or who hold different cultural values to the host culture, or for people who simply do not fit the majority view. People with lived experience of mental health problems additionally face discrimination in therapy services and therapy trainings, in both of which people of minority ethnicities and groups and people from the global majority are also under-represented.

We are ending our chapter drawing attention to this form of intercultural discrimination – between those who have and those who have not had lived experience of mental health problems – because it affects minorities and minoritised people disproportionately and because it remains significantly unattended to. In all the books we have read or looked through on supervision in therapy, with intercultural perspectives or not, we could not find any reference to working as supervisees/therapists or supervisors with lived experience of mental health problems.

What is also bizarrely antithetical is the all-too-common reality that the culture of most mental health counselling and psychotherapy services in the public, private, and third sectors, intentionally or otherwise, exclude people with the greatest mental health needs and vulnerabilities from using them, and their gateways, pathways, service specifications and referral criteria shut out the very people whose entrance they were theoretically designed to enable. A bit like refugees, they end up drowning in the channel that is the last stage of the route to their much-needed refuge. Many individual practitioners in private practice also exclude people with greater needs than the higher functioning "worried well" and "ordinarily neurotic" clients who seek our services. The most common rationales are that people more towards the psychotic and schizoid end of the spectrum (with diagnoses of Personality Disorder [PD] or Borderline PD [BPD], etc.) need "containing" by some sort of institution, and/or that they need expert, specialist and/or psychiatric help. This is perhaps one of the strongest, and least spoken of, bastions of prejudicial and discriminatory practice, one which particularly affects people at the epicentre of intersectionality.[6]

The BACP Ethical Framework also includes in its Ethics section under Values a commitment to "striving for the fair and adequate provision of services" and in its Professional Standards section under "Respect" it commits, amongst other things, to: "f. makes adjustments to overcome barriers to accessibility, so far as is reasonably possible, for clients of any ability wishing to engage with a service" (BACP, 2018). This surely should include people with mental health problems! The UKCP also has a statement about accessibility and non-discriminatory practice (UKCP, 2019).

In supervision, there are parallel processes of both overt and covert/ unconscious discrimination, disease, and exclusion. Supervisees – and supervisors – with histories of mental and emotional ill-health, witness the "othering"[7] that many people working in many counselling and therapy services (which are, or surely should be, mental health services) subject (prospective) clients to and are subjected to.

It is in our view a national tragedy and scandal that there is (a) such a severe lack of understanding of what mental health is (to the extent that it is common currently to talk about people "having mental health," for example, s/he/they have "got mental health" when the very opposite is true if desired), and (b) that the majority of mental health services exclude people with mental health problems, and generally more so if they belong to other cultural minority or minoritised groups.

Supervisors in many organisations contribute to the establishment, maintenance of, and changes in, the cultural norms and practices of the organisations they work in. If we are confident and competent to supervise interculturally and advocate for it, the organisation is much more likely to permit the inclusion of people from previously marginalised and excluded groups. If, as supervisees, we are supported by our supervisors to work outside of our comfort zone/s and expand them, we enable more people to access and benefit from therapy.

Notes

1 We use the word "therapist/s" to refer to counsellors, psychotherapists, counselling psychologists, and other therapeutic staff.
2 "Othering is a process whereby individuals and groups are treated and marked as different and inferior from the dominant social group": Oxford Reference, OUP 2021.
3 *BACP Ethical Framework*
   Our commitment to clients

   1. Put clients first by:

      a Making clients our primary concern while we are working with them.
      b Providing an appropriate standard of service to our clients.

4 2. Work to professional standards by:

      a Working within our competence.

5 All names and identifying features and details have been changed and disguised. Nevertheless, supervisees and clients whose permission we have to use their material may recognise themselves despite the alterations. Any other resemblances are entirely coincidental.
6 "The interconnected nature of social categorisations such as race, class, and gender as they apply to a given individual or group, regarded as creating overlapping and interdependent systems of discrimination or disadvantage" (Google, Oxford Languages).
7 View or treat (a person or group of people) as intrinsically different from and alien to oneself.

References

Ababio, B., Littlewood, R. (2019). *Intercultural Therapy: Challenges, Insights and Developments*. London: Routledge.
Ammaniti, M., Gallese, V. (2014). *The Birth of Intersubjectivity: Psychodynamics, Neurobiology and the Self*. London: Norton.
BACP. (2018). Ethical framework. Available at: https://www.google.com/search?client=firefox-b-d&q=bacp+ethical+framework+2018 (Accessed September 2021).

Broadwell, M. (1969). Teaching for learning XVI. Available at: https://edbatista.typepad.com/files/teaching-for-learning-martin-broadwell-1969-conscious-competence-model.pdf (Accessed September 2021).

Cockersell, P. (2019). Intercultural psychotherapy, intracultural psychotherapy, or just good psychotherapy. In: Ababio, B., Littlewood, R, (eds) *Intercultural Therapy: Challenges, Insights and Developments.* London: Routledge.

Fong, M. (1994). Multicultural issues in supervision, ERIC Identifier: ED372346 Publication Date: 1994-04-00. Available at: https://files/eric.ed.gov>fulltext>ED372346 (Accessed September 2021).

Green, A. (1973). On negative capability: A critical review of W. R. Bion's "attention and interpretation." *International Journal of Psychoanalysis, 54,* 115–128.

Igwe, A. (2003). The impact of multi-cultural issues on the supervision process. In: Dupont-Joshua, (ed.) *Working Interculturally in Counselling Settings.* London: Brunner-Routledge.

Kareem, J., Littlewood, R. (1992). *Intercultural Therapy: Themes, Interpretations and Practice.* London: Routledge

Mckenzie-Mavinga, I. (2019). The challenge of racism in clinical supervision. In: Ababio, B. Littlewood, R. (eds) *Intercultural Therapy: Challenges, Insights and Developments.* London: Routledge.

Oxford Reference. (2021). Oxford University Press, definition of 'othering'. Available at: https://www.oxfordreference.com/view/10.1093/acref/9780191834837.001.0001/acref-9780191834837-e-283 (Accessed September 2021).

Petrucelli, J. (2018). *Knowing, Not Knowing & Sort of Knowing.* London: Routledge.

Rapp, H. (2001). Working with difference and diversity. In: Wheeler, S., King, D. (eds) *Supervising Counsellors: Issue of Responsibility.* London: SAGE Publications.

Rice, A. (1963). *The Enterprise and Its Environment.* London: Tavistock Publications.

Siegel, D. (2015). *The Developing Mind.* London: Norton.

Tummala-Narra, P. (2004). Dynamics of race and culture in the supervisory encounter. *Psychoanalytic Psychology, 21*(2), 300–311. Available at: 10.1037/0736-9735.21.2.300 (Accessed September 2021).

UKCP. (2019). Code of ethics. Available at: https://www.psychotherapy.org.uk/about-ukcp/how-we-are-structured/ukcp-committees/ethics-group/code-of-ethics-updated/ (Accessed September 2021).

Watkins, C. Jr., Hook, J. (2016). On a culturally humble psychoanalytic supervision perspective: Creating the cultural third. *Psychoanalytic Psychology, 33*(3), 487–517. Available at: 10.1037/pap0000044 (Accessed September 2021).

Zarbafi, A., Wilson, S. (2021). *Mother Tongues and Other Tongues, Narratives in Multilingual Psychotherapy.* London: Phoenix Publishing.

Part 2

Supervision and the Social

Chapter 4

The Reflective Group Process for Female Workers

Dilek Güngör

It is difficult to hear traumatic stories from people who are emotionally damaged. This is illustrated with the material from the Therapy Centre which recognised the challenge of this kind of work and developed a creative project for external community professionals with severely traumatised clients.

Firstly, I will begin by describing my role at the Therapy Centre and move on to describe how I engaged with the community and external professionals to set up the project. I will briefly explore what domestic violence is and follow this with a discussion about reflective group practice; illustrated with material drawn from the processes of a reflective group, I facilitated.

This chapter examines the concept of engaging professional help for professionals with a view to enabling meaningful and safe work. The theme of the group was, "working with domestic violence sufferers." Due to confidentiality, the attendees' names and workplaces have been changed to the "Therapy Centre (TC)." I will include my own thoughts, feelings, and the work of the organisation.

The reflective group I present was set up in the late 1990s. I named this group a "reflective group for domestic violence workers" because this title seemed more accessible for many workers.

My role at the centre

Intercultural psychotherapy can help women from the Black, Minority Ethnic and Refugee (BMER) communities who have been through traumatic experiences. I therefore applied for the post of "community development/ analytic psychotherapist" and succeeded in convincing the four Western, white psychoanalytic panellists that I was suitable. I was tasked to offer therapy via information-taster sessions and reflective practice sessions for external staff working with vulnerable women.

My professional participation in diverse trainings and being bi-lingual were useful in ensuring that women from minoritised communities, excluded from psychotherapy due to cultural and linguistic barriers, class, racism, and poverty, were able to access services at the TC. The terrain amongst

DOI: 10.4324/9781003380214-7

therapy providers then revealed a dearth in understanding the needs of BMER women. Therapists were faced with challenges in the delivery of culturally appropriate services to clients from these diverse communities.

I introduced the project via a series of consultation meetings and workshops, providing leaflets and informative papers to explain that reflective practice sessions were designed to offer safe spaces for professionals to engage with and explore the implications of the psychological impact of domestic violence. These were spaces where colleagues could reflect on their own responses to the loss and trauma in the lives of their clients and focus on setting up and embedding structures to support their work.

Initially, it was difficult to gain the trust of professionals and the local communities. The community stakeholders who approached me seemed to expect some sort of magical guarantee about the outcome of the project. I noted a parallel process at play at the TC in the form of my struggles to settle in with my colleagues, who were mainly white – the Eurocentric/ Western psychotherapy culture was dominant, coupled with the assumption of the English language being standard and universal.

"Psychoanalytic practitioners sometimes slip into a position of arrogance, … thinking they know best" (Casement, 2008). The effect of the "external" world and working with differences was not routinely kept in mind in the clinical processes within TC. These considerations formed part of what I introduced colleagues to when I began working at TC.

My outreach work enabled the workers to understand how supervision for themselves was linked to public safety and to protecting their professional standards. It was a free service which they found helpful and enabled them to leave with tools to facilitate their work. It is important to mention that allocating budget lines for the supervision of workers was not in place. Workers shared their personal and professional experiences with me and complained that they could not get supervision due to the absence of resources and policies to support and sustain the structuring of regular supervision. I should add that, due to the absence of a supervision culture, the workers had not considered peer supervision as an option. Some of the reasons they gave when asked about peer arrangements were that they as workers did not have the mental space to allocate for thinking and reflecting about their work. Their workload, according to them, was heavy.

Domestic violence

Domestic violence is a serious crime which has a substantial impact on the health and welfare of adults and children. Hearthstone specialist domestic violence therapeutic counselling services states that:

> An estimated 3 in 10 women will experience domestic violence at some stage in their lives meaning that in Haringey over 3000 women are currently

experiencing domestic violence and over 20000 are living with the legacy of past domestic violence abuse. Only a few of these incidents are reported to the police or to family members and friends. (Hearthstone, 2019)

Domestic violence (DV) is not openly spoken about. An understanding of social and cultural background is vital as a starting point when working with different cultures. The subject may be avoided even more within BMER groups who are highly likely to be subjected to racist and discriminatory acts based on protected characteristics but not exclusively. Due to the oppression of male-dominant patriarchal structures, women from the BMER groups experience double social inequalities. These multiple layers of oppression place them in even more marginalised situations exacerbating their exposure to violence and a lack of access to services. Herman has stated how, "traumatized people are often reluctant to ask for help of any kind, let alone psychotherapy" (Judith Lewis Herman, 1992).

The Department of Health describes "domestic violence," as a continuum of behaviour ranging from verbal abuse to rape even homicide through threats and intimidation, manipulative behaviour, physical and sexual assault. Most of such violence and the most severe, chronic incidents are perpetrated by men against women and children.

More than half the women killed by men in the UK in 2018 were killed by a current or former partner, many after they had taken steps to leave, according to a report on femicide.The fourth Femicide Census, conducted by the campaigner Karen Ingala Smith, found 149 women were killed by 147 men in 2018. The number of deaths is an increase of 10 on the previous year and the highest number since the census began. Of the deceased women, 91 (61%) were killed by a current or former partner. Only 6% of murders were committed by a stranger. (Al-Khalaf and Topping, 2020)

The definition of DV now includes young people under 18s and signals the latest action by the government to tackle violence against women and girls. A change to the official definition of domestic violence used across the government will aim to increase awareness that young people do experience DV and abuse (www.direct.gov.uk/thisisabuse).

At the start, I wondered if a time-limited reflective group would be useful for professionals, who work in the community, in different settings. I had in mind the aim/goal and outcome of the intervention and its completion within the 12-week time frame. I had to think of the selection criteria, techniques, and the outcome of the work. I took a healthy risk due to the limited resources of the TC and chose reflective group members randomly. I did not meet them before the group started. It was a challenging process. However, they were professionals and working in the field for some time, so

I had a basic trust in them. Also, some crucial aspects of the work were supported and held by my theoretical underpinning, as well as by my experience. I deployed curiosity, cultural awareness, containment, and management in facilitating the group. This is echoed somewhat in this quote, "As the matters of technique, the basic principles of an individual psycho-analysis hold good, and it can be assumed that the experienced psycho-analyst should find no difficulty in modifying his techniques to the new situation" (Foulkes, 1984).

> Even mothers have to learn how to be motherly by experience. By experience they grow. If they look at the other way and think that they must work hard at books to learn how to be perfect mothers from the beginning, they all will be on the wrong track. In the long run, what we need is mothers, as well as fathers, who have found out how to believe in themselves. These mothers and their husbands build the best homes in which babies can grow and develop. (Winnicott, 1975)

I decided to be the mother that Winnicott described! I strongly believed; that the community-based pilot project could be sustained over time through an evidencing of its success and consequently, secure funding to sustain the project's medium- to long-term future.

There were challenges with colleagues – some of whom were not familiar with the digital world and were resisting engaging with computers, emails, and phones. There was the notion that the type of community intervention I was initiating might contaminate the TC's analytic work! I insisted and persevered with the 12-week intervention (meeting once a week and sessions lasting for 90 minutes).

Group members

The members of the group I had set up were then working with refugees and DV sufferers. They were from diverse professions, experiences, training, and culture. Boundaries were different to other supervision groups. I was determined to create a healthy environment where anxieties, dilemmas, and challenges could be safely contained. "Without good theory as guide it is likely to be difficult to plan and to be unproductive and findings are difficult to interpret" (Bowlby, 1982; Maguire, 1997). My aim was to provide a corrective and collective learning experience without undermining members' confidence in their skills (Behr, 1995). The process was an important opportunity to examine the cases, clinical practice, and its dynamics. They were aware of the confidentiality and the ethical issues that can arise from the use of clinical material from clients. Main presenting themes from the workers were DV, issues of clients' symptoms of guilt, shame, fear of one's incompetence, irresponsibility, and fear of being blamed by the client's family, friends, and colleagues. They also shared issues situated within their various organisations. I present a description of the group and a vignette below:

Aisha: was a Black British female and a prisoner's therapeutic/welfare project counsellor.
Beatrice: was a multilingual (four languages), family therapist from Turkey.
Carol: was a DV Intervention Project Manager/family therapist and a black woman from the Middle East.
Diana: was a white British volunteer coordinator working for the prison service.
Elaine: was a white-Jewish woman, project manager working with DV issues.
Fiona: was a social worker of mixed (black and white) heritage.
Gill: was a Romanian, multilingual DV coordinator of mixed (black and white) heritage. She was also multilingual.
Hilary: was a DV worker/art therapist of mixed (Pakistani and Indian) heritage.

First session

When I arrived, I introduced myself; this was our first-time meeting face-to-face. Our previous communications were all via e-mail. They followed me and introduced themselves. I was suddenly anxious. "If you are not frightened of the patient who is going to come into your consulting room, then there must be something wrong … " Symington (1993).

Diane started talking about the weather: "It is always raining. I am really fed up! I miss the sun shining."

Beatrice then arrived and was a few minutes late. She immediately started talking without saying "hello." She was breathless and said that she had had a difficult journey to the TC because of road works. She had had to walk for half an hour and the weather was awful. Elaine interposed and said that it was difficult to leave the office due to the amount of paperwork she had to work through.

Beatrice continued and said, "The Receptionist didn't know which room to assign and why we are here!"

I noticed they found it difficult to talk about themselves and reasons for being in the group. "Whenever people talk to me about the weather, I always feel certain that they mean something else" (Wilde et al., 2007). However, by the following sessions, there was a slow, growing interest in the work and a negative transference was developing towards me. They questioned me and the process. Was I a good enough group analyst to facilitate the group? Was I trained sufficiently to understand their work and feelings? Did I know what DV is? They did not think that the group could hold the stresses of their heavy workloads. At what institute did I undertake my training? Where was my accent from? Could they trust me and the group? Why me, why not another therapist? What kind of therapeutic model would I use for the work, analytic, humanistic, or the integrative approach? These were parts of their questions, worries, and concerns.

They expressed feelings towards this unknown initiative: a lack of information and an atmosphere of low trust within the organisation. This stemmed from the centre's history, its poor relationships with the community, their fear of failure and a reluctance to process their hatred towards men.

I was not surprised by their comments but wondered if they would ask those questions, if I was a White European psychotherapist. This is my professional and personal experience in the United Kingdom as a non-European professional with an accent and dark curly hair (now, I have grey and curly hair!). I facilitated a space for the group to realise that the issue was not only about internalised racism but was also intersectional; about being a woman. I encouraged them to connect with their gender issues, what it meant being female professionals and their internalised hatred towards men. After some discussions, they were astonished to find out how much they denigrated themselves and other women.

Gill and Hilary did not disclose that they were from the same organisation; speaking to each other about their work as if they were the only two people in the group. I asked how they felt about being together in this group. I wanted the group to know that they were from the same organisation. I did not want any sub-grouping or secrets in the group. They seemed comfortable about it but, Fiona said, "I wish I had asked my colleagues to be here!"

Suddenly Beatrice changed the subject and said, "Dilek is a Turkish name!"

It was as if she had discovered something special and articulated the unknown. They showed an interest and asked Beatrice how she knew. Beatrice said that she was from Turkey and that Dilek was a Turkish name. Diana was curious that, Beatrice had blue eyes and was blond and asked, "How come you are Turkish?" Beatrice seemed irritated by the question and said, "I am Kurdish, and we can have blue eyes, do you mind?"

There was a long silence. Beatrice then talked about her background and being Kurdish from Turkey as if she was giving a political lecture. She told the group that her parents had immigrated to France when she was four years old. When she talked about being four years old, she suddenly cried. The group was interested in her story but resisted talking about their clients and the psychological impact on themselves. I asked them to think about why they chose to work in the profession they were in. They seemed puzzled to have this question posed to them, but it made them think and reflect. Many of the DV workers were immigrants themselves or their parents had experienced similar losses and traumas described by the clients they were supporting. Some of these workers had themselves experienced DV. The jobs they were engaged in seemed to be their pathway to some form of personal healing.

At the beginning of the process, they were projecting clients' negative feelings onto me or the group. Their clients, who had recounted suffering DV, did not express their appreciation towards the workers; who in turn appeared to reenact the dynamics of their clients in the group.

Elaine said, "I want to sit on that chair (pointing to my chair as she wanted to be the facilitator). I hope one day I will."

The group was pleased to hear her frank opinion. They all thought that if I am doing the job, why could they not do the same? My emotional reaction was anger and to escape, but I just had to sit back and contain those feelings.

Fiona turned to Elaine and said, "Oh my God, you are brave."

While working with envious female clients, the psychotherapist must, then be able to retain an awareness of what is being left outside the therapeutic discourse. Apparently compliant, idealizing clients can then be helped right from the beginning of therapy to recognize their own envy and resentment. Similarly, psychotherapist needs to retain her objectivity in the face of envious devaluation which she may experience as deeply undermining. Ultimately it is helpful to remind the client that their envy relates to admiration as well as with the desire to spoil. Once she acknowledges the profundity of her own envy, the client can then make some realistic decisions about whether she can act on her envious desires to change her own life. Finally, the clinician must tolerate not only her client's projected envy but also, her own unfulfilled wishes, which may be all too painfullyinescapable when she helps other women to enjoy what she will never have. Both client and therapist are ultimately confronted with the fact that some desires can never be realized. (Maguire, 1997)

The group process provided insight for them to get in touch with their envy and competitiveness. Three members of the reflective group decided that they needed individual therapy to work through further unconscious feelings.

Aisha said, "Dilek you are not giving us enough training. I was expecting some articles, essays, and case studies. You are silent and not saying much. We must do the hard work! It's unfair ..."

Diana said,

Yes, but if we want, we can bring cases any way! Dilek is following us. Maybe we are asking too much! I am not sure if she can cope with our awful cases. Can she understand how distressed we are? I understand why Dilek doesn't speak too much. Maybe she wants us to help each other. (She was talking, as if I was not in the room)

Then she turned to me and asked: "What do you think Dilek?"

I smiled and encouraged them that they could say more about the group process and their expectations. Externally, I seemed calm, internally, I was boiling (being a nurse for many years, having worked within surgical wards and theatres, gave me the calm outlook which was useful working with this challenging group).

Following sessions, the group started to describe clients' characters, personalities and events. The members of the group heard each other's stories and gave attention to each other's responses.

How was my style?

Sometimes, it was a confusing process to work with some workers and their traumatised clients. However, I became more curious and worked hard to understand myself as well as others in this group. I was responding to the members and their clinical material, by being calm and curious. I was listening to them wholeheartedly and with a relatively cool head which was important for them. I came across simply, mainly in the background, ordinary but being a dynamic participant in the process. I was conscious of not influencing the group decisions and workers' actions about their work with their clients and organisations. "It is not a clever interpretation of behavior that will most help the patient but rather a process of responsive engagement between the group members themselves" (Winnicott, 1975).

I provided constructive feedback to the group on all aspects of their performance and achievements, which were recognised by the group, including myself. The group felt positive and motivated when they understood and recognised their skills, knowledge, and individual contributions to their clients and workplaces. I offered special attention to the members, who seemed most irritated, more verbal or least verbal, felt left out or most angry. I was also interested in non-verbal behaviour and what it was indicating, how sessions ended and how I felt after the ending. My capacity to contain the group, enabled group members to express emotions, such as anger, hatred, internalised racism, envy and nurturing. Freud said, "The sudden traumatic development of transference creates a distance between the patient and the analyst" (Symington, 1993). It was important to understand the unconscious impulses of the group members and work to mitigate the distance.

Containing the negative transference and staying within the process was tiring, yet paradoxically their openness allowed the work to unfold. The group had the power of using me as a positive or negative object for change.

> The phenomenon of transference is of fundamental importance for all psychotherapy. In the strict and current sense, it describes an unconscious process by which the analyst becomes the representative of properties with which the parents, siblings and other significant figures were credited in early childhood. This is often expressed in symbolic ways. (Foulkes, 1984)

In further sessions, they talked about female clients who were the most excluded in society. In addition to mental and emotional distress, these women experienced poverty, isolation, homelessness, poor housing conditions, an uncertain residency status and were often victims/survivors of rape and DV. They included refugees, asylum seekers, trafficked women, mothers in crisis, women affected by forced marriage, FGC (female genital cutting), older or disabled women affected by poor health conditions and life-limiting illnesses. The workers felt helpless and hopeless and had an overwhelming urge to rescue their clients. Although their need for therapy and emotional support services was high, these clients faced barriers in accessing services which are often not offered in their mother tongue. Members challenged me as I was, for them, a representative of the TC. They referred their clients to the Centre but from time to time, due to long waiting lists, the TC could not offer therapy for all. I helped them to use external networks and other resources to refer their clients to. Some members would make this matter a political issue and say, "the Government does not provide enough funding and they use us like slaves."

Sometimes they would express their admiration towards me but other times, they would be very critical of me. When the group was very critical, Fiona would try to rescue me as if I was her mother although she was still angry with her mother. She would say:

> Maybe this is the way we need to learn, and we must have the same response towards our clients. We can't solve their problems, but we can listen carefully. I think, they only need good ears. But I get very angry with my clients. If we are helping women who are suffering or have suffered domestic violence, take more charge of their own lives. It is essential that we do the same.

Despite the hard feelings which were expressed in the process, the group members achieved a sense of closeness and togetherness by the ninth session. They were able to explore their experiences and inadequacies, despite their fears and vulnerabilities. As the group became more cohesive, they were more open and honest about their work and learnt how to avoid burnout.

Aisha said,

> I have found the group supportive and generous. It is different from supervision sessions which I had in the past. In some ways I feel safer exploring the difficulties that I've had about relating to my clients. But also wondering why, I feel safer. I think Dilek is an outsider. She has nothing to do with our workplaces ...

In the tenth session, I mistakenly attempted to end the session ten minutes before the usual time. Suddenly there was a brief silence. Gill immediately said, "Dilek, we have ten more minutes!"

It felt like a child screaming as if the mother had suddenly stopped feeding them!

I immediately admitted my mistake and apologised but I was mindful of the group's capacity to manage this mistake. My apology was not about sidestepping my error, it was about encouraging them to talk about it and see what they could make of it. They all seemed pleased to see me make a mistake and my acceptance of it. My countertransference was relief. However, this incident gave me the opportunity to explore my guilt and insecurities in my own clinical supervision. "Anyone who is afraid of ever making mistakes may end up not making anything" (Casement, 2008).

Gill said,

No, you can't take our ten minutes away from us! We have more things to say. But I am also wondering if you did this on purpose.

Because it is not possible for analyst to avoid making mistakes, it is important that there is always room for a patient to correct the analyst, and for the analyst not only to be able to tolerate being corrected but also to be able to make positive use of these corrective efforts by the patient. (ibid)

Somehow, Gill could not believe that I could make a mistake! I smiled. There was laughter in the room. In those ten minutes, quite a lot of emotions and thoughts were expressed by group members, particularly those who had been more silent and rigid. This gave rise to a degree of intimacy. I noticed the establishment of group trust and the creation of mutual exploration.

Fiona disclosed that as a child she was fed up with her silent and perfect mother who she believed had been traumatised as a child. She linked this insight to relationship dynamics in the group and to her clients. She acknowledged harbouring strong feelings towards me. Transference feelings were acknowledged by the group. Hilary, who was usually a silent member, challenged Fiona: "Maybe you are a bit like your mother. Trying to be perfect and strong but you are not."

Fiona suddenly burst into tears and shared more about herself. Carol became anxious and changed the subject from personal to professional life and said,

The most violent, most severe and chronic incidents are perpetrated by men against women and their children. Arab women often keep it to themselves, ashamed, embarrassed by what is happening to them, unsure of where to go, what kind help they can get and fearful about doing anything which can make the situation worse. They are frightened of their husbands as they are constantly threatened to be killed or their children being removed.

Beatrice supported this view by agreeing with her and said,

> Divorce is still seen as a taboo in my culture although we have been living in Europe for so many years. My sister is still living with her psychopath husband. I hate this! I hope, one day he won't kill her. My parents are feudal, and they would feel shamed if their daughters divorced. They usually keep it secret from the community and their neighbours. Divorce is seen as a failure and an attack on family honour.

She was in tears. Hilary handed her some tissues. It is typical in such circumstances and parallel to this, that personal feelings materialise in the group where some aspects of the client have not been digested or processed. It was elaborated with group members introducing other parts of themselves such as internal values: conscious and unconscious.

I said, "I wonder if you feel that I am not helpful enough in this group. Fiona is now very upset, and Beatrice, perhaps you feel I carry the values of unhelpful Turkish/Kurdish mothers as I come from Turkey?"

They were puzzled by my comment but ignored it. Instead, they turned to Fiona and said they really understood her. Beatrice appeared more thoughtful after my comment. The group was able to provide a supportive space for each other. They shared their anxieties and realised that others were facing similar cultural issues. Elaine said,

> I feel that I am responsible for offering an environment where the client feels safe to explore each stage in their process and in their own unique way at their pace. If we don't have support for our work and wellbeing, we may have to struggle and burnout and this will not be useful for the work.

I think, sometimes clinging to our rigid professional roles makes it difficult to see the strengths in our clients and our own vulnerabilities as practitioners. As a group analyst, I found this work rewarding and moving as members of the group tried to resolve some of their deep pain and professional difficulties.

The group members thought that the process of a twelve-week group had been the main form of support for them to remain focused on their difficulties. They helped each other to use their resources better, manage their workload and to challenge each other's maladaptive ways of coping. The group had served as a framework for their learning and development and although it was a time-limited process, they were able to internalise the positive learning group process.

Hilary told the group that she thought this was "a very special project" especially as a women-only space. She described how she felt "much more in control," taking decisions more easily, felt valued at work including her male colleagues and other men in her life. "It's helping me in so many ways."

Beatrice followed and said, "It is a big step to be in this group. I am surprised that I am talking about my clients and my feelings."

The group understood that if they ignored the stress symptoms, they would enter a state called: Burnout. Fineman (1986) describes this as "a state of emotional and physical exhaustion with a lack of concern for the job and a low trust of others." The group agreed that accepting their vulnerabilities and not excessively defending against it would be a valuable experience for them and their clients.

When we do not have enough support, we absorb more distress from our clients. Stress is not only taken in from patients or clients but may emanate from work or the organisation in which we work. Many professionals in care jobs such as refugee workers, counsellors, therapists, and DV workers in the community find it hard to face the fact that they might feel a decrease in empathy for, or even become tired, unhappy, and cynical towards, their clients. These reactions are usually not recognised as symptoms of stress. Through our work, at the TC, the question of work-related stress began to be recognised. Indeed, the aims of reflective sessions were as Freud said, "to make what is unconscious conscious" (Sandler et al., 1992). If the worker lacks support in the workplace and denied spaces to enable exploration of their feelings and thoughts, they may end up thinking that, "it is all the clients' fault," especially instances when the clients miss a session.

Carol described herself by saying, "I've never really been good at putting myself first and still I am not good."

She described focusing on the demands of family life and work emotionally and practically in a way that she never gets time to think about herself. "This is the space for me. You know it feels quite safe."

She described how coming to the group helped her to think about moving into management. She tried out this idea at work, even with some male colleagues and the response has been positive: "So, that feels really good." "I was thinking of myself as you were talking."

She then went on to describe eating better and attending a gym regularly and also had positive feedback from clients, "little things, that mean a lot."

I suggested that she was describing the group as being a catalyst for change.

Carol asked, "Is it the group?"

Gill agreed by saying: "Today for the first time I felt no resistance against coming here. I was actually looking forward to it."

She described not giving herself a hard time despite work pressures and seeing this as a space or time for herself. She said,

We don't want it to finish. The group has made a great impact on my professional life. The whole group including you (meaning me) often brought things into my awareness that I might not have thought about as a counsellor. I am fascinated to discover my feelings. I think theory is not enough. Life experience, work experience, group experience and theory all important. It is exciting. It made me think about the complexity of clients' lives, how I can really offer a safe space and a reflective and empathic relationship to accompany clients on their journey. As a counsellor, I work with clients who have experienced racism, as well as domestic violence. They think that racism and domestic violence are the most painful experience in their lives.

Gill went on to describe, telling her manager that she would not take on an unreasonable workload.

I said, "So, you have found your voice to say, no."

She said,

Yes. I used to be afraid of losing my job but now I really don't care. Life is too short to worry about jobs. My mental health is important. Through this group work, I understood that I have lots of skills and I can get another job!

I suggested that there may be some idealisation of the group. However, this was not picked up by any of the participants. There was still some resistance in the group.

Beatrice who had already spoken, referred to last week when Fiona who was not able to attend on this occasion, had become very upset. The room fell silent at this point. Then the woman who had raised the matter commented on how she had worked hard at challenging other people. She had checked out with other members of the group whether she had been too harsh towards Fiona who was upset the previous week. They reassured her and said, "No, you were not harsh."

Aisha asked if others had felt upset by Fiona's absence. I reminded the group that it was Fiona who had become upset, had described a difficult relationship with her mother and this might have been an example of her transferring feelings about her mother onto the group. Also, her absence was planned at the beginning of the group work due to a hospital appointment.

However, there was still some discussion about the fact that Fiona had cried. They did not want to hear what I said. I also said that to cry in front of others is to take a risk and Fiona had taken that risk, showed her vulnerability and allowed others to see this. There was another long silence.

Hilary said that she found hugging difficult and she had wondered if she should have hugged Fiona but had felt unable to do so. She then went on to describe a childhood which was abusive and where there was no love.

She began to cry and the woman next to her touched her arm and gave her some tissues.

At this point, I asked Carol who had not yet spoken at all in the group how she felt and if she wanted to comment. She did not. She was still resisting sharing her feelings. Discussion returned to Fiona again who had cried, and the group needed to know who had had upset her. It seemed easy for them to talk about the absent person.

Beatrice suddenly started talking about her clients at work – women in psychiatric treatment, those fleeing DV and using drugs and alcohol in front of their children and children on the child protection register. She described working with a woman who was very distressed and how she felt for the first time that, she could make a real difference. She again shifted the conversation suddenly by saying that she was very worried about the group ending and how it had been so hard to "find a space for me." "Valuing yourself ... valuing your clients, it's like a chain, a chain I don't want to break. We have learnt to take responsibility." She continued, "If the group was permanent that would be great ... But even if I could hold on to some of what I have learnt ..."

I opened this up to all women: "What about the group ending next week?"

This question was at first, avoided – no one addressed/acknowledged what I had said directly and instead Gill said how hard it is to work with DV and compounded by the absence of support. Suddenly everyone started to say that 12 weeks was not long enough, 20 weeks would be better. Hilary said, "But life is not permanent either. I suppose we have to say goodbye properly!"

Gill said, "This is a textbook response ... I don't want this group to end."

Hilary said, "Dilek, you don't use textbook sentences much. Is it because of your English? I must say, Dilek's interpretations are always very different and surprising ... Maybe it is a cultural thing!"

I was not sure whether she was complimenting me or undermining. I just smiled I did not want to challenge and draw attention to me at that stage.

Elaine said how important it was that the group was diverse. This led to very animated discussions about previous experiences where diversity had not been handled well – women had been at university and on courses – where their ethnicity had been ignored.

I was really relieved to come to this group and see diversity dealt with well. I am White/Jewish. This identity of mine is never acknowledged in other groups but here, I feel I am part of the group with my differences although I may also be representing mainstream, dominant culture.

Gill continued to say:

I just understand that we are doing intense trauma work daily. Some days I feel as if I am beaten up by my clients' or by their partners or by the managers at work. I clearly see this now how awful it was not having support at my workplace. What will happen after this group ends?

I acknowledged those feelings and said we would be collecting feedback forms where they could express their feelings and we would apply for more funding in the future. Thoughts and feelings remained in the room for some time and seemed to impede anyone from moving on.

I received positive feedback towards the end. The only criticism was "why the group is short term." I found it difficult to welcome the positive trans-ference feelings from the group, as I was used to receiving negative trans-ference feelings from colleagues and clients. As an intercultural "reflective group conductor," I found the work both rewarding and moving as members of the group workers learnt to separate what was personal from professional issues. They had good enough insight and capacity to engender respect and trust regarding their differences.

Beatrice said.

Thank you Dilek for your generosity for this group. I genuinely would like to say thank you. Not a plastic one. A Real one. I enjoyed being here and learning in this group. I hope to come back next term.

Gill described attending a psychotherapy course, where the whole assumption was that a white, middle-class perspective was the norm. She described how she was made to feel that counselling and therapy were not for her, and this made her nervous about attending the reflective sessions at the centre. Then she said, "But obviously here things are different."

The discussion then turned to change – some women felt that it was not possible to change institutional racism, that you were left powerless and could not challenge or have an impact in the face of such oppression. Carol challenged this view and used her own experiences to illustrate the point.

There was some acceptance that: "While you might not change anything, you could let people know, what you think and this would be, "doing your bit."

I did not leave the group at this safe space, but asked what would happen if you challenged an authority figure and sought to make changes – what might the fear be? The group did not seem to want to take this on board and were happier to stay with the concept that in these situations they had minimal power.

Last session

They said that all week they were thinking about the group and its ending. The conversation turned to a discussion about how many of them had attended other groups/support groups/courses connected to counselling and therapy and how they felt. In those groups, they were usually in the minority, the only nonwhite woman and felt those groups were not really for them. They compared this group with other groups, including their family groups. "Here, in this room, it feels that this is for me." "Here, it is great to come to a group where race is not an issue."

I turned to Elaine and Diane and asked how it felt to be in the group as a white woman. Diana did not articulate her feelings and looked silently uncomfortable like the rest of the group.

Elaine said,

That's ok. I am fine. I was able to talk in this group. I don't feel guilty that I am white. I didn't choose to be born white. I used to feel guilty. God knows why. I think it was middle class feelings of guilt!

She seemed shy but genuine in her expression of being ok. Carol, who could be abrupt with her expressions, said, "It was bad of me not to recognize you as white."

Beatrice questioned that comment as to why she did not see the colour of a white woman, but they didn't want to make further comments on that.

I said, "It seems difficult to work with differences but somehow you feel safe within your similarities."

My aim was to help the group to get going. I acknowledged their fears and anxieties and then raised the subject of confidentiality. I said, "You may be worried about whether this is a safe place to express some of your feelings. I am aware that this is the last session and you don't want any conflict."

The women then moved on to what felt like safer ground by saying that it was so important that the TC offer free therapy also at a low cost, making it accessible to BMER and working-class women with mental health problems. There was a discussion about how therapy often is for "certain types only" and the domination of therapy groups by white middle-class women.

There was some agreement that BMER women were pushing at the door asking for services, not passively waiting as victims. Talk shifted to the challenging nature of the work regarding DV and how often there are unexpressed feelings of anger present in the work. Hilary described hearing her parents' row often as a child and growing up wanting peace and avoiding conflict, though she acknowledged that as a manager she must deal with conflict and not avoid it.

I raised the fact that the group session was nearly over – she brought the discussion round to the way the group holds women. One woman described it as, "Feeding each other."

Carol said,

Being a member in the group has given me the opportunity to listen to different views, helped me to consider how I experience clients, what it brings up for me and how I contain those feelings/thoughts. After such toxic, damaging work experience, joining this group felt important, enabled me to challenge myself.

Here, we take responsibility for what we do and how we feel.

Beatrice said,

I must confess to the group that, I am learning to be calm like you Dilek. I am really fascinated that, whatever we said, especially negative feelings and thoughts; you listened and reflected on our experience and feelings rather than defending the TC and yourself. You don't try to show how much you know! This group is not easy ... You are too modest ... How can you be calm and modest like this?

Aisha said, "But if you are too modest people may think that you are stupid."
"That's right," said Diane.
 Elaine and Gill were nodding their heads.
 Carol bravely said, "I think this is what I thought about Dilek!"
 They all laughed, and she shared her experience as a professional, how she was very aggressive with one client because the client had no sense of gratitude. When she mentioned gratitude, they all laughed and said, "Like us, we find it difficult to show gratitude to Dilek!"
 This realisation was interesting. The group was actively helping Carol and each other on this matter. They shared their feelings of being angry and defensive towards their clients and their managers.
 As a group, they gained understanding and awareness that failing to contain aggression may create a scapegoating environment in the work or any other place. They appreciated that their aggression was contained in this group.
 Fiona said,

Working within this structure allows me to absorb rather than respond to what was being said. I thought this was a useful, working structure in the process. Reading articles or working on individual cases may not have been as useful as this structure.

Gill said, "I agree with you. Listening to others and reflecting, on specific issues thrown up by client work, has also helped me to gain some perspective and insight on how my clients might feel or understand the therapeutic relationship."

All women decided to have each other's e-mail addresses and contact numbers, to have regular professional contact when the group ended. They decided to keep this group as a "self-management/ reflective group." Carol said, "We can use my office room if you like. I may be able to get it free for us. Aisha also offered her office space for the group."

There was then a long silence before the group ended which felt different from previous silences and "held" comfortably by the group. This felt more real than the idealisation at the beginning of the session.

My general thoughts and feelings about work

All the workers were interested in the idea that reflective practice can positively contribute to the maintenance and development of ethical practice and in return they would be confident and successful in working with their clients. They became clear about their roles, boundaries, and responsibilities; started to explore their jobs and dysfunctional workplaces and whether they have enough resources to do their job well. Dealing with loneliness at work could be very difficult so they felt confident to raise concerns with their organisational managers. They ensured, their work was planned and purposeful and that progress was regularly monitored. They developed a good mental space for better practice and reduced feelings of guilt, shame, and started to look after themselves before they looked after their clients. They were able to talk about race and cultural issues. White therapists stopped worrying about being called "racist," and racially minoritised therapists raised issues and were not inhibited by a fear of being described as having a "chip on your shoulder."

Reflective group processes came from a positive choice rather than one that was forced upon the group and facilitator. A reflective framework provided a concrete example of containment (Bion, 1989). I think the group and the facilitator (me), created a space that made everyone's containing abilities available, as Bion says: "Think the thoughts" (ibid). I was just instrumental in holding the setting, providing a containing presence, and facilitating honest-frank communication.

It was not easy for me to work with some groups, individuals, and organisational managers but I was able to become more curious and worked hard to understand myself as well as others. In the 1990s, I was working part-time with different therapeutic organisations. I had three or four different supervisors in a month. This situation was useful, interesting but demanding. All my supervisors were Western-European psychoanalysts or psychoanalytic therapists. They always found my work interesting, but some were sceptical about whether BMER clients were able to use analytic therapy. When I presented my work, they all had different views.

However, that situation helped me to find my own way of thinking and be creatively independent.

Winnicott, an English paediatrician and psychoanalyst, introduced the concept of the "good-enough mother"– the mother who when her child throws the food back at her, does not react to this event as a personal attack but can hear this event as the child expressing its temporary inability to cope with the external world. Winnicott points out that it is very hard for any mother to be "good-enough" unless she herself is also held and supported, either by the child's father, or another supportive adult. This provides the "nursing triad" which means that the child can be held even when it needs to express his or her negativity or murderous rage. This concept provides a very useful analogy for supervision, where the "good-enough" therapists or other helping professionals can survive the negative attacks of the client through the strength of being held within and by the supervisory relationship (Hawkins et al., 2013). The impact of a traumatic memory continues throughout the client's life and those who witness the survivor's trauma (therapist) may experience some of the pain and might be injured vicariously if help is not offered and received. It is important to help workers facilitate their client's ego maturity. It is about having "good enough" support, one that mitigates the impact of secondary injury and facilitating an increased capacity to enjoy life and work.

Reflective sessions are not only for therapeutic work. For example, the Nursing and Midwifery Council recognises clinical supervision as an important part of clinical governance and a means of maintaining and improving standards of patient care. We work with human beings not with machines.

To be an analytic/intercultural psychotherapist, as well as working with the Centre, was a big challenge but I survived and enjoyed the work. Being an immigrant in the United Kingdom, I learnt to build my own support system with my colleagues, intercultural supervisors or my socially diverse, intercultural friends.

When working with themes of diversity, it is important to be curious and to understand race, beliefs, values, and culture and not make assumptions. My diverse training, ethnicity, accent, and other differences and experiences gave me an opportunity to meet hundreds of people from across the world. I was able to turn my own painful life journey into a positive one. I experienced DV in my twenties as a young mother, separated from my loved ones and especially from my only child. I was a political prisoner in Turkey and had experienced state violence. I had had years of individual and group analysis to heal myself. Positive internal resources, which come from my early childhood, helped me to survive and to enjoy life in the United Kingdom.

The group was able to provide a supportive intercultural space, share their anxieties and realise that others were facing similar issues.

The time limited reflective group facilitated DV workers to improve the quality of their work, develop insight, awareness, and an understanding of their professional style, behaviour, greater capacity to be in touch with expressions and to recognise feelings, skills, ability, and being able to take responsibility for relationships with their clients and colleagues.

I would like to take the opportunity to thank all managerial, clinical supervisors and colleagues that I worked with throughout my professional life.

References

Al-Khalaf, L., Topping, A. (2020). Over half of UK women killed by men die at hands of partner or ex, *The Guardian*. Available at: https://www.theguardian.com/uk-news/2020/feb/20/over-half-of-uk-women-killed-by-men-die-hands-current-ex-partnerac-cessed 17th March 2023

Behr, H. (1995). The integration of theory and practice. In: Sharpe, M. (ed.) *The Third Eye, Supervision of Analytic Groups*. London: Routledge.

Bion, W. R. (1989). *Experiences in Groups, and Other Papers*. London: Tavistock/Routledge.

Bowlby, J. (1982). Attachment and loss: Retrospect and prospect. *American Journal of Orthopsychiatry*, *52*, 664–678.

Casement, P. (2008). *Learning from Our Mistakes*, b*eyond Dogma in Psychoanalysis and Psychotherapy*. New York: Psychology Press.

Fineman, S. (1986). *Social Work Stress and Intervention*. Aldershot, Hants, England: Gower.

Foulkes, S. H. (1984). *Therapeutic Group Analysis*. London: Routledge.

Hawkins, P., Ryde, J., Shohet, R., Wilmot, J. (2013). *Supervision in the Helping Professions*. Maidenhead: Open University.

Hearthstone, Homes for Haringey Limited. (2019). NAFSIYAT intercultural therapy centre, contract for the specialist domestic violence therapeutic and counseling services.

Herman, J. L. (1992). *Trauma and Recovery*. London: Pandora.

Maguire, M. (1997). Envy between women. In: Lawrence, M., Campling, J. (eds) *Psychotherapy with Women. Perspectives*. Basingstoke, Hampshire: Macmillan.

Sandler, J., Dare, C., Holder, A. (1992). *The Patient and the Analyst: The Basis of the Psychoanalytic Process*. New York: Karnac.

Symington, N. (1993). *Narcissism: A New Theory*. London: H Karnac (Books) Ltd.

Wilde, O., Holland, V., Redman, A. (2007). *The Wit and Humor of Oscar Wilde*. New York: Dover.

Winnicott, D. W. (1975). *The Child, the Family, and Outside World*. Harmondsworth: Penguin.

Chapter 5

Nafsiyat Refugee Project
An Intercultural Psychotherapy Supervision Model

Gita Patel

Introduction

Nafsiyat Intercultural Therapy Centre has been offering psychoanalytic psychotherapy to Black and minority communities since 1983. The models used follow the original work of Jafar Kareem outlined in intercultural therapy (Kareem and Littlewood, 1992). In 1995, Nafsiyat set up the Refugee Project to meet the mental health needs of the new refugee communities arriving in the United Kingdom. In this chapter, I will outline the work of the project and then look specifically at how the intercultural supervision model was developed to enable Refugee Centres to deliver psychotherapy within their communities. I will then go on to think about the model of intercultural supervision and how it can be used for marginalised communities to increase the delivery and efficacy of psychoanalytic psychotherapy.

Community-based therapy

One of the first tasks of the Project was to find out about the communities we were serving and carry out a needs assessment. With this in mind, the Project met with local refugee community organisations, the communities we focused on at the time were: Somali, Turkish, Kurdish, Eritrean, Ethiopian, Congolese and people from Sierra Leone. Part of the work was to introduce the concept of psychoanalytic thinking to these communities who might not have an awareness of Western psychotherapy models. In their own communities and particularly in their home country, they may have had many different methods of supporting mental health, such as talking to elders, taking part in community rituals or other community interventions that were accepted and used by individuals. Arriving in a new country, it would become difficult to transport these methods and the efficacy of community rituals would not necessarily survive the migration process. Newly arriving in a country and expecting to talk to a stranger about your problems was not something that many would have considered. There was also the issue for

DOI: 10.4324/9781003380214-8

some asylum seekers about how talking to someone might affect their asylum claims and trusting anyone with their information was difficult.

The Project worked around four main areas of service delivery. Firstly, individual therapy in the Nafsiyat consulting rooms, secondly providing information or psycho-education sessions in community settings. Thirdly, from our needs assessment, we found many clients were reluctant to leave the safety of their community organisations for psychotherapy sessions. To meet this need, we created the Crisis Intervention Project which placed therapists within different community organisations offering one-to-one psychotherapy. The therapists were from the communities that they served and were supervised by Nafsiyat in a weekly group. Soon after the Project was set up, we were overwhelmed with referrals from statutory agencies. We were unable to accept all these referrals and added a fourth aspect of supervision: consultancy and training, to enable professionals such as GPs, teachers, social workers, psychotherapists, and counsellors to deliver services to refugee clients throughout the country.

These various aspects of work provided particular challenges in supervision: the delivery of psychotherapy at Nafsiyat was what therapists had been trained for but supervising individual therapists to deliver psycho-education sessions and one-to-one therapy sessions in their own communities, was more complicated. No therapy courses had prepared them for this work and the supervision played a key role in the success of this approach. Most psychoanalytic trainings did not and still do not, consider the political, social and cultural environment as key to the understanding of the internal world of our clients and this was a learning process for many of the therapists. In addition, therapists with little or no experience of community work had to be supervised to work with the community which was an essential aspect of understanding the context of our clients' lives. During supervision, a constant area of discussion was keeping the balance between the analytic thinking and the social-cultural aspects of the communities. In the Crisis Intervention Project, the therapists were working within their own community organisations and this provided the opportunity for the supervision to examine the personal and professional aspects of their culture and how in psychoanalytic therapy the issues of transference and countertransference interplay with culture. One differing aspect of the intercultural supervision model is helping the supervisee understand the larger socio-political context of their patients' lives and how it links to the work in the consulting room (Gentile, 2010).

Themes emerging in supervision

Culture and identity

The knowledge of a person's culture can have beneficial effects and also bring challenges to the work if the therapist begins to make assumptions about a particular culture. It is essential for therapists to explore the client's personal understanding of their culture, not their own understanding or something that they may have heard or read about. Culture is not a rigid idea but is a dynamic process that interacts with an individual's own ideas, morals and ethics (Kareem and Littlewood, 1992). Intercultural therapy aims not just to get information about culture but to open up the psychoanalytic space in the sessions to explore with the client how their culture is part of their personality and internal world. Often, therapists will assume that the client knows about their culture and identity, but the client may have many mixed feelings and there can be a "splitting" in order for them to cope with racism and prejudices. They may have many unconscious feelings about race, culture and racism, of which they are not aware and the role of the therapist and supervisor is to bring these ideas into the consulting room rather than just asking about concrete aspects of the client's culture. We should apply the same psychoanalytic curiosity and exploration of culture as we would to any other aspect of the client's life. Many clients newly arrived in the United Kingdom may have a lot of ambivalent feelings about their culture and the therapy aimed to allow this exploration within a safe environment.

Vignette

One of the issues that arose in supervision was the idea that the client would know their own views on their culture and their identity. Psychoanalytic thinking informs us that we are always trying to work with the unconscious and a patient's view of their identity and culture could be embedded in the unconscious and only come into play in the transference during the analytic work. For example, the instance of a young person who was being seen by a therapist in the Refugee Project was brought to the supervision group. The client arrived here at the age of 8 and immediately started school, where she thrived. She learnt to speak English within an impressively short period of time and became very comfortable with her school life. She talked about being Westernised and feeling rightly proud of her achievements and her ability to settle into the United Kingdom in her new life. She came to Nafsiyat at the age of 20 presenting with depression, anxiety and panic attacks, she was also self-harming and developing a fear of others which led her to withdraw socially. Her work began to suffer, and she found it hard to function, she sought help from her GP who referred her to Nafsiyat.

During her therapy, she was reluctant to talk about her past refugee experience, focused on her current life and how she was managing at work. She had lost both of her parents in her country and had witnessed a lot of violence around her, finally arriving in the United Kingdom alone and scared. When the therapist tried to raise issues about her refugee experience, she would be dismissive saying it was a long time ago and now "I am just like you". In supervision, we discussed how the client was trying hard to identify with her therapist making comments such as "You know what our community is like" in a derogatory way. She was trying to prove to her therapist that she was different; she was not like others in her community and in doing, so she was denigrating her own identity. The therapist, initially, was praising her for doing so well and managing to achieve all her goals in life. The client had arrived in therapy saying she wanted to feel better about herself and function better at work, and the therapist was trying to support her in this. During supervision, we began to see how the client was drawing the therapist into her world where they could both see the client only as a functioning professional, almost erasing her identity and culture. We discussed how the therapist could begin to address this and allow the client to make associations with what it meant to be a refugee or asylum seeker from her country. When the therapist did this in the session, the client brought only negative associations that she had internalised from the attitudes of people around her to refugees; the image of the "poor little refugee" who could not speak the language, the portrayal of refugees in the media and the racism around that. The therapist found this moving and using the supervision discussed with the client how they could both see her eight-year-old asylum seeker self and allow her to see how she was denigrating herself when she tried to erase this part of herself. Initially, the client began to develop some negative transference towards the therapist; angry with her for bringing in a cultural aspect to the work, instead of allowing them to stay in the false professional identity that she had developed. As we were aware that the responsibility of the intercultural therapist is to address the negative transference in the context of culture (Kareem, 1992), the therapist persisted with raising the issues in a sensitive manner. Over time, the client was able to talk about the trauma and loss, her refugee experience, the violence she had witnessed, and aspects of her life before she came to the United Kingdom, and what these experiences meant to her. The splits that she had created began to ease as she was able to think about various aspects of her life and with them the panic attacks and anxiety began to feel more manageable, and her self-harming considerably reduced. The supervision also allowed the therapist and client to explore her identity and relationship to her country of origin which was impeded by her fear of getting in touch with the vulnerable child part of her. However, over time, they both began to see that as well as loss, trauma and pain, there was something valuable and precious in her memories that she could use to help her in her professional life rather than hinder it.

In this case, the client was struggling with her identity, and this was manifested in her panic attacks and her withdrawal from life. The client felt her panic attacks were purely related to her job and her internal struggles were not conscious. She needed the therapist to be able to see this unconscious struggle and help to make it a conscious idea that they could both work on. She had managed the racism she had experienced by splitting and almost denying her heritage to try to fit in and become more "Westernised". Initially, she was resistant to discussing her culture but once she was able to own all her identities including functioning as a professional and a refugee who had experienced a huge loss of country and culture, the therapist and client were able to explore the complexities of loss and separation and her developing identity.

During supervision, we used the idea of the proxy-self (Thomas, 1998) to think about this client. She was initially presenting her proxy-self devoid of her identity and her ethnicity as she had internalised the idea that this is what was required in a professional setting. Indeed, it was this proxy-self that had served her so well since arriving in the United Kingdom and helped her to achieve her career goals. She was simply using this familiar part of her in the Westernised setting of a therapy session. She was not conscious of any other part of herself, and it was the therapist's role to keep the eight-year-old asylum seeker and her cultural background in her mind and bring it into the session at the appropriate time. Her way of coping was internalised racism (Rose, 1997, Speight, 2007) where she was denigrating her ethnicity and her refugee status in order to survive the challenges she was facing. She had unconsciously taken in the racism and prejudices of others resulting in a "subdominant" identity Littlewood and Ababio (2019). Through the supervision, the therapist was able to understand the idea of internalised racism and internal oppression, which can have a significant effect on the way a therapist conceptualises a client's distress (Agoro, 2019). In this case, it helped the therapist to interpret the negative transference and raise the client's unconscious oppression in the consulting room. The intercultural therapy model embraces the idea that an individual's distress is not always just a manifestation of the inner, psychic world or part of their pathology (Kareem, 1992). In this case, it was related to socio-political factors in her country of origin and the racism, prejudices, and perceptions she experienced as a refugee in the United Kingdom, leading to internalised disturbed thinking, splits, and struggles.

Supervising therapists from Black, Asian and minority communities

Working with therapists from the refugee communities that they serve, raised interesting issues in supervision; the therapist can have a very Westernised view of the expectations in supervision developed from their own training, and their personal therapy, where the issue of race or culture was not considered to be a part of the analytic thinking. It is as though they had been trained to leave behind their cultural identity in order to come into the therapy world and supervision sessions. Therapists from minority communities cannot necessarily hide their identity in the consulting room, they may have identified cultural features such as the colour of their skin, or accent and to ignore this can miss important issues in the transference and counter-transference. The issues of race and racism are very much present in the consulting room with all clients Black and white (Thomas, 1992), yet often they cannot be brought under supervision.

In the Refugee Project supervision group, supervisees were exploring how to work interculturally, which was different to how they had previously been working. The supervision encouraged discussion and self-awareness of their culture and how that manifested in the transference and countertransference issues in the consulting room. Even when supervisors and supervisees are both from minority communities there can still be a struggle to consider the intercultural model of working as most therapists and supervisors have been trained in organisations where there is little or no teaching about working interculturally. The supervision encouraged supervisees to think inter-culturally and bring their understanding of their own or their communities' culture into the supervision and then into the consulting room.

Vignette

Clients may also have different expectations of therapists from Black, Asian, and refugee communities and particularly therapists from their own culture. One male supervisee brought the issue of a client's relationship with his wife and daughters expecting the male therapist to agree with him about the role of the women in their culture. The male therapist and the client were from the same country, religion and culture and spoke the same language. The therapist in supervision was struggling to know how to respond to the client, on the one hand wanting to engage the client, as this group of refugee males rarely access psychotherapy, but also felt that his thoughts about his wife and daughters should be challenged as they were affecting his mental health. The client himself was very depressed with suicidal ideation, finding it hard to engage in daily life, whilst his wife and daughters, to him, seemed to be adapting more easily and engaging with life in the United Kingdom. As a result, he was becoming withdrawn and constantly observing and focusing on his wife and daughters' behaviour leading him to feel more depressed, angry and anxious. The therapist was able to explore this in the supervision balancing the cultural issues and the expectations of the client's family in the new society they were living in; through the exploration he was able to see that the issue that was central to the client was the idea of status and transition in the process of becoming a refugee. In the transference the client was trying to find some familiarity and an anchor, identifying with the male therapist to confirm his status as a man and head of his household. The client had been in a professional post in his country and now found himself working in casual manual jobs for which he was overqualified. In the client's culture the concept of status and honour is a very important part of life and he found himself losing the foundations of his status and honour along with the loss of his career. The family and particularly the women carry the honour of the family, and without honour, the family's place in society is threatened. Now without his career, he felt that his status in the United Kingdom was completely embedded in the behaviour of his wife and daughters. His status and his honour in the community was feeling fragile and unpredictable and this was causing him to become withdrawn and unhappy. The therapist through the supervision was able to interpret the transference and help the client see how he needed his relationship with the therapist to confirm his status as he was feeling a sense of deep loss and trauma. He was able to think about his own feelings rather than seeking to blame his wife and daughters about how they dressed or behaved. He felt that seeing them behaving in a more traditional way was the only thing that could reflect his status as a man in his community. The therapist in this case was exploring how he could demonstrate his understanding of the client and his cultural expectations without colluding and then challenge the re-enactments in the room and address their relationship through the transference. Over the course of the therapy, the client was able to focus on his own feelings and change the way he saw his own status and self-esteem, and began to change his behaviour towards his family, more able to accept his own difficulties with his transitions instead of focusing on the behaviour of others. His symptoms reduced as he was able to think through his struggles. He still felt depressed but no longer had suicidal thoughts and could identify causes for his depression and begin to address them in the therapy. The supervision enabled the therapist to use his own experiences of his community and his view on the traditions and cultural norms not just to understand and agree with the client, but through that understanding, begin to challenge and open up some of the client's thinking about his culture and integrate it into his new life in the United Kingdom.

Language

The therapists in the supervision group spoke many different languages, sometimes sharing a language with the client and at other times working in English. The Nafsiyat Intercultural model has always given the client a choice of seeing someone from their own culture or seeing someone who is not from their culture. One of the issues that arose was how to translate the training and learning into the mother tongue language. Finding words for transference or the unconscious can be difficult, sometimes leading to complex explanations which can leave the client confused. In addition to the technical difficulties is the idea of how emotions are expressed, language can have a primal association and directly connect to emotions which can be lost in translation in the consulting room and can lead to emotional barriers

(Marcos, 1976) and estrangement in the transference. When working in English acknowledging this estrangement with the client is part of the intercultural work. This was openly discussed in the supervision group and brought up the issue of how other languages may express emotional pain in relation to physical pain. Some clients in the Project expressly requested to have therapy in English and not in their mother tongue. This could be seen as a possible defence against expressing primitive feelings and interpreted with the client during their sessions.

Working with boundaries in community settings

A recurring theme in supervision was the issue of boundaries, this is particularly problematic for therapists working within their own communities. On the one hand, offering therapy in community organisations is ideal for accessibility and reaching marginalised communities, but it also presents challenges for therapists and the expectations of us in our own communities. Some of the refugee communities we worked with were very small and that meant that most of the community knew the therapist and might encounter them in their lives outside therapy. The issue of confidentiality was paramount, and some therapists had to become slightly separate from their own communities in their personal lives, having to miss important community events in order to maintain boundaries. Some clients would expect the therapist to support them with other social issues and the centres that employed advice and support workers enabled the therapists to refer clients for other services allowing them to focus on the therapy. This was in a way a learning experience for the organisation about the idea of therapy and the boundaries that were set and enabled them to develop professional boundaries within their organisations. The framework of weekly sessions was also difficult to introduce to clients and to the centres generally, our therapists in supervision would find themselves having to write policies and guidelines for their organisations on the boundaries of therapy.

Qualified and experienced therapists often felt ill-equipped to work interculturally from their training. They wanted to think about intercultural work and how it can be used to enhance the analytic work and how it can be applied to the fundamental tenets of psychoanalysis such as transference, boundaries, attachment and the therapeutic alliance. In supervision, they sometimes felt that it was not possible to apply a Western model of once-weekly 50-minute sessions in the community settings they were based in and found it hard to apply their training to the work they were doing. However, the supervision group with the expertise and history of Nafsiyat, managed to hold onto the idea that this was possible and gave the therapists confidence to apply the model. When Nafsiyat was first established there was an idea that Black, Asian and minority clients could not use psychotherapy (Littlewood, 1992). The same was being said in many mainstream organisations about refugees, Black, Asian, minority, and refugee communities as being least likely to have access to psychotherapy, the main reason being that they do not fit into the "ideal" model based on Western practice, socially, culturally or economically (Gungor, 2019). Perhaps it is the model that is lacking rather than the clients who are unable to use therapy.

Intercultural supervision model

The Refugee Project is a useful, early example of an organisation responding to the needs of the community, and we have seen recent models of this. For example, with the Grenfell fire, newly arriving refugees and Covid-19, where Black, Asian and minority therapists have had to set up models usually in a short space of time to respond to the changing needs of the communities due to the socio-political situations that occur. The intercultural model has always integrated this approach in its work and as a result is a dynamic model that whilst keeping the psychoanalytic frame, uses it in a creative and innovative way to respond to actual needs in the communities it serves. The intercultural model is well placed to be used to work with new situations or circumstances, or groups of clients as it puts the community and its identity at the core of developing services, not just with Black, Asian, minority and refugee communities but with diverse marginalised communities who are not served by mainstream organisations. The starting point is not how this client will fit our services but how can our services understand and respond to the needs of this community. This was always and continues to be an overarching principle within Nafsiyat.

Balint (1948) recognises psychoanalytic supervision as being a hugely significant component of the psychoanalytic education experience. Watkins and Hook (2016) describe psychoanalytic supervision as the crux of the psychoanalytic education process and the single most important contributor to developing psychoanalytic competence. They go on to say that a "culturally inviting" supervision space requires two aspects: firstly, to make culture an indispensable component of their supervisory worldview, and secondly, to recognise that the supervisor is responsible for introducing culture into the supervision and initiating "cultural conversations".

Most training programmes, therapy, and supervision struggle to integrate intercultural work into the curriculum and as a result, supervisors may feel unable to offer intercultural supervision. One example is a team meeting where a therapist and their supervisor were present, the therapist was presenting a client they had been seeing for psychoanalytic psychotherapy for 18 months and was asked about the ethnicity of the client, neither they nor their supervisor knew the client's ethnicity and started describing the colour of the client's skin and eyes to try to tell the team or guess what their ethnicity might be. It is hard for most intercultural therapists to see how we could work with someone for this long without addressing their ethnicity.

If ethnicity had not been addressed by the client, it would be the therapist's and the supervisor's responsibility to raise the issue otherwise a large part of this client's identity is absent from the analysis. This is not an isolated incident, but from an intercultural approach, it demonstrates how aspects of Eurocentric supervision models constrict spaces for the client identity exploration and therefore impacts the quality and efficacy of the therapy. The impact of Eurocentric thinking and racism ripples through to the supervisory relationship and affects the relationship between therapist and supervisor and may get transferred to the client-therapist relationship (Mckenzie-Mavinga, 2019).

It also indicates the low status of race, and culture in mainstream psychoanalytic practice, there may be a concept of a purer form of psychoanalytic work, or "real psychoanalytic psychotherapy" compared to the work delivered by intercultural therapists. This results in the intercultural therapist especially if they are from a minority community being told by supervisors they are not "psychoanalytic enough" when they are thinking about sociocultural aspects of the client's lives.

Supervision can often miss the issues of race and culture within the psychoanalytic frame, or simply see ethnicity or race as a concrete fact rather than a dynamic process. If neither the supervisee nor the supervisor raises the issue, the client will be impacted, even to the point, as in the example above, where the client cannot bring their own ethnicity into an 18-month-long psychotherapy treatment. On occasion, there can be a situation where the client's race can be ignored and the therapy is then justified as providing the same service to every client regardless of their race. The aspect of race becomes simply an interesting additional fact rather than a critical part of the client's internal world, psyche and unconscious inner world and the lack of intercultural supervision can lead to missing the important aspects of clients' lives (Tummala-Narra, 2004). When a supervisor is able to deliver an intercultural stance which includes all aspects of a client's life including issues of race, refugee status, disability, gender, and sexuality then the understanding can be used by the supervisee in the sessions with the client. The intercultural model of supervision can apply not just to race but to other social criteria. Porter and Vasquez (1997) define feminist multicultural supervision as collaborative and mutual, attending to sociocultural processes. It also focuses on hierarchies, gender, race and diversity. Training for supervisors is mentioned by Falendar et al. (2013) stating that feminism and multiculturalism should be more than add-ons to the curriculum, they should be integrated throughout the curriculum in order to address professional competencies. When a supervisor provides "multiculturally competent" supervision, the supervisee is more likely to attend to the issues of the multicultural dynamics in the relationship with the client leading to a more effective treatment (Inman and Kreider, 2013, Ladany et al., 1997).

An important role of any psychoanalytic supervision is to enhance the skills and confidence of supervisees. Supervision that does not address the intercultural aspects can not only impact the client but also impact the supervisee who will not be developing their skills in working with a wide range of clients in a multicultural society. Supervisors who are able to consciously and consistently deliver a multiculturally competent supervision form strong working relationships that facilitate supervisee growth and clinical competence (Burkard et al., 2006, Ladany et al., 1997, Mori et al., 2009, Arpana et al., 2013). Whereas a supervisor's lack of multicultural awareness and competence can limit supervisees' development and self-efficacy within the supervisory and psychotherapy relationship.

The intercultural model is still sadly lacking in most mainstream psychotherapy services. Recently, several psychotherapy organisations have tried to add a policy on race and equality following the Black Lives Matter movement. Although this could be a good starting point, it demonstrates the idea that race is still just an "add on" in the psychotherapy world. The intercultural psychoanalytic psychotherapy and Nafsiyat have been around for decades and other models of therapy addressing race and culture have also been developed, yet issues of culture have still not been integrated into the structure of mainstream psychotherapy services, training and supervision. This will have an inevitable impact on the efficacy of therapists and the treatment that clients receive in our increasingly multicultural society. As mentioned, the intercultural therapy and supervision model is not just a model to examine race but can be used to think about developing an all-inclusive service that can work with gender, race, disability, sexuality and other intersecting identities. It is a model that is dynamic and can be used to respond to socio-cultural changes to increase the efficacy of psychotherapy services.

Conclusion

The Nafsiyat Refugee Project was a response to socio-political world events affecting refugee communities throughout the world. The intercultural model allowed the project to use the psychoanalytic frame to develop a model of supervision that directly addressed the needs of these new communities. It enabled us to supervise therapists using their own cultural awareness and cultural knowledge to contribute to the development of services in the community, and thereby reaching marginalised individuals who would otherwise have found it hard to access therapeutic support. Each community will have its own specific concerns and issues, but the intercultural model is designed to be a dynamic psychoanalytic model that can be used to address any group of clients who need an innovative and responsive model of therapy. There is still a lack of skills and training on intercultural work and supervision, new refugee communities are arriving in the United Kingdom daily and there is still a lack of psychotherapy services for these clients. Developing an intercultural model is still as relevant now as it was when Nafsiyat was first established in 1983. The Refugee Project was used to explore and develop the intercultural model of supervision, not as an add-on to the psychoanalytic supervision but instead, at the core of the client's psyche, their internal world and their unconscious world. It is also central to the development of the supervisee skills, both using intercultural concepts in the delivery of services and being able to use themselves and their own personal intercultural understanding to benefit the clients. Intercultural supervision can only increase the efficacy of the supervision, the supervisory relationship, the experiences and skills of the supervisee's development and ultimately, the efficacy of the therapy that is provided to clients.

References

Agoro, O. (2019). Who's being assessed? Post-modernism and intercultural therapy assessments: a synergetic process. In: Ababio, B., Littlewood R. (eds.) *Intercultural Therapy: Challenges, Insights and Developments*. London: Routledge.

Balint, M. (1948). On the psychoanalytic training system. *The International Journal of Psychoanalysis*, *29*, 163–173.

Burkard, A. W., Johnson, A. J., Madson, M. B., Pruitt, N. T., Contreras-Tadych, D. A., Kozlowski, J. M., ..., Knox, S. (2006). Supervisor cultural responsiveness and unresponsiveness in cross cultural supervision. *Journal of Counselling Psychology*, *53*, 288–301.

Falendar, C. A., Burnes, T. R., Ellis, M. V. (2013). Multicultural clinical supervision and benchmarks: Empirical support informing practice and supervisor training. *The counselling Psychologist*, *41*, 8–27.

Gentile, L., Ballou, M., Roffman, E., Ritchie, J. (2010). Supervision for social change: A feminist ecological perspective. *Women and Therapy*, *33*, 140–151.

Gungor, D. (2019). Group psychotherapy with Turkish Speaking women. In: Ababio, B., Littlewood, R. (eds.) *Intercultural Therapy: Challenges, Insights and Developments*. London: Routledge.

Inman, A. G., Kreider, D. E. (2013). Multicultural competence: Psychotherapy practice and supervision. *Psychotherapy*, *50*(3), 346.

Kareem, J. (1992). The Nafsiyat intercultural therapy centre: Ideas and experience in intercultural therapy. In: Kareem, J., Littlewood, R. (eds.) *Intercultural Therapy: Themes, Interpretations and Practice*. Blackwell Scientific Publications

Ladany, N., Inman, A. G., Constantine, M. G., Hofheinz, E. W. (1997). Supervisee multicultural case conceptualisation ability and self-reported multicultural competence as functions of supervisee racial identity and supervisor focus. *Journal of Counseling Psychology*, *44*, 284–293.

Littlewood, R. (1992). Towards An Intercultural Therapy. In: Kareem, J., Littlewood, R. (eds.) *Intercultural Therapy: Themes, Interpretations and Practice*. Blackwell Scientific Publications

Littlewood, R., Ababio, B. (2019) Process and development in intercultural therapy. In: Ababio, B. Littlewood, R. (eds.) *Intercultural Therapy: Challenges, Insights and Developments.* London: Routledge.

Marcos L. R. (1976). Bilinguals in psychotherapy: Language as an emotional barrier. *American Journal of Psychotherapy.* Oct1976,30, 4.

Mckenzie-Mavinga, I. (2019). The challenge of racism in clinical supervision. In: Ababio, B., Littlewood, R. (eds.) *Intercultural Therapy: Challenges, Insights and Developments.* London: Routledge.

Mori, Y., Inman, A. G., Caskie, G. I. L. (2009). Supervising international students: Relationship between acculturation, supervisor multicultural competence, cultural discussions, and supervision satisfaction. *Training and Education in Professional Psychology, 3,* 10–18.

Porter, N., Vasquez, M. (1997). Covision: Feminist supervision, process and collaboration. In Worell, J., Johnson, N.G. (eds.) *Shaping the Future of Feminist Psychology: Education Research & Practice* (pp. 155–171). Washington, DC: American Psychological Association.

Rose, E. (1997). Daring to work with Internalised racism. *Counselling,* 8, May 1997, 92–94.

Speight Suzette. (2007). Internalized racism: One more piece of the puzzle. *The Counselling Psychologist,* 35, N 126–134.

Thomas, L. (1992). Racism and psychotherapy: Working with racism in the consulting room - An analytic view. In Kareem, J., Littlewood, R. (eds.) *Intercultural Therapy: Themes Interpretations and Practice.* Oxford: Blackwell.

Thomas, L. (1998). Psychotherapy in the context of race and culture: An Intercultural Therapeutic Approach. in Fernando, S. (eds.) *Mental Health in a Multi-ethnic society: A multi-Disciplinary Handbook.* London: Routledge.

Tummala-Narra, P. (2004). Dynamics of race and culture in the supervisory encounter. *Psychoanalytic Psychology, 21,* 300–311.

Watkins, C. E., Jr. Hook, J. N. (2016). On a culturally humble psychoanalytic supervision perspective: Creating a cultural third. *Psychoanalytic Psychology, 33*(3), 487–517.

Chapter 6

Themes in an Intercultural Approach to Supervision

Working with Survivors of Abuse

Waheeda Islam

Working with survivors of abuse has been and continues to be, an experience that takes me to places within myself where there are both shadows and light; places where I am humbled, challenged and from where I grow. The depth of this work and the resources needed from client, therapist, and supervisor cannot be underestimated. Very early on as a counsellor, I realised that this work requires me to delve deeper into myself and has to be approached with greater compassion and heart.

> When survivors of complex trauma enter therapy, they are taking a huge risk, which must be honoured by the counsellor. To risk connection after being repeatedly betrayed is a signal that hope has not been extinguished. However, the fear of intimacy and closeness can create challenges when building the therapeutic relationship. You will need to understand these within the context of complex trauma and work towards providing a '... bridge from the world of trauma where needs were desperate and life threatening to a world where needs can not only be modulated, but also fulfilled (Jonathan Cohen, 1985, cited in Sanderson, 2013: 107).' (Sanderson, 2013, p. 107)

My training as an Islamic Counsellor through Stephen Maynard & Associates, deeply instilled in me the need to tread gently in the lives of others, to create safety through a process that recognised and honoured this huge trust being placed in me by clients. A "bridge from the world of trauma" (ibid) – to create a safe passage across this bridge requires much from the counsellor and essential support in the supervision process. In this chapter, I will draw on case studies from three areas of my work: at Nour – a UK National charity working with survivors of abuse, Women's Health and Family Services (WHFS) working with female genital cutting (FGC) survivors in London, and through work in my own private practice. I will highlight key relational processes that are integral to any supervision process that involves survivors of abuse. These key relational processes were identified through a formative assessment I undertook

DOI: 10.4324/9781003380214-9

when training as a supervisor. I was required to develop my own idiosyncratic model of supervision that was relevant to my field of work. I was surprised at the results that my research yielded. My surprise was not at the key relational processes that were highlighted, but at how many of these processes run parallel in a supervisory triad, when working with survivors of abuse.

Traditionally, parallel processes were viewed as unidirectional. Searles (1955) described what he termed as "reflection process," unconscious processes that are enacted in the supervisory relationship as a result of the therapist's work with the client. This idea of parallel processes developed over time; Bernard and Goodyear (2019, p. 74) present an aspect of its evolution as "a reenactment in one dyad (supervisor – supervisee or supervisee – client) of processes that are occurring in the other dyad"; a multidirectional flow, emanating from any individual within the supervisory triad, rippling outwards to the others. Parallel processes are a broadening of the concept of transference (Crowe et al., 2011), expanding to the transference and countertransference of supervisee and supervisor. Transference/countertransference is one relational dynamic, but there are many more that should be consciously harnessed in the supervision process for the best outcome for clients who are survivors of abuse. It is essential that any supervision model working with survivors of abuse has an intercultural, trauma-informed approach and sits within a wider social justice framework; "counselors and psychologists need to integrate a social justice perspective within the model so that counseling can serve to deconstruct injustice and oppression" (Martín-Baró, 1994, cited in Goodman, 2013, p. 400). An integrative, relational model of supervision, with heart, compassion, and justice at its core; where understanding of oppression and liberation of people form part of the ethical codes (Brown, 2016). A model that recognises the attunement and warmth that is needed when working with survivors of abuse. "To counterbalance the dehumanising abuse experience, you will need to be human in your responses rather than clinical, cold or distant" (Sanderson, 2013, p. 9).

Whilst it is beyond the scope of this chapter to share the entirety of my research in its richness and depth, what I hope to demonstrate are the key relational processes that run parallel in a supervisory triad; processes which require an intentional engagement from the practitioner when working with this client group (see Figure 6.1). These key relational processes are cultural competence; trauma-informed lens and practise; safety and trust; power dynamics; transference, countertransference and parallel processes; shame; self-efficacy; learning, growth and reflexive practice and social justice. These themes are interwoven and will be demonstrated through the narratives of two case studies (identifiable details have been changed to protect their anonymity).

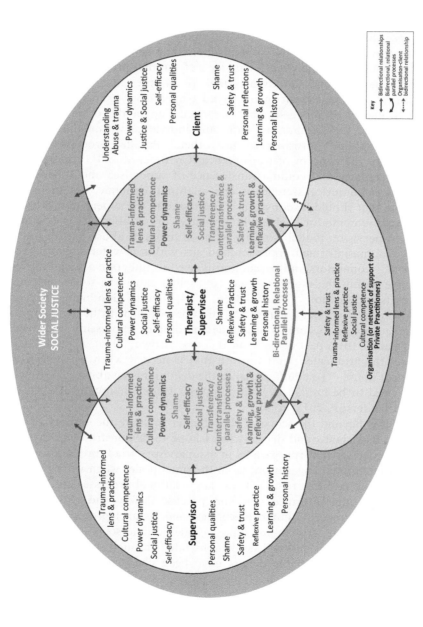

Figure 6.1 Relational parallel processes model of supervision for therapists working with survivors of abuse (Islam, 2021).

Case study one – Salma

Salma was a woman in her late 20s, born and brought up in the United Kingdom, with a Kashmiri mother and an Afghan father. She had two older brothers and two half-siblings from her father's side. Salma's parents separated when she was six. Her father was addicted to drugs and alcohol, and growing up, Salma witnessed her father abuse her mother and older brother, this included physical abuse. Salma described her mother as cold, disconnected and emotionally, physically, and psychologically abusive. Her mother was highly critical of her from a very young age, finding fault in her interests, what she wore and who she was as a person. Salma recalls a deeply painful and bewildering childhood memory of being called a "prostitute who hangs around on street corners" by her mother. In her early childhood, Salma was sexually abused by a close male, family member who was often entrusted with her care when her mother worked. This abuse sustained over a long period. She had been bullied at school and ran away from home on several occasions in her teenage years. A divorcee, single mother of two children, she had previously been in two abusive marriages, including incidents of marital rape in her second marriage. Salma had a history of self-harm and suicidal ideation; her children and her faith were her protective factors. Salma had seen several counsellors over the years but had felt unable to connect with them. She presented in counselling with thoughts about ending her life, feeling disconnected from everything and described feeling overwhelmed, confused, and lost.

Salma had disclosed the abuse in her second marriage to members of her family, including her mother, and was angry and felt deeply let down by their responses. She had expected her mother to support her and confront him; however, she felt unprotected by her mother, even when her mother had witnessed the bruising on her face, she did not support Salma in leaving the relationship. Salma was often shamed for being a divorcee by her mother and other family members, and she felt like there was something deeply wrong with her. She was angry at her mother and at a culture that she experienced as deeply misogynistic and patriarchal. As a woman, she was expected to shoulder the responsibility for her marriages falling apart with no acknowledgement of her abusive experiences. As a therapist, I had to hold and validate these feelings for Salma from the place of her lived experience of them, without my own feelings and experiences impacting her processes.

One of my earliest memories of domestic abuse was at about seven-years-old, witnessing the process a female cousin had to endure when she came to our home to escape her abusive husband. Although my parents wanted to support her, the decision was made by a group of male, family elders that she should return to her husband. I remember her anger, distress, and fear. I remember my own anger at this injustice. I could not understand why this group of men were making this decision for her. In supervision, dialoguing and exploring my anger at my culture, particularly the misogyny and the shaming of survivors into silence, enabled me to keep the focus on validating Salma's anger in therapy, and to hold the discourse within an intercultural and social justice context, which is particularly important when working with trauma (Goodman, 2013). This created safety and enabled Salma to explore the issues on a deeper level. In the same way, when supervisors demonstrate cultural competence, it creates safety for supervisees (Jones et al., 2019; Thomas et al., 2019); I had a supervisor who had the cultural competency to facilitate my exploration, and who could support me in my work with Salma. I felt safe to explore my values and culture, to explore my feelings about Salma's experiences, thereby separating my anger from hers. This enabled me to facilitate Salma's exploration of her values and her feelings, to focus on her self-efficacy and how she wanted to manage her feelings towards her mother, rather than me placing her as a victim and being her rescuer. The trauma from abuse can impact survivor's sense of self-efficacy, how they perceive themselves and their sense of autonomy (Sanderson, 2013). It was important to foster that self-efficacy in Salma, to also understand the dynamics of power and how it could impact her and to bring these aspects of the therapeutic work to supervision.

I was very conscious of the power dynamics in the therapeutic work with Salma. Powerlessness has often meant devastating, horrific experiences for survivors of abuse and this was certainly the case for Salma; the power of the perpetrator and the power of the wider social structures that condoned and sanctioned this abuse. Supervisors and therapists in their respective roles hold the balance of power. Feminist models of supervision advocate for a more egalitarian relationship (Brown, 2016) and this is essential when working with survivors of abuse. Berger and Quiros (2016) advocate balancing this with the expectations of the service and the guiding role of the supervisor. It is important to note the impact of feminist models of supervision on male supervisees; Mackinnon et al. (2011) raise the issue of male diversity and assert that psychological paradigms, including the feminist paradigm, can be ethnocentric in their approach. An important area of discussion that I felt was essential to note but is beyond the scope of this chapter to explore.

To redress the balance of power, it is important to work in a way that is collaborative and empowering for clients (Arczynski and Morrow, 2017; Berger and Quiros, 2016; Ellis et al., 2019; Green and Dekkers, 2010), it is connected to building safety and trust, and can enable growth for the client (Berger and Quiros, 2016; Thomas et al., 2019). In practice, sometimes, this meant holding back on powerful reflections or connections I was making in our therapeutic encounters, so Salma could be empowered to arrive at those herself, to affirm her position as the expert on her life. Minimising power differentials can also be modelled by a supervisor in supervision, where they can empower the supervisee to formulate the work with the client and not always provide answers readily or speed up the process. Time constraints in supervision may hinder this. However, when practised, this can foster agency and self-efficacy in the supervisee. My supervisor's trust in me to formulate the work with Salma created feelings of safety and enabled me to dialogue and explore complex and difficult areas of the work in supervision, without fear of judgement. I felt competent in my work with Salma and supported in navigating the power dynamics of our relationship sensitively and collaboratively.

Powerlessness also featured in the intergenerational trauma in Salma's family and explorations of this was critical to Salma processing her anger at her mother. Salma's mother was a migrant from Kashmir, an area that has been besieged by war and conflict for many decades. Her grandmother had also been very disconnected emotionally from her mother as a child and her mother and grandmother were both survivors of domestic abuse. Byers and Gere (2007, p. 388) describe the "chain of pain" that can be passed on through generations by individuals or groups, particularly when the trauma has not been acknowledged and is dissociated. Intergenerational trauma is a relational process (Isobel et al., 2019) and Salma had been impacted by this in her relationships with both parents. During our work together, when exploring her feelings around the abuse and the bullying, Salma described how sad, lost, and confused she felt as a child. We may be working with adult survivors of child sexual or physical abuse, but in this process, we are also working with the child who experienced these atrocities: the lived experience of the inner child of each person we work with. A child who was scared or terrified, a child who was betrayed, a child who was confused and a child who was powerless to prevent the perpetrator. A child who was silenced, even if for a moment. A child who may carry the shame, as if somehow, they deserved it or asked for it. Salma's inner child was very present and this evoked in me, a very powerful need to protect this deeply, lonely, and distressed child she described. In the transference, I felt she was looking to me to be that protective mother and I wanted to protect her. I wanted to be her rescuer (Walker, 2004). In supervision, we explored how these feelings of protection were manifesting in me and how they could hinder the process; I might unconsciously want to protect her from pain and therefore may not be able to sit with her pain or facilitate her exploration of it. It could also lead to me relaxing the boundaries such as extending the time of the sessions, make contact between sessions or during holidays, etc. (Walker, 2004). During these dialogues, I felt moments of anger. Anger that my supervisor was not being protective. Anger about a child not being protected. However, this was my own countertransference from a history of child abuse. At that moment, my supervisor's feedback was perceived by me as being critical, although she had communicated it very supportively. It felt like a dismissive, critical parent. This was a parallel process to how Salma felt with her mother. Reflexive practice was important as it allowed me to step back and realise what was happening. I was angry at those who did not protect me, as a child. I was angry at Salma's mother and angry at my supervisor who momentarily represented these people. I wanted my supervisor to be the protective mother for Salma and I. My countertransference was a powerful concoction, a reaction to Salma's transference and originating in my own personal history.

> It is useful to focus on what is created between client and therapist, or between supervisee and supervisor. Because of the intersubjective nature of human beings, we use ourselves as a therapeutic tool, both in therapy and in supervision. A contemplative stance helps us be aware and notice what is going on from moment to moment. (Faris and Van Ooijen, 2012, p. 144)

Work with adult survivors of child sexual abuse can be intense, erratic, disorganised, and particularly potent in rapidly shifting transferential and countertransferential enactments, which can lead to strong parallel processes in supervision (Frawley-O'Dea, 1997). The reflexive practice enabled me to disentangle myself from this powerful enactment; I was able to come back to a place of safety within myself, where I was not fearful and did not need protection. In holding that space with gentleness and compassion, I stepped back from my anger at her mother and my own anger rooted in my own personal history, thereby fostering for Salma a space that was open and non-judgemental. In this space, Salma was able to explore the impact of the intergenerational trauma, her feelings about her mother's trauma and her mother's reactions to her trauma. Her father was not very present in her life after the divorce, and her anger was focused more on her mother and the lack of protection and empathy from her. She could explore her anger towards her mother without shame, in the safety of the therapeutic relationship. She felt that her mother was the product of a misogynistic and patriarchal upbringing and society and has not been able to process her own trauma and that her inability to advocate for her and protect her, as well as her behaviour towards her, were connected to her mother's personal history. She was able to recognise this, whilst also learning to set boundaries to protect herself from further abuse from her mother. This work with Salma highlights how important it is for therapists to "become more aware of the socio-political histories and forms of transgenerational and systemic oppression trauma that their clients may have experienced" (Goodman, 2013, p. 399).

Trauma work has seen a significant paradigm shift in the last fifteen years with more focus on the neurobiology of trauma, adverse childhood effects and somatic experiencing. Behaviours viewed through a trauma-informed lens focus on *what happened to a trauma survivor* rather than *what is wrong with a trauma survivor*, and there is a greater understanding that behaviours that have previously been viewed as problematic, are in fact coping mechanisms for survival and adaptive ways of responding to trauma (Sweeney et al., 2018). Working with survivors of abuse is multi-layered work; survivors of abuse can have complex histories of trauma (Frawley-O'Dea, 1997; Sanderson, 2006; Sanderson, 2013). Another layer of this work was enabling Salma to understand how trauma manifests to enable her to find safety and expand her window of tolerance. Even her relationship with silence was connected to her abuse. Salma struggled in periods of silence in our sessions as it made her feel unsafe. Silence can feel dangerous for survivors of abuse, as the abuse can often take place in silence and they may have been silenced from disclosing the abuse. As therapists, we need to be able to identify what is the purpose and meaning of the silence as it could also be suppressed anger, disassociation, or avoidance (Sanderson, 2013).

Salma was very anxious and often overwhelmed, whilst other times she felt dissociated from her feelings. We were able to explore the processes of fight, flight, and freeze and how these manifested for her and the nature of hypoarousal and hyperarousal. This psychoeducation provided learning and growth for Salma, it enabled her to reflect on her triggers and learn to manage them through various grounding techniques. This can be broken down for clients in a way that they can understand and connect to their experiences. Salma was able to explore feelings of deep shame about not being able to leave her abusive relationships early on, for finding herself in abusive relationships again and for not fighting back to protect herself, particularly during the physical violence and marital rape. Seeing an illustrated representation of the cycle of abuse was a turning point for Salma. She was able to see how she had been drawn back into the cycle, and how it repeats. Survivors of abuse have been dehumanised, degraded, and forced into compliance, which can create shame from feeling powerless and unable to stop the abuse (Sanderson, 2015). Trauma-informed approaches have an awareness of how the survival mechanisms activate the fight, flight, and freeze response. Shame can be sustained and internalised through a misunderstanding of freeze responses, which are involuntary responses, and if compliance and secrecy are not understood as survival mechanisms (Sanderson, 2015). We explored how the freeze response was linked to her survival mechanism, and that this response was designed to protect her in a situation where fight and flight were not a safe option. Compliance is a part of the freeze response, and for Salma, understanding this enabled her to develop self-compassion, which is key to trauma recovery and for overcoming shame. "Self-kindness can have a calming effect on autonomic hyperarousal, common humanity is an antidote to hiding in shame, and balanced, mindful awareness allows us to disentangle ourselves from intrusive memories and feelings" (Germer and Neff, 2014, p. 45).

It was important to be aware of how compliance may be playing out in our therapeutic relationship. Survivors of abuse can struggle to trust or self-disclose (Ellis et al., 2019) or they may trust too easily because they want to be liked, this can also lead to them displaying compliance and appearing as the "model" client (Sanderson, 2013). Supervisees also need safety and trust

(Berger and Quiros, 2016) and may feel unable to show vulnerability for fear of judgement or not being liked by the supervisor (Ellis et al., 2019). Supervision should be a place of trust and safety where they can explore impacts of any personal history of trauma (Jordan, 2018) and transference/countertransference (Courtois, 2018). I was able to reflect on my own healing journey in relation to trauma, shame, and felt particularly grateful for the compassionate approach of my therapist and our therapeutic work in relation to healing from trauma and overcoming shame. My therapist fostered the growth of my self-compassion, and this was transformative and healing. Scoglio et al. (2015) carried out a study on women seeking treatment for post-traumatic stress disorder. The study explored the connection between self-compassion, resilience, emotion dysregulation, and the severity of post-traumatic stress disorder (PTSD) symptoms. Results suggest that self-compassion is negatively related to the severity of PTSD symptoms and emotion dysregulation and that it is positively related to resilience.

> Self-compassion is strongly linked to emotional well-being, is an important mechanism of change in psychotherapy, and touches the core of trauma related symptomatology. Our modern, scientific understanding of self-compassion opens the possibility of developing uniquely effective self-compassion-based treatments designed specifically for survivors of childhood and adult trauma. (Germer and Neff, 2015, p. 55)

Shame was a topic that I was able to explore deeply in supervision, and this enriched my work with Salma; therapist's awareness and processing of their own historical shame may depend on how consciously this was addressed in their personal therapy or training and may be evoked in the therapeutic encounter; this can be paralleled in supervision, particularly given the power imbalance, and supervisors also need to be aware of their unprocessed shame (Sanderson, 2015).

Salma had internalised her abusive experiences as meaning that there was something inherently wrong with her and that she was to blame for the abuse (Sanderson, 2015). Salma's shame was also connected to her experiences of marital rape. She struggled to name it as rape; her ex-husband insisted that as a Muslim wife, she was obliged to always comply with his sexual advances, no matter how abusive he had been, or how she felt. This is a dangerous, harmful assertion, utilised by many abusers. Faith was important to Salma, and she was struggling to reconcile this with her horrific experiences of marital rape; experiences which had been presented, through spiritual abuse, as being part of her faith. It was important for her to feel her faith was not under attack or being judged as she explored this. Even when a counsellor shares their client's ethnicity and culture, the issue of race is rarely absent (Kareem and Littlewood, 2000), and the same is true of faith and spirituality. Our shared faith was very much present in the room; I was very conscious that as a hijab-wearing,

Muslim therapist, I may represent those from whom Salma had experienced spiritual abuse. It was important to state that I did not condone such views and that she could speak openly about her experiences, without fear of judgement. To have her experiences of spiritual and sexual abuse met with empathy and validation was deeply healing for Salma. She could recognise where she was taking on the shame that had been projected or bypassed by the perpetrators (Sanderson, 2015). A trauma-informed approach encompasses understanding of interpersonal trauma and socio-political trauma, thus it is orientated within a social justice framework (Berger and Quiros, 2016). This approach recognises the intersectionality of the trauma with racism, sexism, ageism, oppression, homophobia, and classism (Quiros and Berger, 2015; Sweeney et al., 2016).

Salma had struggled with previous therapists when exploring domestic abuse, feeling like they did not understand her experience and judged her culture and faith. Domestic abuse happens in all cultures and all communities and should not be reduced to what is perceived as cultured forms of violence. For example, according to the Office for National Statistics Data on *Domestic Abuse Prevalence and Victim Characteristics* (Year Ending March 2020), there were 274 domestic abuse homicides where victims were women (aged 16+) in a two-year period (March 2017–March 2019). According to the Honour-Based Violence Awareness Network (HBVA), there are 12 estimated honour killings per year in the United Kingdom. Based on these statistics, "honour" killings would form an estimated 1.55% of total Domestic Abuse Homicides, where the victims were women aged 16 plus in the two-year period of March 2019–March 2019. Yet, this forms a strong part of the narrative around domestic abuse in minoritised communities – othering gender-based violence in these communities. Challenging the narratives on domestic abuse is not akin to dismissing the horrific injustices such as "honour-based' killings, FGC, or forced marriages. We need policies and practices that address these and address the systems and structures that condone or perpetuate such injustices. However, we must contextualise the narratives we have and ask *how are those felt and received by the communities they are about?* Domestic abuse happens in all communities, and any narrative that does not reflect this is implicitly saying, *your perpetrators are not like our perpetrators, your abuse is not like our abuse.*

Violence against women is a universal problem, affecting women at all levels of society; however, differently situated women have unique experiences with violence. Theoretically, this calls for the necessity to balance universality with intersectionality. Analysing EU policy texts, we argue that the recognition of different forms of violence has led to an increased tendency toward culturalization, i.e. articulating culture as the only explanation behind certain forms of violence or focusing exclusively on culturalized forms of violence. While largely ignoring the gendered

nature of violence, cultural framings of violence also create a dichotomy
between "insiders" (non-violent Europeans) and "outsiders" (violent
others). (Montoya and Agustin, 2013, p. 534)

The therapeutic work with Salma demonstrates how critical cultural competency is to creating safety and trust with survivors of abuse. It highlights
the need for trauma-focused lens and practice when working with survivors
of abuse (Knight, 2018), that encompasses the well-being of the supervisory
triad and incorporates an understanding of vicarious trauma (Berger and
Quiros, 2016) and compassion fatigue (Miller and Sprang, 2017).
Therapists working with survivors of abuse are often engaging with deeply
distressing accounts that place them at risk of compassion fatigue, secondary traumatic stress and vicarious trauma (Brown, 2016; Sanderson,
2006; Sanderson, 2013). As a survivor of trauma, and as a therapist
working with trauma, it was important that my supervisor was focused on
my well-being. Supervisors should ensure that they impart knowledge on
trauma and vicarious trauma and also encourage supervisees to expand on
this knowledge (Berger and Quiros, 2014). The self-care of therapists and
the prevention or management of vicarious trauma (Jordan, 2018) are
crucial elements of the restorative function of supervision models, and core
to any supervision model working with survivors of abuse. Reflexive
practice is vital for reducing compassion fatigue and vicarious trauma
(Jordan, 2018; Miller and Sprang, 2017) and is also very important for the
cultural competence of supervisor and supervisee (Jones et al., 2019;
Thomas et al., 2019), all essential aspects of work with survivors of abuse.

Case study two – Mala

Mala was a woman in her mid-30s of Somali and Ethiopian origin. Mala's
mother was under 16 when she was born, and her parents separated when
she was two years old. Her father married multiple times and she had half-
siblings through both parents. Her father remained in Ethiopia. Her mother
left Mala and her sibling in the care of her maternal family in Somalia
and moved to the United Kingdom; Mala joined her mother in the United
Kingdom at the age of 12 with her sibling. Mala accessed counselling at a
time when she was struggling to sleep and was finding it difficult to cope
with everyday life. She had a fraught relationship with her mother, who she
described as emotionally absent and highly critical. She was always working
to gain her mother's approval and love. Mala had an FGC procedure at five
years old and was struggling with the physical and psychological impacts
of the FGC. Mala's counsellor, Hannah, was in her late 30s and of North
African and French origin and was a trauma survivor. Hannah was my
supervisee and this case study will focus on my work with Hannah and my
reflections as a supervisor.

Hannah found her work with Mala both rewarding and challenging. She felt like sometimes they connected well and made progress, and that other times Mala was resistant to the therapy. During supervision, Hannah expressed that she needed more interventions for her work with Mala. As we explored this deeper, Hannah realised that Mala had been expressing dissatisfaction at her progress in therapy and was demanding "practical" tools she could use. Hannah was able to see the parallel process that was taking place. She wondered if the practical element was rooted in Mala's culture. Somalia has seen many wars, and many of the FGC clients we work with have experienced multiple traumas from childhood through to adulthood. Many FGC survivors from this region who are part of the Somali diaspora have lived in survival mode for most of their lives. I remember one survivor, when speaking about her FGC, said to me, "The FGC is just a blip in my life, it is nothing because I have experienced things far, far worse." However well-intentioned, when we reduce someone's experience of abuse to a narrative around culture, tradition, faith, ethnicity, or specific forms of abuse, we are detracting from the human experience. The horrific human experience of abuse and the associated trauma. Thereby, othering communities that are already marginalised, facing barriers to accessing services and struggling to have a voice. Erturk (2007, p. 13) in her report to the United Nations Human Rights Council on "Intersections between culture and violence against women" asserts that:

> While this agenda has helped to identify types of violence against women formerly not recognized and mobilized international and local constituencies for their eradication, it also contributed to essentializing certain cultures as the source of the problem. As one writer put it, the harmful traditional practices agenda "unfortunately reinforced the notion that metropolitan centers of the West contain no 'tradition' or 'culture' harmful to women, and that the violence which does exist is idiosyncratic and individualized rather than culturally condoned (Winter et al., 2002)."

Whilst trying to understand Mala's need for a practical approach, it was important that Hannah and I were not making assumptions about Mala's culture but rather seeking to understand her lived experience. Reflexivity plays an important role in the cultural competency of supervisor and supervisee (Jones et al., 2019) and in exploring bias and assumptions (Varghese et al., 2018). What was important was for Hannah to explore with Mala *what her experience of her culture is*, rather than exploring *what her culture is*. The same culture can be experienced very differently by two people of the same ethnicity and similar backgrounds. Cultural competence creates a safe and open space for the supervisee, and when race, culture, and identity are not openly discussed it can impact the supervisory working alliance (Kapten, 2020). I knew that broaching discussions on race, identity, and culture is a key aspect of my supervisory role and my cultural competence (Haans and Balke, 2018; Jones et al., 2019). It was also important to note that Mala's experience of her mother had been of someone who was very practical in her care but disconnected emotionally. Her mother had to detach from her very young children and move to the United Kingdom. She had faced her own traumas and the generational trauma can be seen in the relational trauma Mala experienced. Relating on a practical level was what she was familiar with.

Mala's approach to therapy made Hannah question her competency. Therapists' personal history and experiences can also impact their sense of self-efficacy (Ellis et al., 2019), and Hannah's personal history was feeding into her feelings on this. When therapists feel ineffectual, it can make them feel useless, helpless and small. This can be accompanied by feeling attacked by the client and reflects the split between abuser and victim roles One consequence of abuse is that the survivor can experience the world as being divided between victims and perpetrators; being sadistic or being persecuted, and unconsciously recreates this. Helping the survivor to discover the space in between and to integrate the many splits is a complex therapeutic task (Walker, 2004, p. 178).

Transference and countertransference mark a strong feature of work with survivors of abuse (Sanderson, 2006; Sanderson, 2013). Familiarity with possible relational re-enactments by survivors of abuse can help supervisor and supervisee to manage the transference, countertransference, and parallel processes and can prove particularly insightful for understanding the client's relational dynamics (Frawley-O'Dea, 1997), the unconscious processes and the therapeutic relationship (Courtois, 2018). Reflexive practice was required for Hannah to recognise the countertransference in herself, which was to feel like the victim and to feel like she was not competent. She was enacting the freeze response, feeling overwhelmed, and disconnected from Mala. It was important for her to acknowledge this countertransference so she did not stay engaged in this dynamic or shift to the role of perpetrator in some way; this could potentially reinforce the binary view of victims and perpetrators for Mala and make her feel rejected, as if she is too much, or that she is dangerous (Walker, 2004).

Hannah was also feeling shame at being what she perceived as ineffectual; a therapist's historical shame can be triggered by clients, this shame can manifest when clients communicate feeling a lack of progress (Morrison, 2008). This can be a particular feature of working with survivors of abuse, which can require long-term therapy, but clients want to see more immediate results. Mala wanted more immediate results; her window of tolerance was very small, and she struggled to sit with pain, often attempting to bypass it through *doing* and keeping busy and focusing on her career. There may also have been power dynamics at play: survivors of abuse can relate to power by seeking control, being compliant, or oscillating between the two and these are often re-enacted in the therapeutic process (Sanderson, 2013); transference and countertransference can be paralleled in the supervisory process (Aasheim, 2012). Our supervision dialogues explored whether there were unconscious dynamics around Hannah being a woman of North African and French ethnicities and light-skinned, and Mala being a Black African woman. Particularly when considering the colonial impacts on Somalia and the rest of Africa. Agoro (2019) suggests that therapists need a high-level awareness of power dynamics, the absence of which could result in a form of cultural imperialism within the therapeutic process, even if unintentional. Kareem and Littlewood (2000) describe how differences in race between client and therapist, connected to wider power dynamics that are institutionalised, can lead to a counter-therapeutic effect.

During these dialogues, I realised that I had not explored how Hannah identified in terms of her ethnicity. My North African friends and family often identified as "Arab" and I realised I had assumed that Hannah felt the same. However, Hannah felt strongly about her African identity but disclosed that her French identity felt more prominent in academic settings. Hannah felt that Mala connected with her on their shared African and Muslim identity and their use of the Arabic language, but she also acknowledged that race may play a part in the power dynamics of their therapeutic relationship. Mearns and Cooper (2005, p. 39) suggest that "in this relationship, the therapist's Otherness is called forth by the Otherness of the client, and this requires a deep, empathic understanding of the very essence of the client's experiencing." There was still so much for me to learn about Hannah and explore about myself, in relation to identity, power, privilege and oppression, and the interplay of these in our supervisor-supervisee relationship. Blasini-Méndez (2019) suggests an interpersonal, postcolonial approach to supervision would encourage these discussions in supervision and thereby, also encourage a reflection on how the therapeutic relationship with the client is impacted by power dynamics. A postcolonial approach is one that broaches discussions on issues around privilege, power, and oppression as a way of building towards fairness and justice (Hernandez and McDowell, 2010). In relation to supervision, a postcolonial perspective goes beyond multiculturalism, as it challenges the very foundations on which many theories of supervision and therapy are built; foundations that are a product of colonisation, leading to individualistic theories and practices that are Eurocentric (Hernandez and McDowell, 2010). A critical postcolonial approach seeks to establish new frameworks for supervision and therapy that can attend to and integrate cultural diversity, diversity of experiences, and diversity of knowledge (Butler-Byrd, 2010; Hernández and McDowell, 2010).

When supervisors address cultural identities in the supervisory relationship, they model for supervisees how to use similar interventions with their clients and the supervisor's cultural competence has been linked to a stronger supervisory working alliance and enhanced outcomes for clients (Jones et al., 2019). When cultural competency is not part of the supervisory process, it "may contribute to supervisees' feelings of frustration as well as supervisees' possible reluctance to openly sharing their feelings and concerns" (Hird et al, 2001) (Green and Dekkers, 2010, p. 297). This proposed model focuses on the various relational parallel processes in supervision and counselling, and it is important that there is clarity on the functions and boundaries of each setting. However, Frawley-O'Dea (1997) points out that relational models of supervision have a therapeutic element and are not just educational.

Hannah needed a supportive and safe place in the supervision to explore all these aspects of her therapeutic work and to find her way back to a place of self-efficacy; for her to recognise the importance of *being* in the therapeutic process, and not always feel like she had to be *doing*, again a parallel process with Mala who was always *doing* and found it difficult to *be*. Hannah felt this distinction was helpful and enabled her to feel more competent in her work with Mala. I encouraged Hannah to come back to her trauma lens and practice, so she could recognise the fight, flight, freeze responses in Mala and herself. Trauma-informed lens and practice by supervisors can: develop a better understanding for supervisees on the impact of trauma on clients and how they can heal from the trauma (Berger and Quiros, 2016). It fosters supervisee growth and skills development (Ellis et al., 2019); provides insight on the varying triggers that may cause trauma to surface in clients (Knight, 2018). It acknowledges and works with vicarious traumatisation and compassion fatigue in therapists working with traumatised clients (Berger and Quiros, 2014; Courtois, 2018; Jordan, 2018; Knight, 2018; Miller and Sprang, 2017). There were also times when modelling coregulation was important when Hannah seemed overwhelmed. The process of coregulation occurs when two people experience a connection with each other, through which their autonomic nervous systems find safety (Dana, 2018). So, for example, through eye contact, touch, tone of voice or the regularity of breathing, safety can be communicated to another in that co-created experience. Trauma that occurs through an unsafe interaction with another can make coregulation feel dangerous, so the nervous system will start to regulate independently and disrupt the social engagement system (Dana, 2018); this can continue beyond the time needed, leading to ongoing distress cycles and dissociative patterns (Heller and LaPierre, 2012). The polyvagal theory developed by Stephen Porges provides deeper insight into the role of the social engagement system in parasympathetic recovery (Porges, 2011); the theory "emphasizes sociality as a core process in mitigating threat and supporting mental and physical health" (Porges, 2021, p. 1). When applied to supervision, coregulation can be used by the supervisor to help the supervisee to manage affect and activation of the autonomic nervous system, helping their autonomic nervous system find sanctuary and safety. The modelling of this by the supervisor can provide experiential learning for the supervisee and increase their levels of competence and skills for working with survivors of abuse.

The challenging nature of work with survivors of abuse can feel disempowering and deskilling; Socratic questioning can be utilised to encourage supervisees in their case formulation and applications of this to client work and supervisors who are willing to be learned from the supervisee and defer to their formulations can enable trainees to develop competence and self-efficacy (Ellis et al., 2019). To foster her self-efficacy, I encouraged Hannah to develop her own formulations and we worked collaboratively with these. This also enabled me to consciously address the power dynamics in our supervisory relationship; by modelling this in our supervisory work, Hannah could feed this back into the therapeutic process and relationship with Mala. A strong supervisory working alliance can lead to supervisees feeling more content with their supervision and greater feelings of self-efficacy are fostered (Crockett and Hays, 2015). We explored whether there was also a countertransference in Hannah to be the rescuer who could meet all of Mala's unmet needs (Walker, 2004), triggered by the feelings of her own inner child. Hannah felt that this could sometimes be the case. Through the supervisory process, Hannah was able to understand that her task was to foster an environment that felt contained and holding, a "good enough" therapeutic relationship which would enable Mala to experience a corrective emotional experience (Lapworth and Sills, 2010). A safe supervision space was important, where Hannah could explore her feelings of shame, the transference and countertransference and parallel processes without fear of judgement. Shame can be triggered in the supervisory process where the supervisee may feel judged by the supervisor or find it difficult to present work where they feel less effective (Morrison, 2008).

Reflexive practice was also key for me, to understand that I could respond to Hannah's feelings about her competency with my own sense of shame. Morrison (2008) asserts that there is an avoidance to examine shame by therapists and suggests that countertransference shame in therapists and supervisors requires further study. Reflexivity is an important part of counselling work, and more so in the often intense and challenging work with survivors of abuse. Reflexivity can be used as a tool to minimise negative impacts of supervisory power, enhance collaboration, create transparency (Arczynski and Morrow, 2017) and be a source of experiential learning (Courtois, 2018). I had to be aware of whether, I too, was falling into the dynamics of being either victim, perpetrator, or rescuer. It was essential that I was enabling Hannah's self-efficacy, rather than attempting to rescue her.

A note about social justice

The case studies have demonstrated the intricacy and interwoven nature of all these relational parallel processes in the supervisory triad. They have demonstrated the need for an intercultural trauma-informed model of supervision when working with survivors of abuse; a model that sits within a broader framework of social justice. Supervision should consider how social justice and wider social issues impact survivors of abuse, who can have strong feelings about justice; they can struggle with wider systems that are not trauma-informed, such as the justice, housing, and welfare systems. Refugee survivors of abuse may have cumulative traumatic experiences, including in the country they have migrated to, where they can experience marginalisation, feel powerless, and face discrimination (Kastrup and Dymi, 2020). One criticism of the Domestic Abuse Act 2021 is that it does not go far enough to afford the same level of protection to migrant domestic abuse survivors, including children, who do not have a secure immigration status. A therapeutic process that does not holistically consider the lived experience of a person is one that is fragmenting (Kareem and Littlewood, 2000); this lived experience is inclusive of race, culture, gender, religion, spirituality, sexual orientation, and social values, and supervisors/supervisees should play an active role in social justice advocacy (Brown, 2016; Burnes et al., 2013). We cannot do this work with survivors of abuse and be neglectful in our role of advocating for social justice, neither can we encourage a voice for survivors of abuse, and be resistant to fighting for, and championing that voice.

References

Aasheim, L. (2012). *Practical Clinical Supervision for Counselors: An Experiential Guide*. New York: Springer Publishing Company.

Agoro, O. (2019). Who is being assessed? Postmodernism and intercultural therapy assessments: A synergetic process. In: Ababio, B., Littlewood, R. (eds). *Intercultural Therapy Challenges, Insights and Developments*. London: Routledge.

Arczynski, A. V., Morrow, S. L. (2017). The complexities of power in feminist multicultural psychotherapy supervision. *Journal of Counseling Psychology*, *64*, 192–205.

Arnaud, K. O. St. (2017). Encountering the wounded healer: Parallel process and supervision. *Canadian Journal of Counselling and Psychotherapy*, *51*(2), 131–144.

Berger, R., Quiros, L. (2014). Supervision for trauma-informed practice. *Traumatology*, *20*, 296–301.

Berger, R., Quiros, L. (2016). 'Best practices for training trauma-informed practitioners: Supervisors' voice. *Traumatology*, *22*, 145–154.

Berger, R., Quiros, L., Benavidez-Hatzis, J. R. (2017). The intersection of identities in supervision for trauma-informed practice: Challenges and strategies. *The Clinical Supervisor*, *37*, 122–141.

Bernard, J. M., Goodyear, R. K. (2019). *Fundamentals of Clinical Supervision* (6th ed.). Saddle River, NJ: Pearson Education.

Blasini-Méndez, M. (2019). Interpersonal postcolonial supervision: Facilitating conversations of countertransference. *Training and Education in Professional Psychology*, *13*, 233–223.

Brown, L. S. (2016). *Supervision Essentials for the Feminist Psychotherapy Model of Supervision*. Washington: American Psychological Association.

Burnes, T. R., Wood, J. M., Inman, J. L., Welikson, G. A. (2013). An investigation of process variables in feminist group clinical supervision. *The Counseling Psychologist*, *41*, 86–109.

Butler-Byrd, N. M. (2010). An African American supervisor's reflections on multicultural supervision. *Training and Education in Professional Psychology*, *4*, 11–15.

Byers, J. G., Gere, S. (2007). Expression in the service of humanity: Trauma and temporality. *Journal of Humanistic Psychology*, *47*, 384–391.

Cassedy, P. (2010). *First Steps in Clinical Supervision: A Guide for Healthcare Professionals*. Berkshire: Open University Press.

Courtois, C. A. (2018). Trauma-informed supervision and consultation: Personal reflections. *The Clinical Supervisor*, *37*, 38–63.

Crockett, S., Hays, D. G. (2015). The influence of supervisor multicultural competence on the supervisory working alliance, supervisee counseling self-efficacy, and supervisee satisfaction with supervision: A mediation model. *Counselor Education and Supervision*, *54*, 258–273.

Crowe, T. P., Oades, L. G., Deane, F. P., Ciarrochi, J., Williams, V. C. (2011). Parallel processes in clinical supervision: Implications for coaching mental health practitioners. *International Journal of Evidence Based Coaching and Mentoring*, *9*, 56–66.

Dana, D. (2018). *The Polyvagal Theory in Therapy*. New York: W.W. Norton & Company.

Dixon-Woods, M., Cavers, D., Agarwal, S., Annandale, E., Arthur, A., Harvey, J., Hsu, R., Katbamna, S., Olsen, R., Smith, L., Riley, R., Sutton, A. J. (2006). Conducting a critical interpretive synthesis of the literature on access to healthcare by vulnerable groups. *BMC Medical Research Methodology*, *6*(35), 147–2288.

Ellis, A. E., Gold, S. N., Courtois, C., Araujo, K., Quinones, M. (2019). Supervising trauma treatment: The contextual trauma treatment model applied to supervision. *Practice Innovations*, *4*, 166–181.

Erturk, Y. (2007). *UN Human Rights Council Report of Special Rapporteur on Violence against Women, Its Causes and Consequences*. Intersections between Culture and Violence against Women, A/HRC/4//34.

Etherington, K. (2000). Supervising counsellors who work with survivors of childhood sexual abuse. *Counselling Psychology Quarterly*, *13*, 377–389.

Faris, A., Van Ooijen, E. (2012). *Integrative Counselling and Psychotherapy: A Relational Approach*. London: SAGE Publications.

Frawley-O'Dea, M. G. (1997). Who's doing what to whom? *Contemporary Psychoanalysis*, *33*, 5–18.

Germer, C. K., Neff, K. (2014). Cultivating self-compassion in trauma survivors. In: Follette, V., Briere, J., Rozelle, D., Hopper, J., Rome, D. (eds) *Mindfulness-Oriented Interventions for Trauma: Integrating Contemplative Practices*. New York: Guilford Press.

Giordano, A., Clarke, P., Borders, L. D. (2013). Using motivational interviewing techniques to address parallel process in supervision. *Counselor Education and Supervision*, *52*, 15–29.

Goodman, R. D. (2013). The transgenerational trauma and resilience genogram. *Counselling Psychology Quarterly, 26,* 386–405.

Green, M. S., Dekkers, T. D. (2010). Attending to power and diversity in supervision: An exploration of supervisee learning outcomes and satisfaction with supervision. *Journal of Feminist Family Therapy, 22,* 293–312.

Haans, A., Balke, N. (2018). Trauma-informed intercultural group supervision. *The Clinical Supervisor, 37,* 158–181.

Heller, L., LaPierre, A. (2012). *Healing Developmental Trauma: How Early Trauma Affects Self-Regulation, Self-Image and the Capacity for Relationship.* Berkley: North Atlantic Books.

Hernández, P., McDowell, T. (2010). Intersectionality, power, and relational safety in context: Key concepts in clinical supervision. *Training and Education in Professional Psychology, 4,* 29–35.

Hird, J. S., Cavalieri, C. E., Dulko, J. P., Felice, A. A. D., Ho, T. A. (2001). Visions and realities: Supervisee perspectives of multicultural supervision. *Journal of Multicultural Counseling and Development, 29,* 114–13010.1002/j.2161-1912.2001.tb00509.x.

Islam, W. (2021). Synthesise supervisory and learning theories and apply them creatively to complex supervisory processes and practice. Assignment for *7CL530, Postgraduate Certificate in Clinical Supervision,* University of Derby. Unpublished.

Isobel, S., Goodyear, M., Furness, T., Foster, K. (2019). Preventing intergenerational trauma transmission: A critical interpretive synthesis. *Journal of Clinical Nursing, 28,* 1100–1113.

Jones C. T., Welfare L. E., Melchior, S., Cash, R. M. (2019). Broaching as a strategy for intercultural understanding in clinical supervision. *The Clinical Supervisor, 38,* 1–16.

Jordan, K. (2018). Trauma-informed counseling supervision: Something every counselor should know about. *Asia Pacific Journal of Counselling and Psychotherapy, 9,* 127–142.

Kapten, S. W. (2020). Power, powerlessness, and the parallel process. *Journal of Psychotherapy Integration, 30,* 147–154.

Kareem, J., Littlewood, R. (2000). *Intercultural Therapy,* 2nd edn. London: Blackwell Science.

Kastrup, M. C., Dymi, K. (2020). *Intercultural Psychotherapy: For Immigrants, Refugees, Asylum Seekers and Ethnic Minority Patients.* In: Schouler-Ocak, M., Kastrup, M. C. (eds). Cham: Springer Nature Switzerland.

Knight, C. (2018). Trauma-informed supervision: Historical antecedents, current practice, and future directions. *The Clinical Supervisor, 37,* 7–37.

Lapworth, P., Sills, C. (2010). *Integration in Counselling and Psychotherapy: Developing a Personal Approach,* 2nd edn. London: SAGE Publications.

Levine, P. A. (2010). *In an Unspoken Voice: How the Body Releases Trauma and Restores Goodness.* Berkley: North Atlantic Books.

MacKinnon, C. J., Bhatia, M., Sunderani, S., Affleck, W., Smith, N. G. (2011). Opening the dialogue: Implications of feminist supervision theory with male supervisees. *Professional Psychology: Research and Practice, 42,* 130–136.

McKibben, W. B., Cook, R. M., Fickling, M. J. (2019). Feminist supervision and supervisee nondisclosure: The mediating role of the supervisory relationship. *The Clinical Supervisor, 38*(1), 38–57. 10.1080/07325223.2018.1509756

Mearns, D., Cooper, M. (2005). *Working at Relational Depth in Counselling and Psychotherapy*. London: SAGE Publications.

Miller, B., Sprang, G. (2017). A components-based practice and supervision model for reducing compassion fatigue by affecting clinician experience. *Traumatology*, *23*, 153–164.

Montoya, C., Agustin, L. R. (2013). The othering of domestic violence: The EU and cultural framings of violence against women. *Social Politics*, *20*, 534–557.

Morrison, A. P. (2008). The analyst's shame. *Contemporary Psychoanalysis*, *44*, 65–82.

Morrissey, J., Tribe, R. (2001). Parallel process in supervision. *Counselling Psychology Quarterly*, *14*, 103–110.

Porges, S. W. (2011). *The Polyvagal Theory: Neurophysiological Foundations of Emotions, Attachment, Communication, Self-Regulation*. New York: Norton.

Porges, S. W. (2021). Polyvagal theory: A biobehavioral journey to sociality. *Journal of Comprehensive Psychoneuroendocrinology*, *7*, 1–7.

Quiros, L., Berger, R. (2015). Responding to the sociopolitical complexity of trauma: An integration of theory and practice. *Loss and Trauma*, *20*, 149–159.

Sanderson, C. (2006). *Counselling Adult Survivors of Child Sexual Abuse*. London: Jessica Kingsley Publishers.

Sanderson, C. (2013). *Counselling Skills for Working with Trauma*. London: Jessica Kinglsey Publishers.

Sanderson, C. (2015). *Counselling Skills for Working with Shame*. Philadelphia: Jessica Kingsley Publishers.

Scoglio, A., Rudat, D., Garvert, D., Jarmolowski, M., Jackson, C., Herman, J. (2015). Self-compassion and responses to trauma: The role of emotion regulation. *Journal of Interpersonal Violence*, *33*, 2016–2036.

Searles, H. F. (1955). The informational value of the supervisor's emotional experience. *Psychiatry*, *18*, 135–146.

Sweeney, A., Clement, S., Filson, B., Kennedy, A. (2016). Trauma-informed mental healthcare in the UK: What is it and how can we further its development? *Mental Health Review Journal*, *21*, 174–192.

Sweeney, A., Filson, B., Kennedy, A., Collinson, L., Gillard, S. (2018). A paradigm shift: Relationships in trauma-informed mental health services. *BJPsych Advances*, *24*, 319–333.

Thomas, F. C., Bowie, J.-A., Hill, L., Taknint, J. T. (2019). Growth-promoting supervision: Reflections from women of color psychology trainees. *Training and Education in Professional Psychology*, *13*, 167–173.

Van Oojien, E. (2013). *Clinical Supervision Made Easy*, 2nd edn. Monmouth: PCCS Books.

Varghese, R., Quiros, L., Berger, R. (2018). Reflective practices for engaging in trauma-informed culturally competent supervision. *Smith College Studies in Social Work*, *88*, 135–151.

Walker, M. (2004). Supervising practitioners working with survivors of childhood abuse: Counter transference; secondary traumatization and terror. *Psychodynamic Practice*, *10*, 173–193.

Winter, B., Thompson, D., Jeffreys, S. (2002). The UN approach to harmful traditional practices. *International Feminist Journal of Politics*, *4*, 72–9410.1080/14616740110116191.

Developmental Perspectives

Chapter 7

Passing as White – Colour Blindness in the Journey of a Multiracial Psychotherapist

Ravind Jeawon

Introduction

The Republic of Ireland of 2021 conjures the image of a modern, European, progressive society celebrated with great fanfare in 2015 with the legalisation of same-sex marriage. Issues around ethnic diversity are increasingly being amplified as Ireland reversed its historical narrative of emigration to become a country of destination for migrants, both forced and economic. The rapid transformation of this narrative in the 21st century is felt broadly throughout Irish society, and psychotherapy like many disciplines is faced with the reality of these changes. Almost ninety-two per cent of respondents in the 2016 census identified as white (CSO, 2017) but psychotherapy in Ireland is interacting with an increasingly diverse set of clients, some Irish born with migrant parentage like myself. The Irish government has recognised this reality by publishing two *Intercultural Health Strategy* documents spanning 2007–2023. These highlight the need for cultural competency and awareness training to be delivered to all relevant staff providing services (HSE, 2018).

Psychotherapy often explores the theme of change but like many disciplines is entrenched in its own history; theories and models formulated by white, western practitioners with individualistic cultural outlooks, immersed in the attitudes, prejudices and language of their era. The past 40 years may have introduced exciting new models and protocols, but modern research indicates very little in terms of improved client outcomes (Prochaska et al., 2020). Is this what clients from minoritised backgrounds need? What type of practitioners are psychotherapy courses producing? Where does clinical supervision sit within this? This chapter examines the experience of an accredited, multi-racial psychotherapist and supervisee, qualified within the last decade working in private practice in Dublin. It explores how relationships with clients and supervisors have evolved alongside my identity as a multicultural practitioner, and the challenges and insights this has released. It also highlights the role culturally responsive supervision inhabits within the therapeutic working alliance, insulating against unhelpful ruptures, and enabling

DOI: 10.4324/9781003380214-11

cultural opportunities (Watkins et al., 2019) whilst enhancing relational depth with clients from all backgrounds. It also suggests a role in professionally supporting minoritised practitioners outside of client work, navigating potential systemic prejudice and bias in the institutions of psychotherapy itself.

Passing **prior to training**

Race is a dynamic construct and the criterion for what is considered white is ever-changing. Various nationalities including the Irish have had difficulties being admitted to the club especially as migrants (Diangelo, 2018). Over time, the process of assimilation changes this and even if your internal identity is different, if you can *pass*, a white experience externally is available. Passing as white is a seductive privilege available to some multiracial therapists. Its genesis lies in the daily experience of a microaggression described by Sue and Sue (2016) as Colour Blindness which infers both implicitly and explicitly, that we assimilate to the dominant culture. This starts occurring from birth is influenced by relationships with our key attachment figures and our environment and is reinforced along developmental milestones through relationships within social, sporting, recreational, educational, and employment settings. The children of migrants have a unique experience in this regard, often born into a different society to that of their parent(s) or guardian(s). They begin exploring their identity by interacting with attachment figures and observing their challenges and triumphs within potentially minoritised communities. The impact and outcomes of these struggles are often transmitted to the next generation including learnt coping mechanisms such as code-switching (*passing*) which can interact with other microaggression in the environment such as *the myth of meritocracy* or *being an alien in one's own land* (Sue and Sue, 2016). As a result practitioners from minoritised backgrounds are at significant risk of presenting for training and supervision with a developed false self (Winnicott, 1960) or with fractured sub-personalities (Assagioli, 1965). From the humanistic perspective, this could be described as introjected values or *conditions of worth* (Rogers, 1961), that drive an external locus of evaluation, and thus incongruence in the practitioner or student.

In my own case, I borrowed generously from observing my own father's struggle with his environment. Born in South Africa, he was the descendant of indentured Northern Indian labourers. Like his ancestors, he too was forced to migrate as a young person due to racist limitations on education and opportunity and developed a large portion of his adult identity in the white catholic Ireland of the 1950s and 1960s as a student and junior doctor. I now wonder, was his ability to be more "Irish than the Irish" honed in apartheid South Africa where passing was a life skill that could open and close doors very quickly? I find myself curious about the role his own ancestors from Northern India may have had in modelling *passing* to my father.

Ababio (2019) describes how colonialism interacted with educational structures to encourage this type of behaviour in a West African context. It certainly was the case for my father who was only semi-literate in Hindi, completely unable to write but highly literate in English. I recall him mentioning how his accent helped him gain UK-based summer telephonist jobs over Irish applicants in the 1950s. Further evidence for this hypothesis is present in a book he gave an interview for, entitled *The Irish Raj* (Kapur, 1997). The book celebrates the stories of members of the Indian community in Ireland and my father's sections are littered with elaborations and omissions facilitating a comfortable read for a white or *passing* Asian audience. There are practical benefits to passing., my father contributed to Ireland as a doctor, a taxpayer, and a parent. I have heard it said he was an example of *a good migrant – a credit to his race*, why would not I continue to emulate this example myself professionally?

Then there is my Irish identity - my mother, her country, religion and culture. As can happen within multicultural unions the impact of code-switching was evident here too. My mother, born in rural Ireland married my father just before my birth and embarked on a multicultural journey of her own. Revisiting videos and photos from my childhood years I am struck by images of my mother wearing a sari at public events, a bindi between her eyebrows, and humming Hindi ghazals with her children. It is in stark contrast to the devout white catholic lady I meet today who talks with fondness of her rural upbringing and Irish identity. She too was putting great effort into passing as she leaned into her husband's world and culture, one face in public another at home. No doubt gender dynamics were at play here too. In school, I had no knowledge of what communion or confirmation were, I had never been to mass, and I watched cricket and soccer not Gaelic football, or hurling. I recall using Hindi words for certain items, particularly foods which caused much confusion. My mother's efforts to pass had created silence around important cultural content from her own identity. Passing was being modelled as a way of being, particularly when interacting outside of the home environment and it transcended the constructs of race or skin tone.

Ababio (2019) calls attention to the amount of psychic energy this "passing" maintenance takes within relationships. Sue and Sue (2016) describe culture as something we *do* rather than something we are. The practitioner's cultural narrative, including unconscious bias, internalised oppression and associated coping behaviours, is relevant to their professional identity and poses a risk of incongruence (Rogers, 1961) in both supervisory and client relationships. This professional identity emerges through experiences prior to training, within training and across other professional developmental markers like client work, clinical supervision and personal therapy. Consciously, I may believe I am providing a secure base (Bowlby, 1988) for my clients to explore their experience and emotions but unconsciously, through passing, I risk turning my consultation room into a microcosm of society, potentially wrought with prejudice, microaggression and oppression. Research highlights disparities in mental healthcare delivery to ethnic minority groups with many practitioners having better outcomes with white clients (Drinane et al., 2016; Hayes et al., 2015). Research also points to high rates of racial–ethnic micro-aggressions in sessions, with as many as 53% to 81% of clients reporting an experience of at least one micro-aggression (Hook et al., 2016). If, as therapists, we are not aware of these issues within ourselves, if race or other aspects to cultural identity are minimised because "we are all the same under the skin" or "all part of the one human race", significant risk is present to therapeutic relationships with clients from different cultural backgrounds. If not attended to, therapists may see early dropout rates from clients from diverse backgrounds or enable enactments (Chused, 2003) between client and therapist that mirror the above issues. If handled sensitively, these enactments present an opportunity for growth and healing. However, if handled recklessly, they have the opposite effect, reinforcing negatives in the external environment, making psychotherapy a tool of oppression, rewriting narratives and instilling the kinds of impulses that may have influenced my father's interview in *the Irish Raj*.

Passing in training – the supervisee and education

The educational setting has historically been used as a tool of oppression. History has been rewritten, minimised and appropriated to suit the majority culture (Diangelo, 2018). My father's education took place in the build-up to the *Bantu Education Act of 1953,* an overt, racist, legalisation of educational segregation in South Africa. Diangelo (2018) highlights contemporary forms of oppression are much more nuanced than the blatant acts and hate crimes associated with white supremacy. There have been changes to the types of racism societies will tolerate but education is still a setting where it can thrive. St Columba's College, a prestigious private South Dublin boarding school, launched an investigation into disturbing examples of racism shared by multiple past pupils (Lally, 2020). This contemporary Irish example suggests that underneath modern Ireland's progressive facade lies a much more complex relationship with differences tinted with a painful colonial history that predates the formation of the state. The rapid pace of change – from a conservative catholic nation, a country of emigration to a seemingly liberal, progressive country of destination – may explain why many courses that develop professionals omit intercultural contexts to training.

Am I passing in this chapter? Could it be more than just the rapid pace of change? - Whilst I have never faced anything like the educational obstacles my father faced, I believe my educational experience regularly interacted with prejudice. This started with the difficulty my parents had in the 1980s accessing admission to local schools due to my "not being Christian". I was ultimately placed in a non-denominational school with a Quaker ethos to help insulate me from this reality; a minority experience within a minority educational setting became my actual reality, one available only due to socio-economic privilege. This same privilege ultimately afforded me the opportunity to train as a therapist and a core part of my Integrative Psychotherapy training was based on the work of Carl Rogers. I find it interesting that over the years no mention was ever made of his training videos with a black client or the book exploring these sessions by Moodley, Lago and Talahite (2004). These sessions' explored anger and hurt, emotions I was soon to experience interacting with the profession in Ireland. Anger and hurt, feelings carried throughout my own journey in formal education were kept in check by passing. Passing was rewarded; occasional outbursts or acts of rebellion labelled disruptive, unfocused or below my potential were not. On reflection, the toll this passing maintenance was taking on me is clear and established a real challenge for me working as a therapist.

In the majority of Irish psychotherapy training courses, the issue of race and ethnic diversity is not an explicit part of the curriculum, easily demonstrated by the absence of reading lists. This syllabus harks back to the evolution of psychotherapy in Ireland, its inherent catholic world-view and the eventual fallout from the demise of this worldview (O'Morain et al., 2012). For a country with a volatile history of colonisation, assimilation, and rebellion I find it striking that in my training ethnicity was never explored directly with experiences relegated to lunchtime corridors amongst students with non-Irish identities. These students also happened to be white so even in these discussions the conditions were ripe for colour blindness to thrive. The majority of tutors in my training and many of the contributors to the syllabus were respected clinical supervisors. This points to systemic issues within psychotherapy, mirroring challenges in educational settings in general when it comes to diversity. Silence on the topic was the norm in both small and large group work with experiential training on difference focusing on sexuality, gender, and to a lesser degree disability and age. Diversity was welcome but only certain types - when it came to race and ethnicity assimilation to the dominant culture was the way to go. I remember an article on culture that we were encouraged to read; its title was *Growing Up Irish* (Greene, 1994). Not only did I find this article out of date, but its content and language signalled a focus on a particular type of Irish experience, *their* experience.

There were other cultural opportunities (Watkins Jr. et al., 2019) across my years of training, and holding and exploring these could have benefitted all students in terms of intercultural learning.

A tutor noticed me using a shorter version of my name and asked me what I would like to be called. My group responded by calling me by my full name for the rest of my training and the experience stayed with me. I was happy to reclaim my name in an educational setting, grateful enough to not make it too uncomfortable for anyone. I had a vested interest in passing in education going all the way back to early school experiences and this fed the enactment from my side. This episode was a significant cultural opportunity that repeatedly re-emerged over my years of training but was never explored by supervisors or trainers. The present incarnation of my names spelling points to colonial damage and internalised oppression within my father, who shortened it to Ravind (from Ravinder or Ravindra) to make it easier for "the Irish to pronounce". Over the years I continued making these concessions answering to Ray, Ravi, Raj, Raymond, Rav, and even Roy.

During a 20-minute skills practice session with a non-Irish student, in which they were having difficulty expressing something personal about themselves, I got the notion to invite them to use their native language. The intervention was effective, and they privately thanked me after, but while commended for my use of Rogerian (1961) empathy by the tutor, this session could have been opened up and explored for the benefit of all students' learning if viewed through a multicultural orientation lens of cultural humility, comfort and opportunity (Watkins Jr. et al., 2019). I see this session now as the genesis of my attempts at cultural responsiveness (Muñoz, 2007) Ignoring opportunities like this in supervision outside of a college setting could leave a client and therapist missing an opportunity to deepen their work even by the standards of popular models of supervision like the Seven-Eyed Process model (Hawkins and Shohet, 2012).

These lost potential learning experiences, overseen by white Irish tutors reinforce the bias in learning evident in all my formal educational experiences to date. The destruction of my name, assumptions about religion, denegation of sporting preferences, insensitive teaching of history and ignorance of cultural topics have been reoccurring experiences. In my view, this highlights a denial of racism, prejudice, and discrimination – terms being reserved for extreme examples of white supremacy (Diangelo, 2018). When therapists, teachers or supervisors support this denial, they abdicate responsibility and ignore the more nuanced ways racism is pervasive in our institutions and society while maintaining the comfort and associated privileges passed down through the ages. I believe there is an urgent need to review the training of practitioners aiming to work with some of the most vulnerable people in society as a matter of urgency. I can imagine my college's response to my observations – that time is limited and that some process left unexplored belongs in personal therapy, a mandatory part of training. This would conveniently ignore the structural issue, again, underscoring the diversity problem in Irish psychotherapy. Over one thousand therapists registered with Ireland's largest professional body answered a membership survey the results of which indicated that 88% were Irish-born, 78% were female and 77% were over 45 years old (Kelly, 2019). In personal therapy, I was attuned to my difference and aware of challenges within my training course but focused on other issues, particularly grieving the death of my father which occurred the year I started training. This bereavement took up a lot of space and deflected from other processes. Later, through work in private practice, these processes were rekindled revealing another dimension to my loss, the demise of a great source of cultural richness, and last substantial link to my non-white identity, to South Africa, to India, and my ancestry.

"I had emerged from psychotherapy training as a white therapist for white clients."

Passing in Supervision – an extension of the training experience?

Training exists within the context of a group setting with the needs of many students and course demands present. This context creates the potential for a majority culture approach to diversity. As training evolves, the start of intensely supervised clinical work becomes a crucial stage in the development of a therapist, the integration of theory, process, practice, and the exploration of a professional identity. Supervision provides a setting for issues not fully covered in training to be addressed as they emerge between client and therapist. It is the firewall for the concessions needed in a group or classroom setting and crucially a safety net for the clients presenting for therapy with clinically inexperienced practitioners. My training and pre-accreditation clinical work was with white Irish-born clients and my supervision reflected this caseload - issues of race and culture were never to the fore and nothing stood out in terms of learning about intercultural practice. Looking back, I find it remarkable that my own ethnicity and its potential relevance in the room was never explored at all in supervision. Evidently, supervision was fertile ground to continue passing, the clinical work mirroring my supervisory relationship. Constantine (1997) describes psychotherapy supervisors as a group who have often received less multicultural training and are less demographically diverse than their supervisees. Research continues to uncover evidence of the deleterious effects of unresponsive or inappropriate handling of cultural themes in supervision (Burkard et al., 2006; Mori, Inman, and Caskie, 2009; Ng and Smith, 2012; Nilsson, 2007). Gatmon et al. (2001) suggest this may help explain the finding that supervisors are less likely than supervisees to initiate conversations about culture in supervision.

Looking back on earlier client work, cultural opportunities come to mind which may have been worth casting a multicultural lens upon.

I recall repeatedly dissolving interest around my name and "where I was really from" in initial sessions – allowing myself to be called a variety of versions of my name. This hints at my unwillingness to address microaggression in the room and demonstrates my intent of assimilating to the dominant culture. I never mentioned any of this behaviour in supervision, ultimately showing incongruence within my own identity as a multiracial individual and practitioner. Both in the sessions and in supervision I was working hard for comfort through passing.

Another potentially missed cultural opportunity was when a client repeatedly commented on being surprised about having a positive experience with a male therapist, sharing that initially they had serious reservations about working with me. I mentioned this as positive during supervision, but never explored this further with the client from the perspective of intersectionality, being an Asian male or a younger, multiracial male. The opportunity was there to take the client's lead to explore our difference but I was intent on maintaining comfort in the room, happily taking positive feedback and missing the opportunity. My confirmation bias around all this could have been queried had I culturally responsive supervision at the time. I feel it would have enabled me to go further than the limitations I was framing around the work. Difference *and silence were presenting issues for this client and within our relationship my own silence fed an enactment which I now feel restricted the depth of our work.*

I continued this trajectory toward assimilation as a therapist and went full steam into private practice where I was surprised by quick success in terms of demand. I was no longer being allocated clients by a counselling centre or college setting, they were self-referring directly and the demographic changes were noticeable. I was receiving repeated enquiries from people born outside of Ireland and Irish-born clients from multi-ethnic backgrounds. *Agencies contacted me for help working with vulnerable asylum seekers and undocumented clients. Passing* became unsustainable, clients directly named racism as a presenting issue. Some clients explicitly wanted to see me due to my ethnic background, often curious about my Irish birth and what languages I spoke. I was also told on a few occasions that interventions I had made sounded very "white". Some clients shared difficulties with other therapists when the topics of race and cultural differences were mentioned. I was finally being forced to confront my own identity and it started to consciously impact my work. I believe this was driven in part by increased self-disclosure. Putting myself "out there" on the internet involved a biography, a picture and my name being visible which provided curious clients the opportunity to look me up on other platforms. This invited projection of various cultural dynamics onto me before any sessions occurred. Sue and Sue (2016) cite therapeutic use of self-disclosure as being one aspect of research that has shown some clients from diverse backgrounds appreciate in counselling, and it is possible I accidentally tapped into this.

If self-disclosure was one part of the shift the other was a change in supervisor. For the first time, I was not involved with a practitioner linked to my old training institution, and this proved more liberating than I realised at the time. Issues of race and culture were initially not a focus in our work, but I do recall noting he was a well-travelled person with experience working with non-Irish clients in his career. Cultural issues and race began being addressed directly in supervision. Generally, the presenting issues were familiar, anxiety, depression, somatic manifestations of trauma and relationship issues. The fact we could even talk about these issues from different cultural perspectives in our sessions was new, it signalled permission to explore, and it also signalled permission for me to be more honest in the room, more congruent as a practitioner. This was a very delicate phase in my professional development, with a significant risk of regression possible. I found the culturally responsive environment now present in supervision allowed me to take the risk and share a vulnerable part of myself, increasingly key to my professional identity. This supervisory working alliance was instrumental in removing the shackles ignored in my training and associated clinical supervision, shackles that had existed around formal educational experiences since I was four years old.

Supervision – Supporting the minoritised practitioner's voice

My interest in social justice encouraged me to start speaking more on the subject of culture with my fellow practitioners. I was invited by an accrediting body to give a short presentation where I introduced the idea of culturally sensitive counselling and explored topics like working with an interpreter. The success of this led to me offering a day's workshop the following year introducing the topic of multicultural counselling.

I invited different organisations representing marginalised sections of society to speak at the event, consciously giving the room a day rich in diversity. After lunch, I noticed some attendees struggled to stay alert and a lack of time resulted in me not being able to deliver an important section of material. As I processed this afterward, I became aware of a strong emotion, anger. I had silenced myself again – I had packed in too much content for one day and it struck me later that my whole design of the day may have been unconsciously focused on keeping me in a comfortable place by letting others speak. Soon after this event, I attended the AGM of my accrediting body during which I challenged a comment made by a therapist who disparaged younger practitioners (a minority in Ireland), their training and their lack of life experience. This therapist sought me out during a break and without even introducing herself let me know she had attended my training on multicultural counselling where I had demonstrated my own lack of experience. She explained how what I was exploring was nonsense and that it was all about "the client". I countered asking do we not need to look at ourselves before we can journey with clients, are we not in the room? She disagreed and added vehemently that my presentation was terrible, that the only part of interest was the section delivered by a member of the Irish travelling community and that the video I had shown, the documentary short "Black Sheep", was irrelevant. Was it a coincidence that the member of the travelling community she praised was the only white speaker? I expressed my sorrow that she felt that way and off she went into the crowd. Later, I discovered she was a supervisor as

I saw her mixing with the top brass of the accrediting body, on first name basis; I felt very uncomfortable.

Had I just met the personification of a larger problem engrained within the institution of psychotherapy training itself? A system of professional education suspicious of change and difference, that was consciously influencing new practitioners including those highlighting different experiences. To add fuel to my discomfort I was later informed by a peer linked to one of my course tutors, that I had been "protected" from certain trainers throughout my own training, not as I suspected because of gender, but because of the intersection of my ethnicity and gender. Since then, I am conscious of sitting on feelings of frustration when interacting with these institutions. These feelings are what *Passing*, has been protecting me from all along; my website, public presentations, my challenge to ageism all point to an abating reliance on this way of being. Without passing, I am aware of a new discomfort I feel in my daily life which in turn invites curiosity about how some of my clients may feel in theirs. Luckily, I have received support with this from clinical supervision which has prevented regression. For practitioners of diverse backgrounds experiences like these may well point to specific hurdles in place, in training, in practice and the professional world outside our consulting rooms. The role of culturally responsive supervision is essential for those of us emerging from trainings, accredited by institutions producing and sanctioning biased practice. Without this to support and encourage diversity amongst therapists it is often the most minoritised and vulnerable clients who will be silenced or who will face oppressive enactments (Chused, 2003) within their interactions with professionals. The result will be poor outcomes, early dropouts and ultimately the reinforcement of oppression, prejudice and racism, the very things that may have brought them to therapy in the first place.

Conclusion

I now view this incident at the AGM as a gift. I walked straight into what I feared was in the profession, highlighting for me the risks both clients and therapists face when addressing power, privilege, race and cultural differences. As practitioners emerge from training and move toward accreditation interaction with a more culturally diverse set of clients is inevitable and it is here that supervision remains a secure base for both clients and practitioners who face racism and oppression within their daily lived experiences and potentially in their therapeutic alliances. The topic is uncomfortable particularly for those of us who have the privilege of passing. Silence is tempting and all cultural manifestations of passing must be explored in supervision, not just around race, but also gender, class, age and so forth.

Supervision is widely regarded as critical to the development of psychotherapy trainees (Bernard and Goodyear, 2014; Falender et al., 2013;

Watkins, 2014; 2017). The preceding paragraphs represent my own sub-jective experience focusing on the key development phase of training and the beginning of clinical practice. For supervisees, effective super-vision necessitates exploration of culture when working with clients from all backgrounds. There are many challenges to working effectively in supervision using a Multicultural Orientation (Watkins et al., 2019). My own early experience indicates an engrained lack of cultural humility, an ignorance of cultural opportunity and a generous portion of cultural discomfort on all sides. A lack of intercultural, experiential process throughout training produces "culture blind" alumni, who in turn provide individual therapy and supervision to many future practitioners. If diversity is not embraced from the start, it is a self-perpetuating loop keeping the status quo intact. The current training reality raises the distinct possi-bility the supervisory relationship may be the venue these issues are ad-dressed in detail for the first time. It is often the client's voice that enables this cultural opportunity, and it is one that supervisors must take seriously. *The triangle with curved sides* (Lago and Thompson, 1997) not only faces the unconscious bias and prejudices engrained in broader society but in training institutions, accrediting bodies and traditional psychotherapy theory. Unchecked, this amalgamation risks reinforcing a pattern of intergenerational robbery for clients of diverse cultural backgrounds.

References

Ababio, B. (2019). Not yet at home: an exploration of aural and verbal passing amongst African migrants in Britain. In: Ababio, B., Littlewood, R. (eds.) *Intercultural Therapy: Challenges, Insights and Developments*. London: Routledge

Assagioli, R. (1965). *Psychosynthesis: A Collection of Basic Writings*. Synthesis Center, Hadley, MA: Commonwealth Printing.

Bernard, J. M., Goodyear, R. K. (2014). *Fundamentals of Clinical Supervision* (5th ed.). Upper Saddle River, NJ: Merrill.

Bowlby, J. (1988). A *Secure Base: Clinical Applications of Attachment Theory*. London: Routledge

Burkard, A. W., Johnson, A. J., Madson, M. B., Pruitt, N. T., Contreras-Tadych, D. A., Kozlowski, J. M., ...Knox, S. (2006). Supervisor cultural responsiveness and un-responsiveness in cross-cultural supervision. *Journal of Counseling Psychology, 53*, 288–301.

Chused, J. F. (2003). The role of enactments. *Psychoanal. Dial., 13*:677–687.

Constantine, M. G. (1997). Facilitating multicultural competency in counseling supervision: Operationalizing a practical framework. In: Pope-Davis, D. B., Coleman, H. L. K. (eds.) *Multicultural Aspects of Counseling Series, Vol. 7. Multicultural Counseling Competencies: Assessment, Education and Training, and Supervision* (pp. 310–324). Sage Publications, Inc.

CSO. (2017). *Census 2016: Ethnicity and Irish Travellers*. Central Statistics Office, Cork Retrieved from https://cso.ie on the 25th October 2020.

Diangelo, R. (2018). *White Fragility, Why It's So Hard for White People to Talk About Racism.* United Kingdom: Penguin Random House.

Drinane, J. M., Owen, J., Kopta, M. (2016). Racial/ethnic disparities in psychotherapy: Does the outcome matter? *Testing, Psychometrics, Methodology in Applied Psychology, 23,* 531–544.

Falender, C. A., Burnes, T. R., Ellis, M. V. (2013). Multicultural clinical supervision and benchmarks: Empirical support informing practice and supervisor training. *The Counseling Psychologist, 41,* 8–27.

Gatmon, D., Jackson, D., Koshkarian, L., Martos-Perry, N., Molina, A., Patel, N., Rodolfa, E. (2001). Exploring ethnic, gender, and sexual orientation variables in supervision: Do they really matter?. *Journal of Multicultural Counseling and Development, 29,* 102–113.

Greene, S.M. (1994). Growing up Irish: Development in context. *The Irish Journal of Psychology, 15*(2 & 3), 354–371

Hawkins, P., Shohet, R. (2012). *Supervision in the Helping Professions* (4th edn.) Berkshire: Open University Press.

Hayes, J. A., Owen, J., Bieschke, K. J. (2015). Therapist differences in symptom change with racial/ethnic minority clients. *Psychotherapy, 52,* 308–314.

Hook, J. N., Farrell, J. E., Davis, D. E., DeBlaere, C., Van Tongeren, D. R., Utsey, S. O. (2016). Cultural humility and racial microaggressions in counseling. *Journal of Counseling Psychology, 63,* 269–277.

HSE. (2018). *Second National Intercultural Health Strategy 2018-2023.* National Social Inclusion Office, Health Service Executive, Dublin Retrieved from https://www.hse.ie on the 25th October 2020.

Kapur, N. (1997). *The Irish Raj: Illustrated Stories About Irish in India and Indian in Ireland.* Antrim: Greystone Books.

Kelly, E. (2019). IACP *Member's Survey 2018 Summary Report.* Retrieved from https://iacp.ie/files/UserFiles/Publications/IACP-Member-Survey-2018-Report.pdf on the 25th October 2020

Lago, C., Thompson, J. (1997). The triangle with curved sides: Sensitivity to issues of race and culture in supervision. In Shipton, G. (ed.) *Supervision of Psychotherapy & Counselling* (pp. 119–130). Buckingham: Open University Press.

Lally, C. (2020). Dublin Boarding School reviewing racism allegations from pupils. The Irish Times (Online) June 7th.

Moodley, R., Lago, C., Talahite, A. (eds.). (2004). *Carl Rogers Counsels a Black Client.* Ross-on-Wye: PCCS Books.

Mori, Y., Inman, A. G., Caskie, G. L. (2009). Supervising international students: Relationship between acculturation, supervisor multicultural competence, cultural discussions, and supervision satisfaction. *Training and Education in Professional Psychology, 3,* 10–18.

Muñoz, J. P. (2007). Culturally responsive caring in occupational therapy. *Occupational Therapy International, 14*(4), 256–280.

Ng, K., Smith, S. D. (2012). Training level, acculturation, role ambiguity, and multicultural discussions in training and supervising international counseling students in the United States. *International Journal for the Advancement of Counselling, 34,* 72–86.

Nilsson, J. E. (2007). International students in supervision: Course self-efficacy, stress, and cultural discussions in supervision. *The Clinical Supervisor, 26,* 35–47.

O'Morain P, McAuliffe, G. J., Conroy, K., Johnson, J. M., Michel, R. E. (2012). *Counseling in Ireland Journal of Counseling & Development.* July 2012,Volume 90 371

Prochaska, J. O., Norcross, J. C., Saul, S. F. (2020). Generating psychotherapy breakthroughs: Transtheoretical strategies from population health psychology. *American Psychologist, 75,* 996–1010. Retrieved on the 25th October 2020

Rogers, C. R. (1961). *On Becoming a Person: A Therapist's View of Psychotherapy.* Boston: Houghton Mifflin.

Sue, D.W., Sue, D. (2016). *Counselling the Culturally Diverse Theory and Practice* (7th Ed.). New Jersey: Wiley.

Watkins, C. E. Jr., Hook, J. N., Owen, J., DeBlaere, C., Davis, D. E., Van Tongeren, D. R. (2019). Multicultural orientation in psychotherapy supervision: Cultural humility, cultural comfort, and cultural opportunities. *American Journal of Psychotherapy, 72*(2): 38–46

Watkins, C. J. (2014). The supervisory alliance: A half century of theory, practice, and research in critical perspective. *Journal of Contemporary Psychotherapy, 41,* 57–67.

Winnicott, D. W. (1960). Ego distortion in terms of true and false self. In: Winnicott, D.W., (ed.) *The Maturational Processes and the Facilitating Environment: Studies in the Theory of Emotional Development.* London: Karnac Books, 140–152.

Chapter 8

An Attachment Approach to Working with Issues of Difference in an Intercultural Setting

Caroline Adewole

This chapter offers a description of a supervision group within a placement organisational setting. It highlights three essential tasks of supervision and explains the theoretical thinking and models that inform my supervisory process. To this end, I draw on a psychodynamic, intercultural, and attachment framework in conjunction with the seven-eyed supervision model.

Three phases of the supervisory process and treatment are explored, I consider group formation, therapeutic dyad, process, and ending. In the formation phase, enabling safety is discussed through the perspective of the Attachment Theory. I attend to exploration as linked to the process phase in the supervision. Referencing case examples from the therapeutic dyad and the relationships within the supervisory group, I discuss *disruptions*, a pivotal and unavoidable part of human experience. I argue that a secure attachment in supervision, facilitates explorations in the thematic areas of separation, loss and trauma. I present Four vignettes to explicate differences listed as: race, religion, gender, and review the differentiation process within the group.

The concept of reparation is important from an attachment-based perspective. Meanings and interpretations of reparation are varied. Could it be a restoration to a lost but desired state, or might it be the ability to mourn and embrace the emergent with a newfound ability to carry on? The reparation process enables separation and loss to be engaged and worked through.

Finally, the chapter discusses endings and links it to the therapeutic dyad, the supervision group and the organisational setting. The placement organisation operates from an intercultural/psychodynamic perspective and was developed to address issues faced by racialised and minoritised communities. I present a description of the group below.

The group

The supervision group consists of three females and one male. Jack is a white South African raised in England and male. Marisha is black and of Jamaican

DOI: 10.4324/9781003380214-12

heritage; Aleema and Salah derive their heritage from Pakistan and Bangladesh respectively. Marisha, Aleema, and Salah were born in the United Kingdom and identify as British. Aleema and Salah are practising Muslims, Marisha and Jack are not particularly religious. They are all students on training placements, pursuing post-graduate degrees in Psychotherapy or counselling at different universities and interested in the psychodynamic framework. Two members are from integrative training institutes. I, their supervisor, trained as an attachment-based, psycho-analytic psychotherapist. I am a black, female, born in the United Kingdom and raised in West Africa.

Hawkins and Shohet (2012) posit the following three functions as key in supervisory work. They are developmental, supportive, and qualitative in nature. As a supervisor in the group, I promote self-care and provide educational support to enable supervisees develop their psychotherapeutic skills and familiarise themselves with promoting supervisee self-care.

Hawkins and Shohet commenting on the processing levels at play in the supervision, say, "At any time in supervision, there are many levels operating. At a minimum, all supervision situations involve at least five elements ..." (ibid) p.86. This, they term, the seven-eyed model, which they posit, operates on seven processing levels in most supervision groups. The levels are addressed in more detail toward the end of this chapter. The model, in my view, helps the supervisor recognise areas in the trainee's work which might require strengthening – tracking their progress to appropriately offer support where and when required. Now to the three phases of the supervision process, beginning with group formation.

Group formation

Prioritising safety is key in enabling group formation. Castellino's "*The Principles*" (2013) applied in his Womb Surround workshops is apposite. I reference these principles to facilitate a sense of safety in the groups I supervise. The group's awareness of these principles enables their client-therapist relationships to be of primary importance in an evolving experiential positioning. Each group member's relationship with clients of their peers is revered albeit secondary to their own clients. It encourages the group to develop a somewhat healthy attachment to each other's clients, meaning members experience being held, (including their client work) by their peers. To put it another way, a therapist would naturally be their client's first layer of support and the supervision group the second.

The principles postulated by Castellino are mutual respect, choice, brief-eye contact, self-care, self-regulation, touch and attention, and confidentiality. They are foundational to the formation of the supervision group.

Mutual respect involves group members relating to each other and their clients with thoughtfulness and consideration. A principle enshrined in the ethical framework of the different training models of the supervisees. Respect is associated with choice, in this regard supervisees may in the supervision decide which clients to work with. It is exercised if a therapist realises that they could potentially be in a dual relationship with an allocated client. For example, a referred client is also a relative of Marisha's friend. The client in question is reallocated to another therapist in a different supervision group. Similarly, every group member decides how much of their personal stories, if relevant to client material, they choose to disclose in supervision sessions.

Supervisees' ability to be appropriately open about their personal stories, especially regarding countertransference, has a positive effect on the supervisory process and outcome. However, they do so because they feel safe, and where they discover this appropriate but too uncomfortable, supervisees take it to therapy. There is a link here to self-care, a principle the group explores throughout their time in the supervision group. They are clear about the difference between supervision and personal therapy. A pre-requisite for a training placement in the organisation is for supervisees to have personal therapy. Self-care is held in supervision and therapy; the supervisees and the supervisor consequentially share the responsibility of care.

Self-regulation as a principle benefits the group, particularly when the pace of the material under discussion quickens inappropriately. In such instances, it requires a slowing down to increase the group's ability to identify what might be going on in the countertransference and enable reflection. Respect and attentiveness extend to the clarity of the induction process of new members to the placement organisation, this is fundamental to the group formation process. New members spend their first three weeks in familiarising themselves with the service: a group induction and ongoing access to technical and administrative support enhances this process, as does the introduction to organisational policies, the supervision group, its goals and mode of operation.

Respect and the integrity of an individual's space and their boundaries are connected. Physical touch is not recommended within the psychodynamic supervision model. However, warmth, attunement, brief yet consistent eye contact, the use of the trainees' names, mirroring and curiosity can facilitate the experience of this principle of respect. Confidentiality, the seventh principle, is already woven into every psychotherapeutic organisation's ethical framework. It suggests supervisees could bring and reflect on, in supervision, aspects of themselves touching on their client work, both positively and otherwise. These seven principles are adapted to form part of the usual contracting at the start of supervisory group relationships and are used continuously throughout the group's life.

The process

The second phase of the supervision is the process. Clients, by and large, seek therapy due to disruptions in their lives, and it is the sporadic enactment of this disruption in the therapy that the supervisee in part explores in supervision. I illustrate this process phase of the actual supervision through four case examples (related to, race, religion, and gender) under the rubric of difference, diversity and the differentiation process within the group.

Race

Falila a client, 47 years old, of Indian heritage, was subjected to severe physical abuse as a child by her father and had had a complicated relationship with her mother. Falila was in an arranged marriage at the age of 16, in her country of origin, to a British citizen. She joined her husband two years later in the United Kingdom. The marriage was childless for the first five years during which Falila was subjected to domestic violence. Her husband was alcohol dependent. Falila was severely depressed when she commenced therapy. The second of her two children, a son, had left home for university while the first, a daughter, was married. Her father had died suddenly in India, and she had not attended the funeral. She had not had therapy before and had no idea how it worked. She chose to work in her mother tongue, Punjabi.

Aleema is bilingual and Punjabi is one of her therapy languages. She presents her client, Falila. She says Falila has missed quite a few sessions and has also been late several times. Falila, according to Aleema is not accustomed to therapy because she does not say much. Aleema seems disappointed, desperate. There is a hint of frustration, possibly anger, in her voice.

My curiosity about Aleema's countertransference prompts an exploration with her. She confirms her frustration. She says she is training because of her desire to help her community, to educate them, but she experiences her community as unavailable, not engaging, like Falila. She sounds heroic, but her desire to "educate them" feels uncomfortable. I invite her to analyse this desire and I wonder how this desire might play out in the therapy. What does she think would happen if she does not "educate"? Aleema then says she thinks her community is far less civilised compared to others. They behave differently and seem to live in a different world.

Her agenda to fix, which she conveys through a critical lens, seems at odds with her client's needs and expectations. Aleema exudes an air of superiority. I verbalise my observation and ask if any of it resonates with her. There is silence as she reflects, and I continue to be curious and wonder aloud what she imagines clients from her community would look like after fixing. The silence continues, then a smile of recognition. She says she is aware she has had a deep reluctance to bring clients from her community to supervision. It has been shameful, she says, for her to share the painful aspects of individuals from her ethnic community with the supervision group.

She continues the self-reflection and deploys the BAMER identity model (Agoro, 2019) she situates herself as somewhere between the conformity and dissonance phases. She does not only prefer white British values but expects her ethnic community to conform to her ideal (proximity to whiteness). She connects with an awareness of the motivation of her choice of an intercultural training placement. Which, in part, was a combination of a curiosity about herself and the desire to "fix" others. Her self-reflection facilitates a discussion on internalised racism and oppression and the strategy of using caregiving as a means of perpetuating an insecure response of *silence and withdrawal* in a less dominant group, in this case, members of her community. Aleema also recognises her continued efforts with her client as reminiscent of *over-working*, another characteristic of internalised oppression which was contributing to the activation and maintenance of an avoidant pattern of attachment in their relationship. She could see how this was counter to the therapeutic task of supporting Falila to safely deconstruct in therapy distressing events that occur within the therapeutic relationship and life generally.

In attachment terms, the impasse between Aleema and Falila is illustrative of an ineffective caregiving interaction between therapists and their clients. Heard on this matter says (Heard et al. 2012):

> The care seeker communicates despair nonverbally and provides very little content; caregiver avoids naming the affect and asks questions; care seeker responds minimally to the questions; caregiver continues to ask questions; care seeker continues to respond minimally; both become silent and withdrawn.

Now back to the impasse, Aleema, continuing with her self-reflection, notices that the caregiving part of her is also fuelled by shame in the sessions with Falila. She realises this caregiving is a defence against the shame she feels in the group regarding clients from her community. She recognised that the shame was also linked to her early life experiences. I highlight that shame is the hallmark of trauma, testifying to the traumatic nature of race-related, psychic injuries. She takes these emerging insights to her therapy.

In subsequent sessions, Aleema is open, reflective and warm. Something has shifted in the therapeutic relationship with Falila, who begins to attend regularly and punctually. She is also more open and communicative. Falila delves into her story, and Aleema begins to see how Falila's external environment – culture and attachment-figures – have impacted Falila. Aleema's frustration lifts, and she begins to look forward to her sessions with Falila and present her with openness in the supervision.

Religion

Heard et al. describe three types of effective caregiving interactions with a careseeker. Next, I describe one of these interactions concerning the intersection between religion and race in elucidating aspects of process in a supervision session. You will see how embedded I am as supervisor in the following case example. On effective caregiving interaction, Heard et al. observe:

> *The careseeker presents as highly aroused and gives an incoherent account of concerns involving a lot of seemingly unconnected detail; the caregiver responds verbally and nonverbally, down-regulates the affect, and confirms, contains, and encourages; the careseeker continues to expand on their issues; the caregiver continues to respond - matching their vitality affects to the vitality affects of the careseeker, and contains, orientates, and provides a context for exploration; careseeker and the caregiver are seen to be mutually responsive.*

(Heard et al. 2012, p. 131)

Case example

The last twenty-four hours for me (supervisor) have been particularly problematic. I have witnessed racist assaults against Muslims. As I walk to the service this morning, I feel the tension in the atmosphere.

In the supervision session following the Finsbury Park Mosque (in north London) attack on 17 June 2017, Salah and Aleema, two Muslims in the group, look absent and numb. Their manner recalls the tension I had experienced in certain spaces in the last twenty-four hours. I have a feeling the strain in the supervision room is related to the mosque attack, but I could be wrong, so I sit with the tension. I notice a need to look away and down. Body language comes to mind, so I check their body language. Salah and Aleema are looking down while Aleema fidgets with her fingers. Jack and Marisha look perplexed. Then, Salah starts to speak. She did not feel like coming in today, she feels tired, somewhat unwell. She has struggled to attend and might not seem present, she says apologetically.

The Finsbury Park Mosque terror attack seemed retaliatory in the context of the previous London Bridge and Manchester terror attacks. This was a challenging and disconcerting time for the two supervisees and other Muslim clients who access the service and I wonder with the group what it must feel like to be here right now in supervision. Perhaps Muslim colleagues feel they will be judged here, too, as in broader society. I intentionally pay attention to the prosody in my voice and my body language, make brief eye contact and am mindful.

The relief is palpable. Aleema looks up and speaks of the shame of being vilified, stigmatised and stereotyped as a Muslim. She is aware of wanting to hide as it has felt unsafe lately. I highlight how her posture had previously portrayed that, and how it links to her trauma. She is still slightly slouched, so I ask if she would like to experiment with elongating her back. Everyone in the group, including me, assumes a more upright sitting position. Listening to Aleema seems to have helped Salah, whose earlier response sounded somewhat dissociated. She joins in. She now seems more in touch with her anger. "It is not fair", she says. "Most Muslims like other communities are peaceful and not terrorists", "condemning and ostracising us will not help," she added.

Naming the elephant in the room also seems helpful for Marisha and Jack. Jack speaks about his mixed feelings. He, too, has been feeling unsafe and angry. Marisha is also empathically present for them, and she is aware of just wanting to sit with them in their pain.

Exploration

In the exploration, we begin by analysing the range of feelings present in the group. This was linked to what feelings Muslim clients and allies might bring to their therapy sessions. The group connect with an experience of the dynamics and impact of racialisation processes and the effect of external world events on the intrapsychic and, invariably, human interaction. We consider the consequences of individual responses in the group (including mine as supervisor) on Aleema and Salah and the potential re-enactments between supervisees and their clients.

At the next session, the whole group reports feeling 'more present' and able to contain and deal with the different ways in which the racialised, social-cultural climate had influenced their clinical work.

Gender

The following case example discusses the dynamics of gender in the process phase. It describes a different type of interaction and outcome between the care seeker and caregiver. Heard et al. remark that:

> The careseeker is demanding; caregiver's responses are cognitive and fail to regulate careseeker's affect; careseeker becomes more demanding; caregiver continues engaging cognitively; careseeker becomes more aroused; caregiver, careseeker, or both attack one another or withdraw.
>
> (Heard et al. 2012, p. 132)

In the group, Salah's presentation seems to indicate her unease and of being activated by her client Aya's narrative. Aya has been in an abusive relationship with a man. She is distraught by the breakdown in her relationship with her father. Her decision to live with the abusive man seems to have precipitated the problem with her father who has not been part of her life whilst she was growing up. She has been feeling angry, bewildered and highly anxious at the possibility of losing a relationship with him again. She is twenty-two years old and her mother berates her for not going to university even though her A-level results were good enough. Her mother could not understand why she was depressed and stuck because of an abusive man and an absent father.

Aya is three years younger than Salah her therapist, who has developed a sibling countertransference toward her which she reciprocates in the transference. Salah in supervision describes Aya's yearning for her father. She has questioned why Aya is so preoccupied with these two men. Salah points out that Aya is very resourceful and has survived without her father, and she has what it takes to get an education and improve her life. Salah in supervision is frustrated and does not understand Aya's desire to have a relationship with an unreliable father and an abusive partner. Salah says she has tried to be the voice of reason, and that Aya continues to bring the same issues to the therapy each week as if they have never been addressed.

I notice Jack is somewhat agitated and distant during the supervision, and I say so and wonder with him what is going on. He is apprehensive and cautious, so I observe the principle of the pause operative and encourage him to take time and pay attention to his inner world. He says he feels there is something in the material and supervision which is denigrating of men and makes him feel uncomfortable. He says he is less vocal when male clients are being discussed because he feels attacked.

I point out a similarity with how Aleema had felt in the group when race was being explored. I ask him to describe what he is feeling. He says he feels he has to be the container for the projections in the room. He visibly regulates his affect, which I observe and acknowledge. He relaxes and agrees. I then check if he is okay before moving my attention back to Salah. He says that he feels better voicing it, and I promise to return it to him.

Back with Salah, I highlighted a parallel process, her lecturing Aya on what she could and could not do, a repetition of what Aya said her mother did with her. Salah recognises the repetition and is shocked to recognise her repetition of Aya's trauma in her treatment. I asked her to say more about her process. She had, on reflection, become aware of her identification with Aya. Salah had experienced similar challenges with her father. She had been experiencing her client's challenges through her values, trying to impose her solution on her client. Salah became aware in our exploration, that her approach to her own issue had not eradicated the problem she had with her own father. She could also see how she had become empathically disconnected from her client while being enmeshed with her material.

I go back to check on Jack. He says he is fine, and he discloses that he is aware of how aspects of his past have also influenced his earlier reaction.

Also, it is difficult, he says, to sit in the group as the only male and hear stories of ineffective and sometimes unavailable fathers as well as the reactions to the material from the female members in the supervision. However, listening to Salah's process has helped him get in touch with something developmental in himself. I reflect that in addition to being male, he is also the only white person in the group (he says he is surprised that he had not considered it). I encourage the whole group to take the events in the session to therapy to consolidate the work.

Differentiation within the group

In looking at this process phase in supervision, I reference the previous point I made regarding the facilitative role Castellino's seven principles play in building and maintaining an essential secure base in the supervision. Developmentally, this is crucial for exploration to commence. Differentiation accelerates the group's move to the next developmental level. At face value, attachment and differentiation seem to be mutually exclusive. However, differentiation usually occurs when there is a sense of safety, and it is also essential to a secure attachment in that to be genuinely seen and accepted is to be seen and accepted in the totality of one's uniqueness. The differentiation process enables the emergence and celebration of all these distinct qualities.

In the group, the supervisees start showing their strengths, abilities and areas for development. Also, their idiosyncrasies begin to emerge, visible and invisible differences become apparent, and contradict, clash, or resonate. This dynamic is not limited to the group, their ideas, actions, and interactions, but also to their clients.

Like attachment, differentiation is an innate tendency of humans; we are born unique yet simultaneously attaching and seeking to express and celebrate our difference throughout the life cycle. Having access to our attachment system facilitates our capacity to negotiate the inevitable and sensitive differentiation process.

As the group bring to supervision, initially, their view of their performance, constantly seeking validation and approval, their sense of safety increases, their focus shifts outward, and they begin to show curiosity about their clients and not just how well they are looking after them and meeting organisational requirements. They also begin to show interest in other group members in ways that highlight their identities and idiosyncrasies.

Curiosity and interest in the other are very healthy but can also easily give rise to issues around roles and perceptions about the other. Wallin (2007) asserts that "… the intersubjective approach highlights the opportunity to learn through attention to enactments about the conflict the patient experiences when it comes to making use of the empathy and containment" (p. 188).

Likewise, using mentalisation Allen et al. (2008), the caregiving process facilitates intrapsychic and interpsychic differentiation.

Differentiation could also be defined as the interface between the secure base and exploration experiences. Members of the group begin to see the Secure base of supervision as a tool – a springboard from which to engage in their explorations. Internal world exploration results in self-definition, an assured self-reflective stance and a robust sense of self. When external exploration finally begins, it is interspersed with frequent attachment system activation and a return to the base as a safe haven. Subsequently, activations become less frequent leading to the last phase of the work, Ending and Mourning, which will be discussed shortly.

Let us, briefly, return to the earlier case examples. In the vignette on race, Aleema's task is to uncouple herself from her client's material, and it is not till she can see her values as separate from the client's that exploration properly begins. In the discussions on gender, we see an active "I am male" with Jack (*also white*) and "I am female" with Aleema (and brown). Again, as they begin to see themselves separate from the client and their material, their exploration begins to deepen, and supervisees become more available for each other and the client.

Differentiation can be fraught with anxiety, conflict, and rupture, due to separation anxiety, these dynamics can reverberate in the supervisory relationship and are usually felt in an earlier developmental stage of the group. It is pertinent here to reference an experience from the case example on race not included in its previous discussion, Aleema and I have a disruption. It takes a couple of sessions before I access an understanding of what was taking place. Prior to this, Aleema in supervision has portrayed considerable anxiety around her performance and continued to receive caregiving to contain her unease. She, however, begins to display a change, she interjects intermittently and challenges my comments and interventions. The challenges are appropriate, but I experience her interjections as protest in the countertransference. After interjecting and putting her point of view across, on one occasion, I say that I think she is trying to tell me she is ok, and that I can step back a little now. She physically calms when her developmental growth is acknowledged, and she hears that she is more able to hold her clients. I had missed when to step back in *my* anxiety to ensure she receives optimal caregiving. When I eventually do, the interjections cease altogether.

Marisha, 21, is the youngest member of the group. Her issues around her age first surfaced at the interview stage but has continued into her clinical work. She has not been able to retain any of her clients beyond the third session. She is presenting in the group and informs us that her third client has not attended twice in a row. She sounds constricted as she speaks and holds back her tears. She says two of her clients have raised her age as an issue, and she believes it informed the client's decision to discontinue. Marisha, it appears had not explored with clients their concerns about her age. She blames the Organisation for denting her confidence during her interview by raising concerns about her age.

Marisha expresses her feelings and explores what else might be going on. She thinks the supervision group also views her as young and inexperienced. She feels other group members are more capable. She notices her three supervision peers retain all three clients they were allocated. She makes a shift in owning her resentment and anger toward the Organisation, me (supervisor) and the group. She also recognises that she had been worried about her age prior to taking up her placement. She conveys her wish to work through this with a view to becoming more available for her client and with an increased capacity to help clients work through similar issues. Marisha takes it to therapy, and we work in supervision to help her with her subsequent clients around this specific issue. Marisha begins to separate from her age difference and relate to it differently. She continues to take responsibility for it in her clinical work and the supervision group. Eventually, she retains her fourth client and builds a healthy caseload of three clients like her peers. Her contributions in supervision also become more insightful, and she experiences [a shift in her perception of] being respected by her peers.

The implication of the supervision group's interaction with other functioning parts of the organisation in the differentiation process is worth noting. Consider the referrals and Allocation Team which has responsibility for allocating clients to therapists. They have sometimes intentionally 'overlooked' clients' specific requests or preferences to work with a particular kind of therapist and instead thoughtfully and intuitively matched them differently. For example, some clients at consultation might request for a therapist of a particular culture, race, gender, or religious persuasion and end up being allocated to a different therapist altogether. The supervisory relationship becomes tense when this has occurred in the group.

The initial sessions in such cases are usually anxiety-ridden for the therapists and their attachment system is activated. Therapists in such instances are closely supported to work through the disappointments of the client and their own anger at the "mismatch." However, as therapy progresses, careseeking and the accompanying anger begin to soften. The therapist learns to use and finetune their intercultural skills (working with differences in transference and countertransference). Therapist and client challenge each other's fears and biases and facilitate the client to work on their problems. Thus far, I have with case examples examined the dynamics of group formation, process and differentiation and will at this juncture in the chapter attend to the ending phase.

Mourning and ending

Bowlby (1980) emphasised the link between loss and mourning through an attachment paradigm. The supervision group drawing on this paradigm can identify areas in their clinical work and supervision where mourning and loss occur. The attention and recognition enabled in the group focuses on phases such as end of sessions, breaks, gaps in the therapy, and the end of each therapeutic relationship. An understanding of client responses to themes of mourning is expanded, for example, how some clients with an avoidant attachment pattern might always promptly remind the therapist of the time being up at the end of their sessions. From experience, clients exhibiting avoidant patterns are more likely not to miss their therapist when there are gaps, breaks and at the end of therapy. On the other hand, clients with a preoccupied attachment pattern might tend to prolong their sessions, and breaks and therapy termination would probably heighten their distress, a form of separation anxiety. Individuals in the group may discern parallel processes in how they prolong their time when presenting clients with preoccupied attachments in the supervision. This contrasts with time spent presenting their avoidant clients, which is managed by therapists keeping well within the time boundaries or avoid bringing them at all for discussion.

The following case example elucidates an aspect of these dynamics. Jack's first client Yara was approaching the end of her therapy. She was in her late 20s, an only child and immigrant who with her family fled Syria to settle in the United Kingdom, when she was five years old without time for goodbyes. The family's journey to the United Kingdom meant putting up in temporary camps, where friendships were transient. As asylum seekers in the United Kingdom, Yara and her family lived in short let accommodations and eventually settled in the Midlands. When she was ten years old her father left the family home with no explanation, she was devastated. Mother was frequently hospitalised and treated for mental health problems. Her absences meant that other people took care of her. As an adult, Yara's relationships were short term and she reported being described by the partners who left as "weird" and "being too much."

In a supervision, Jack says he was happy for his time to be taken up by other colleagues as he did not have much to explore. After presentations by peers, there was time left for Jack. He then proceeds albeit with some reluctance to present Yara, who has thus far attended eight sessions. Jack says Yara had ended her current relationship after a "minor" argument and subsequently cut ties with an only friend. After the ninth session, he reports she had handed in a resignation letter at work because of another "small" disagreement. The pattern of her relationships is highlighted in supervision in the context of the therapy nearing completion. Jack was concerned about her history of losses and her fear of the pain of being abandoned. Yara appears to manage this lack of control over relationships by severing relationships, Jack feared this pattern might play out in the ending stage of the therapy because of Yara's avoidance of a fear of being rejected in the therapy. Jack reflects on this formulation and explores it in the subsequent session with her. She reflects on Jack's comment and connects her rejecting of the "good objects" in her life to her anxieties regarding the ending phase of her relationship with Jack. The themes of severing and helplessness are explored and linked to endings in her life. Yara described how torturous it felt to have something she cherished taken from her as a child and how difficult it has been to trust. She connected her therapeutic relationship to her intimate relationships. She could see that her anxiety over losing a partner meant that she would often initiate the rejection.

In the next session, Yara reports she has initiated the process of working through the rupture with her partner and reports to have exchanged messages with her friend who she had disconnected from. She reports asking to withdraw her resignation letter. She is emotional in the final session – she concludes that therapy had been painful, insightful and helpful and that she would seek long-term therapy.

The group supervision ending

Placement agreements in the organisation are signed for a year and can be extended subject to review. The end of the group emerges in discussions by the ninth month, and it seems a healthy time to explore the process. There is anticipation, excitement, anxiety, denial, regret, relief and hope.

The following example elucidates Marisha's ending experience. The Organisation has a policy that trainees can apply for honorary status after completion of their training and one-year placement agreement with the centre. It is interesting why trainees may want to extend their time in the supervision and the organisation, as it might indicate a struggle associated to working through the ending, anxieties with separation. Marisha applied in the tenth month of her placement to extend. She says she wishes to gain more experience. She also applies for a paid position. In the meantime, the group's grieving process is well underway, this involves mourning their losses and celebrating their accomplishments. She does not seem perturbed. Instead, she speaks of her expectations from the Organisation, and it becomes clear that the application for an extension might be serving a defensive function against the painful loss of her placement and the supervision group.

The Organisation advises her that the offer of an honorary position would be subject to her completing her placement and her training and that there were no openings for a paid position at present. The consequence was the beginning of a contentious period between Marisha and management. In supervision, she experiences the Organisation as a withholding object; not offering her a paid position, which she attributes to her age. She focuses on this and glosses over the pain and her upcoming loss of the group. Her disappointment and anger at me – emerge, she feels I am not advocating for her to secure what she is asking for. The intensity of this issue seems to hijack the group's mourning process.

John Bowlby (1980) highlights three stages of separation - protest, despair, and detachment. We had, as previously discussed, perhaps been able to help Marisha relate differently to her age difference but had overlooked her relationship with the Organisation. The "rejection" by the Organisation triggered unresolved issues. I acknowledge and explore the implications of these losses – this served as a path to enabling Marisha process and mourn these losses (including the end of the group supervision) with the group.

Marisha begins to engage and the absence of an interest in the group ending dissipates. She talks about the pain and shame of her slow beginning in the supervision group and its consequences for her training. She had secured an additional placement to make up for the time lost at the beginning. There was frustration and anger in the countertransference, I wonder, if she feels I could have done more. Marisha insists supervision has been excellent; and sees management as her problem. I point out her split between the supervision group and the Organisation and she begins to work through her idealisation of the supervision group and her denigration of the Organisation. I comment that it probably feels like I could have used my power and privilege to support her more. She agrees and now owns her suppressed anger and verbalises that she has felt marginalised in an organisation and supervision group which has a focus on intercultural work.

Marisha mourns her losses and can ultimately accept that the Organisation's policy was followed and that having no vacancies is a constraint beyond anyone's control. She could recognise her experience of historical rejection, among other things at play, and how her preoccupation with the Organisation as a withholding mother was acting as a distraction from the grief of the ending. As she works through this in therapy, she engages with the ending in the supervision group.

The group in this phase names the communal, organisational, personal losses which have affected them over the year. They acknowledged the conflictual and uncomfortable nature of their experiences. As peers and as supervisors, we sat with these memories and feelings in honesty and openness. A recollection of professional and personal stories, appreciating their relationships with clients who were so much a part of their growth and development.

Conclusion

I have in the chapter discussions, highlighted my supervisory theoretical approach as drawing on attachment theory and intercultural therapy principles.

Inter-cultural therapy and attachment theory both consider the client's, therapist's and supervisor's external reality as being crucial to the supervisory and therapeutic process. The interpsychic and intra-psychic environments being equally critical to the process.

Regarding an attachment perspective, Bowlby (1988) emphasises how early attachment relationships shape and influence how safe and secure we feel in the world, impacting interactions within relationships. These attachment systems and experiences of attachment relationships are influenced by cultural and socio-political structures. Similarly, referencing intercultural therapy, Kareem (1978) highlights the significance of the client's whole being and communal life in the world, the wider society and culture in confluence, within historical and current contexts.

My supervisory style also benefits from the seven-eyed model. It enables my evaluation and consideration of areas to address in the supervisory process. The model advances seven areas to examine, which are: Focus on the client and how they present; exploration of the strategies and interventions used by the supervisee; exploration of the relationship between the client and the supervisee; focus on the supervisee; focus on the supervisory relationship; the supervisor focusing on their process; focus on the wider contexts in which the work occurs. The case examples have explicated the phases of group formation, process, mourning and ending through the application of the seven-eyed model in conjunction with attachment theory and intercultural perspectives. This pluralist approach concerns itself with the supervision group, the supervisor and supervisee relationship, the supervisor, supervisee, client relationship and the assumptions located in all the individuals as well as the assumptions and the cultures within the institutions where the work happens.

Group formation is predicated on the degree of safety fostered, and provides a secure base, Holmes (2001) for the supervision group. Safety is important as the group in its initial formation stage is concerned with itself, its members, its survival and safety. This sense of safety enables curiosity and creativity between members in the group.

For some clients experiencing a secure base within the therapeutic space is critical to enable the sort of exploration which facilitates growth and development. This is a key task of the therapist and by extension a critical task for the supervisor to facilitate, sustain and hold.

Differences and diversity in the group relationships pertaining to gender, age, religion, race, the type or nature of their post-graduate training, and personal history are constituent dynamic elements affecting the relationships within the group. The case examples illustrate the ruptures which occurred as a consequence of differences and how the recognition of these differences in turn inaugurates the differentiation process phase in the group. The differentiation phase leads to an enhanced capacity to engage in exploration. We saw how this capacity translates to negotiating disruptions. The disruption between Aleema and me (supervisor) was explored, leading to a repair.

The anecdotal presentations of the therapists in the cases have provided insights into the intersections between their personal histories and their supervision and engagements in therapy with clients. Wallin (2014) posits that therapists are shaped by their own unresolved histories, leaving them with residues of disorganised attachment which might play out in the therapy with clients. The supervisees in navigating the various therapeutic and supervisory encounters have shown that we cannot escape the fact that like our clients, we bring all that we are into the therapeutic space.

Marisha's experience provides an insight into her relationship with the placement organisation which reverberates in the case example towards the end of her placement in the organisation and initialises her mourning, grieving and separation which connects to similar processes in the group. Bowlby describes mourning as a natural healing balm for the psyche. The responses of numbness, angry protest, displaced anger and frustration, yearning to stay on, despair, and detachment as elaborated are all normal responses to ending with supervisees and clients alike, Holmes (2001). The group in the explorations in the ending phase were able to engage with a capacity to mourn their losses and celebrate successes.

The pluralist [intercultural and attachment] supervision approach I espouse and describe with case examples in granular detail, is a resource for therapists addressing race and culture and its intersections in their work. It creates a space within which (cultural and racial) enactments and impasses can be identified and explored. It builds and enables security which gradually unfolds, with incremental shifts sometimes taking place in specific areas, in the therapist's life-long professional journey of self-examination and development in processing (race and culture) in their work. The therapist's experience of security supported in the supervision, translates to the client who in turn connects with safety as the work evolves. A lack of therapist security in working with differences and diversity leads to a disconnect from the client and an inability to be present for the client.

References

Agoro, O. (2019). Who is being assessed? Postmodernism and intercultural therapy assessments: A synergy process. In: Ababio, B., Littlewood, R. (eds.) *Intercultural Therapy Challenges, Insights and Developments*. London. Routledge, pp. 23–39.

Allen, J. G., Fonagy, P., Bateman, A.W. (2008). *Mentalising in Clinical Practice*. Washington, DC: American Psychiatric Publishing Inc.

Bowlby, J. (1980). *Attachment and Loss. Vol. 3*. New York, USA: Basic Books.

Bowlby, J. (1988). *A secure Base*. New York, USA: Basic Books.

Delboy, S. (2020). A country of two: Race and social class in an immigrant therapeutic dyad. *Psychoanalytic Dialogues, 30*, 90–101.

Hawkins, P., Shohet, R. (2012). *Supervision in the Helping Professions*. Fourth edn. London: Open University Press.

Heard, D., Lake, B., McCluskey, U. (2012). *Attachment Therapy with Adolescents and Adults Theory and Practice Post Bowlby*. London, UK: Karnac Books.

Holmes, J. (2001). *The Search for the Secure Base: Attachment Theory and Psychotherapy*. East Sussex: Brunner-Routledge.

Kareem, J. (1978). Conflicting concepts of mental health in multicultural society. *Psychopathology, 11*(2), 90–95.

Wallin, D. (2007). *Attachment in Psychotherapy*. New York: The Guilford Press.

Wallin, D. (2014). Because connection takes two: The analyst's psychology in treating the "Connection-Resistant" patient. *International Journal of Psychoanalytic Self Psychology, 9*(3), 200–207.

Part 4

Supervision as Intercultural Training (Potentialities and Pitfalls)

Chapter 9

Interplays of Visible and Invisible Differences in the Intercultural Supervision Frame

Eda Avcioglu

Clients have different stories and backgrounds that they bring into the room with them; similarly, we as practitioners, also bring our own stories and histories. As a trainee, my first experience in the consulting room was with a client of a different "racial" group, a 20-year-old black woman who had requested to see a counsellor from a similar "racial" group as herself. However, she ended up with me, a white female counsellor of Turkish and German heritage. She did not show up again. From this experience (and many more), I was left with one question: were these clients anxious that they would not be understood when working with people from different heritages and, or cultures? As mentioned, that was my first ever experience in the consulting room therefore, I felt (in my countertransference) insecure and a lack of confidence about addressing the "differences" between her and me, even though my personal therapist is black. I freely discussed these "differences" with her. Once I learnt that this first client had chosen not to return, it generated feelings of failure in me, and I became hyperaware of this perceived difference between us, as though there must have been an elephant in the room that was not brought up by me. Since then, talking about any anxieties surrounding being different to each other is one of the most important elements in my counselling practice and supervision experience. This chapter explores the meaning of differences in a therapeutic context and how they may be understood and worked with through a psychodynamic framework. I specifically explore the function of intercultural therapy when it comes to working with differences and diversity and its elucidation within the supervision matrix. From a supervisee's point of view, I use my own understanding of intercultural aspects and psychodynamic psychotherapy, as well as adopting Kareem's (1992) concept of intercultural psychotherapy. I draw on my own experiences as a supervisee and trainee counsellor and provide case examples that highlight themes such as multiculturalism, cross-culture, interculturalism and language differences. I also show how these themes have played out in my clinical work with clients and in supervision.

DOI: 10.4324/9781003380214-14

My background

My own interpersonal and cultural roots are derived from my maternal German grandmother and Turkish grandfather. This makes me partly German and part Turkish, which I believe plays an important role in the therapy room as well as in a supervision group, given that this consists of people from a range of ethnicities. It perhaps, enables me to have a greater understanding of the different cultures, "races" and heritages, whether in the therapy or in the supervision room, than I might otherwise have. When introducing myself and my background, I do highlight my German heritage, despite never having lived in Germany. Growing up in Istanbul, with a mother who grew up in Germany, gave me the opportunity to consider and explore my own roots within personal therapy. I do not think that my decision to continue working with the black therapist that I was previously referred to, was a coincidence. I never searched for a therapist who could speak Turkish, as I wanted to conduct my therapy in English, and perhaps, subconsciously, I wanted to work with someone who was unfamiliar with my culture. I preferred to explain my intercultural personal dilemmas and culture from my own perspective to someone who was unlikely to be prejudiced about (or biased towards) my culture. Having a different perspective and not being of a similar "racial" group as my own therapist gave me a sense of understanding "how to work on differences and still understand clients" in the therapy room (Lowe, 2013, p. 2). As already mentioned, as a supervisee, each case is "different" and each counsellor comes from various backgrounds, which has meant that in supervision, I have explored the experience of receiving a range of comments from each of my clients, from diverse cultural and "racial" perspectives.

This chapter contains a case study of working from an intercultural perspective and how this plays out in the supervision. I also explore how I locate my identity as a white, Turkish woman with German roots, as the duality in this intercultural self also plays an important role in my work. For example, my Turkish-speaking clients usually comment: *"You don't look Turkish, you look like a foreigner? Where are you from originally?"* Often, I interpreted this question as stemming from both curiosity about me as well as anxiety arising from their concern of whether I would be able to understand their "cultural traumas." This leads me to consider my own identity, race, language and culture. I do locate myself, in this intercultural "self," as a bit German and a bit Turkish, as I do like to acknowledge and appreciate my German roots. Yet growing up in Turkey, and speaking the language better than German, makes me feel more Turkish. In this "split," I locate myself in the "depressive position" (Klein, 1946), accepting both sides of my heritage as equally important, as I work towards feeling a sense of "wholeness" in my identity. However, I find I possess different upbringings, cultures and identities even with most of my Turkish-speaking clients, yet this does not mean we cannot develop a common understanding. If we cannot develop this understanding, perhaps there is also significance and meaning within that. To conclude, behind a Turkish, white woman, there are German roots, which prompt me to try to understand and explore the various anxieties clients from a "different" or "same" "race" may experience and express within a supervision context.

My understanding of intercultural perspective and our supervision group

I remember my placement application to the Nafsiyat Intercultural Therapy Centre. First, perhaps it is useful for me to explore why I decided to apply. I thought that it was a conscious action to do so; I simply came across the advertisement on social media and "liked" the name of the centre. I think there was an unconscious feeling that drew me to this place. I was only able to recognise why I was there, in a supervision session in which I began talking about "my Turkish and German sides," and the supervisor and supervisees warmly welcomed me to the Intercultural Therapy Centre. I was like the rest of the group: "different." So, my understanding of working through an intercultural perspective highlighted the idea of being understood in therapy, for and with, clients from either the same or a different culture to myself. At the core of this intercultural aspect, there is the deep-rooted desire to understand and be understood, and the anxieties that may arise as a result.

Given that individuals within my supervision group also originate from different countries, with varied backgrounds and training, I felt that we possessed different assumptions and understanding of the world as well. From the onset of supervision, it was evident that I was to be the only white person in the group, and I remember wondering how this may have felt for the rest of the supervisees, as they were already a "group" before me. Would I be accepted or rejected, for instance? This difference has never been raised. However, within the supervision framework, our differences have all become eminently obvious when discussing the case studies. I feel this intercultural supervision group is not like other therapeutic groups I have been in (this is more like a professional setting as it welcomes everybody), although it took some time for me to understand the dynamic of the group and the centre itself. Despite this, with time, I now see how this group works, where we all respect each other, and are all able to talk about the different perspectives of cases; open to any comment, interpretation or idea. I think the most important experience in this supervision group is the coming together, despite our differences.

Case study (detailed intervention of a case and some dialogues in supervision)

One interesting case study that I felt particularly invested in, from the very beginning, involved twelve therapy sessions with a woman from mixed heritages along ethnic, "racial," cultural and language lines. In our sessions, she was able to discuss the "visible" and "invisible" differences within herself, society and indeed with me. Together, we worked with those differences; I aim to reveal how it was that she and I got along, and how I worked within her transference, supported in my supervision with this cross-cultural approach. I should say that supervision gave me a new way of thinking about my clients, especially regarding working cross-culturally, and developed my thinking on intercultural counselling. This case is perhaps evidence of this development. In this case study, and indeed this entire chapter, I use the supervision framework and some keywords such as "multicultural," "cross-culture," and "intercultural supervision," which are all terms employed to study the interaction between people of different cultural backgrounds. The term, "multicultural" indicates the study and practice of supervision in and for different cultures (Dokter and Khasnavis, 2008, p. 111). The term intercultural therapy also highlights working with difference (Kareem, 1992), through which I explore my clients' inner struggles of culture, race and identity.

"Intercultural therapy also has encouraged clients and therapists from different backgrounds and cultures to find a way of working together" (Thomas, 2019, p. 138).

Client "Maida"

I was allocated a 20-year-old woman who was born in London in the United Kingdom, although her family is from Algeria. She does not even remember when and how her family migrated to London. She only knows her father was exposed to a lot of racism when he came to the United Kingdom. Having four older siblings and being the fifth (and youngest) child in the family, gave her the feeling that her family was "different" to her. She also experienced feelings of rejection and struggled with her confidence, perhaps because she was bullied in secondary school. She came to therapy to explore her past traumas and childhood experiences, despite possessing very little information about her roots. Before me, she had been allocated to another female therapist, who she did not successfully engage with (due to miscommunication). When we met, she was distant and came across as quite angry, yet determined to work on her traumas. Maida was quite clear about what she wanted to talk about but did not know why she had childhood traumas or why she still carried them.

The sessions started on the online platform "Zoom," and she began by talking about her family structure (a very conservative one), her social life, school, and friends; yet her conversation remained somewhat superficial. I could see that trusting a stranger was not easy, especially after her first therapy experience. I brought that possible fear to the "Zoom room":

E: *Perhaps it is not easy for you to talk about traumas to a stranger and to a very different person than you after your previous, perhaps unexpected*

*experience. I wondered how you feel about it? Wanting to explore traumas
yet not ready to trust a stranger?*

M: *Yeah, definitely a very bad experience ... that's okay, this is a
professional stage, setting.*

During the first session, she highlighted her conservative family structure
and described her family – especially her father – as being very "different"
to her. Yet I was "different" to her as well. She shares the same "race,"
language, and culture with her father, but at the same time, she said she
feels very distant from him, as though the culture she had inherited from
him was alien to her. In my countertransference, I found myself wondering,
that with all of those acknowledged differences, whether we could find a
common understanding. I asked her how far she thought being the "same"
mattered. She said she was apprehensive that we may not find common
ground as a result of our different backgrounds; both from a Western
culture, ostensibly at least, she felt we may differ in some vital ways
that may generate miscommunication and misunderstandings. Yet at the
same time, she also felt distant from her Algerian culture. I found it interesting how she used the word culture; whilst the word *ethnicity* still refers
back to people's putative "racial" origins, and their distinctive physical
appearance as it is perceived by themselves and others, the term *culture*
describes the process of living within a system of values and practices
shared by a particular group of people. Thus, *ethnicity* then remains a
concept for the individual culture by distinction (Acharyya, cited in
Kareem, 1992, p. 74). However, Maida did not feel she belonged to the
same cultural system as her parents.

When I brought the first couple of sessions to supervision, I was encouraged to talk more about this cultural aspect and the differences
between us. This included how Maida saw me as a white therapist and how
she might have connected with me, as well as how I attempted to connect
with her. In supervision, I was able to discuss the visible and invisible
intercultural differences that existed between us. For example, in one of the
sessions, it was clear that we both had a different cultural upbringing,
language and "racial" heritage, yet we felt so close, and I was able to
understand where her traumas came from and some of her complaints
about her culture.

There was notably one session that I think was very important in terms of
her progression in describing her identity and cultural self, and perhaps the
split of two selves (British and Algerian). I will explore this further in this
chapter.

The session prior to this pivotal one was impactful; that session began with
Maida discussing taking her driving test but failing – again – as a result of
anxiety. She said she knows how to do things correctly yet is not able to
execute this in practice when feeling nervous. I interpreted this anxiety as

though she feels the need to put on a performance for the test, perhaps like in all aspects of her life. At work, she needs to be a modern person, and at home, she needs to be like her family (perhaps more conservative). In all of these "performances," she feels she fails, all the time, with the driving test indicating just one of these perceived failures.

In my countertransference, I felt she might believe she needed to also put on another performance – this time with me, in our sessions. This was perhaps confirmed when she said she does not like it if she cannot read people's body language. This suggested to me that, as she could only see half of me on Zoom, it was hard for her to connect. Furthermore, at work with her female Western boss, she could talk about herself, because her boss also talks about herself as well, which does not happen during our sessions. I think this meant it was a struggle for her to talk about our visible and invisible differences. Not knowing me in her conventional sense of *knowing* was difficult. The session finished with her acknowledging and processing her wish to have approval from her conservative family.

Session

Maida usually came to every session having "processed," "digested" the previous one. I believe she used the therapeutic space to spend more time thinking about her processed thoughts. Lowe (2014, p. 11) states that "the thinking space sought to promote curiosity, exploration and learning about difference by paying as much attention to how we learn (process) as to what we learn (content)." She usually took her sessions at the office as she felt she was able to talk more freely there. She left our previous session with one question and perhaps, during the gap of a week between sessions, there was a shift in our work together. She wanted to discuss her wish to discover who she was in terms of race and the purpose of being in this session, as well as who she was at home and in the session with me. She used the word 'chaotic' to describe the feeling of having Algerian roots but feeling Western and modern in her identity. Such a split was very clear in the way she sees and presents herself at work versus in her family: her British side versus her Algerian side. Within this chaotic split, she was lost, and came to therapy to "find" herself.

I felt that Maida seemed uncertain as to where she belonged and that perhaps in our remaining sessions, there was still time to work towards achieving a depressive position for Maida – to see herself as a "whole," instead of splitting her identity into parts (Klein, 1946). She wanted to get to know herself better and understand her roots but felt there was insufficient family input to support this process. During the session, Maida said that she holds back from showing all of her different "selves" to other people, as she believed that no one would understand her mixed background and the "cultural trauma" she experienced on a daily basis. For this reason, she decided to write poems, and joined a poetry group, stating that even though (or perhaps because) there were people of different ethnicities in the group, she felt safe enough to express her true self there, perhaps a reference to her sessions with me at the time. We had a discussion about her fear of showing vulnerability to her family and in society more generally, something that she agreed with, stating that she finds writing easier as it allowed her to show all of her different selves. This discussion of "selves" meant that Winnicott's (1953) conceptualisation of the true and false self was one of the main tools I drew on when working with Maida (Winnicott, 1965).

Maida's anxiety stemmed from the fear of being judged by society, her family, and at work. I asked her if she felt understood by me, given that my physical appearance as a white woman was very different to hers. This question appeared to make Maida feel uncomfortable at first, but in the unconscious communication I perceived that she felt understood as we continued to spend time together, as our sessions also became open, honest and perhaps straightforward. Maida's main fear was of opening up and showing her different sides to her family, as she believed she would not be welcomed/well-received or understood; for instance, she indicated that in Algerian culture, writing poetry was perceived to be useless. She was scared that her family would not accept her authentic side and instead would want and expect her to follow the traditional path of marriage and motherhood. She wished to be free of these expectations yet felt stuck in what she perceived to be cultural clichés and stereotypes.

During the session, Maida expressed her anger towards her family, especially towards her father, and I believe overall towards her culture and her background (which represents her family). I felt the same anger in my countertransference. Maida stated:

> *I want to understand my intergenerational, cross-cultural traumas - how I carry it and it's never resolved. My parents had their own experiences … I don't know what happened in their life, but it affects the way they treated and raised me. So now I am carrying those toxic qualities and I am trying to identify what they are and who I am.*

Maida expressed both anger as well as curiosity towards her heritage:

> *I don't really know about my family; they grew up in Algeria. My mum experienced lots of racism … and our country was in civil war, we were trying to become independent, they were very young, and this is something that I can't understand. Lots of conflict probably, and racism from the West … and the way they raised us, my parents telling me to be careful, they don't trust me with people outside of the Algerian community. They don't want me to go out at night.*

In supervision, when listening to my colleagues discuss intergenerational trauma, I was reminded of how Maida recognised her family trauma, too. Thomas (2019, cited in Ababio and Littlewood, 2019:138) stated that people are affected by traumas experienced by their parents or grandparents, who may have survived something traumatic, and perhaps may then draw other family members into a cycle of traumatised behaviour as a result. I thought Maida may be acknowledging trauma from her family's past, perhaps subconsciously, despite not possessing full details of what happened. Volkan (1997, p.43) described the mechanism of transmission of trauma very clearly: the older generation externalises their traumatised self onto a child's personality, wherein the child becomes a container, absorbing the unresolved parts of the previous generation's trauma.

The issue of trust was prevalent between us; I was not perceived as "trustworthy," an enactment of her family's view, which had established an internalised mistrust in her, this manifested itself at the beginning of our sessions:

E: *I am wondering what your family would think of this session you are having with me and what do you feel? Where I come from, what's my race, which culture do I belong to; we are very different, do you think your family would be able to understand our dynamics?*

M: *They don't talk about emotions, people who have … they come from a culture that does not accept mental health, they don't understand. My aim here is to make peace with my traumas and not pass it on to my own children.*

She continued to talk about her father, stating that he was not a good person, due she said to his antipathy towards white people, black people, intolerant of anyone from a different religion (or no religion), and that he was misogynistic. Maida therefore struggled to understand and accept her father. This conversation led her to talk about how she sees her community, as she said her friends are not from Algeria and that they were mostly from different heritages except Algeria. She claimed that when it came to her community, there was only one person with whom she could share her cultural difficulties and that she appreciated the Algerian food and flavours. I interpreted this as a form of emotional connection with Algeria. I wondered if perhaps she wanted to keep her Algerian side and the emotional warmth it generates but struggled with the prejudice and xenophobia exhibited by her father. With friends from different ethnicities, Maida felt free to introduce herself in the way she wanted, yet the split still manifested itself even with her friendships, as she seemed to want to, both be visible as well as invisible (culturally).

I was also encouraged in supervision to deepen the explorations around her identity. In the subsequent therapy sessions when the theme of identity emerged Maida said:

M: *I identify with being British-Arab. I have my own experience of life, which doesn't identify with most people. I am very lucky to have the job that I have, and the money, the space … lots of people from Algeria live in poverty, they have a different accent. I grew up in west London. I have a different way of speaking and living, so it shapes the way I identify with them, so I don't always understand them.*

E: *'Them' means … your community? I think what you are trying to say is you are different from them even though you come from the same background, but there is a huge difference. Where are you from – what would you say … ?*

M: *I am from London; my parents are from Algeria. And that's my heritage, but not necessarily my culture, but like you said the food, perhaps the emotional connection and the language.*

E: *You are splitting from your parents, but at the same time want to keep some bits of your heritage.*

M: *Yes, and I am lucky because my colour of skin is lighter than theirs and I look more western, if I go to Algeria, they wouldn't know I am from there. I would feel like a foreigner because of my physical appearance.*

She felt privileged to have therapy sessions because if she lived in Algeria, she would not have had this opportunity, to seek the support that could help her change.

Overall, therefore, this client gave me much to ponder, and in supervision, when we were discussing her, I began to wonder whether Maida was also subconsciously racist – towards her Algerian heritage. She grew up with a father who she described as "prejudiced" towards other groups. My supervisor suggested that I explore the concept of "internalised racism." Perhaps Maida had internalised the racism directed at Algerians living in Britain (mobilised in part by father's biases towards other communities [including her Britishness] designated by him as "outgroups"). Her ambivalent – alienated experience of Algeria combined with her father's distrust of the British part of her may have forged a perception of herself as being different from her Algerian community, which might explain why she wished to be cut off from the Algerian community at times. Davids (2011) states that a relationship between the self and "racial" other exists universally in the inner world; he also asserts that splitting (like my client) and projective identification (her father projected prejudice and she, in turn, became defensive towards her Algerian heritage) are components of internal racism, which can be observed in relation to how individuals situate themselves in social "in groups" and "out groups." There was also the question of her positioning with me – my white identity one formed outside Britain, and she of Algerian heritage, born and raised in Britain. The issues of hierarchies in white communities, of language and accent were present.

How supervision helped, and the kind of supervisor I would like to be

Supervision helped me to think of my clients more in terms of our inter-cultural relationship, in order to be able to understand our transference and countertransference. With this specific client, supervision helped me realise that I needed to challenge myself to think about my own counter-transference. I realised that despite our differences, there were some ele-ments of this client that reminded me of my own cultural difficulties and complexities. Even though our culture, language, heritage and "racial" identities were different, there was a common, if unconscious, under-standing. In our sessions, I usually felt something akin to: "I know what you mean, this is what we have in our country, and I do feel the same about my own community in London sometimes." In supervision, I sometimes felt guilty, feeling the same way Maida did, about my own community, as if my feelings were somehow "wrong." However, I was reminded by the supervisor that in our supervision sessions, we are encouraged to discuss our feelings openly. The comments from my colleagues helped me to re-cognise that issues of race, colour, culture, community and identity were very important for my client and have always been prevalent in our group discussions.

Thus, in amongst this "otherness," I felt a sense of "sameness" in my countertransference, which I was only alerted to when talking about her with colleagues in supervision. As Morgan (2014 cited in Lowe, 2014 p. 84) stated, we should acknowledge how we may use the "other" – in particular, their difference – to contain our own anxieties about ourselves.

The group dynamic aspect

As previously stated, in the supervision group, all supervisees are different, and there are sometimes different approaches to a specific client issue. Sometimes we, as supervisees, had discussions about our opinions, and about being understood clearly (or not, as the case may be). I feel that being understood was not only important in the consulting room but also in the intercultural supervision group. From my perspective, groups are never easy to understand and navigate. Supervision groups, in particular, are different to other groups given the unconscious presence of a competitive spirit, the feeling of wanting to be the "best." I realise now that this competitive nature resided in me, hidden, until discussing openly the idea of difference. Perhaps, therefore, talking about client material alongside understanding the intercultural group dynamic will be beneficial for the group. This is something that I would be keen to understand if I were a supervisor and would be motivated to offer up for discussion with my supervisees. The relatively underplayed exploration of "racial" and cultural locations between my peers and my supervisor in supervision with regards to racialised internalisations, hierarchies, language and religion may have been paralleled in aspects of my work with Maida.

Conclusions and recommendations

The intercultural supervision group is unlike any other supervision group given that in the nature of the work, there is something aligned to working with "difference." I have learned to address and process many new cross-cultural issues over the course of a year. When I started my therapy training, I was only involved in a psychodynamic supervision group, which I found difficult to be myself in. On meeting this new intercultural supervision group, the difference in each member was palpable; yet despite the differences in approach, this became a group that could share anything without judgement. Learning how to work cross-culturally was something that I enjoyed, and I hope to continually grow in this process.

I believe it is very important, in any field, to work with people (in therapy and clinical supervision) from different cultures and backgrounds, speaking diverse languages and hailing from various parts of the globe. This openness to and appreciation of "difference" in this respect not only allows practitioners to see their invisible sides; it also gives great insight to therapeutic work. Discussing difference and "sameness" – regardless of where a client is from – enables us to understand both visible and invisible differences, absorbing the meaning of working with "difference" in a meaningful way. Intercultural therapy may awaken something in the counsellor that they could find pertinent or important to work on in themselves, which could then be explored within the supervision matrix.

References

Ababio, B., Littlewood, R., (eds.) (2019). *Intercultural Therapy: Challenges, Insights and Developments*. London: Routledge.

Davids, M.F., M., (2011). *Internal Racism: A Psychoanalytic Approach to Race And Difference*. London: Macmillan.

Dokter, D., Khasnavis, R. (2008). *Supervision of Drama therapy*. London: Routledge.

Kareem, J., Littlewood, R., (eds.) (1992). *Intercultural Therapy*. 2nd ed. Oxford: Blackwell science.

Klein, M. (1946). Notes on some schizoid mechanisms. *International Journal of Psycho-Analysis, 27*, n, 100–150.

Lowe, F., (ed.) (2014). *Thinking Space: Promoting Thinking About Race, Culture, And Diversity in Psychotherapy and Beyond*. London: Karnac.

Morgan, H. (2014). Between fear and blindness: The white therapist and the black patient. In Lowe, F. (Ed.). *Thinking space: Promoting Thinking About Race, Culture and Diversity in Psychotherapy and Beyond*. London: Karnac.

Thomas, L. (2019). Intercultural psychoanalytic psychotherapy and generationally transmitted trauma. In Ababio, B. & Littlewood, R. (Eds.). *Intercultural Therapy: Challenges, Insights and Developments*. London: Routledge.

Volkan, V. (1997). *Bloodlines: From Ethnic Pride to Ethnic Terrorism*. Boulder, CO: Westview.

Winnicott, D. (1965). *The Maturational Processes and the Facilitating Environment*. London: Hogarth Press.

Chapter 10

My Journey with Omar in Supervision

Ali Donat

Introduction

My therapeutic work with Omar had a profound effect in shaping my work as a training psychotherapist. The work highlighted how differences can play a defining role in the therapy room and the supervision group and emphasised some key intercultural issues which came out both with Omar and my group.

I aim to present how cultural differences manifesting themselves in the transference and the countertransference in the therapy room, influenced the therapeutic work with Omar. I will also show how my participation in supervision and my work with Omar were shaped by the supervision group, my cultural and political orientation and the ongoing political situation at the time. Finally, I make some recommendations that may be of assistance to training psychotherapists as supervisees and supervisors.

Client history

Omar is a Kurdish man in his fifties who was born and raised in the Middle East. Omar grew up in what he described as a "a low-income area" where his father was a shopkeeper and his mother a home maker. Omar experienced hostility from a very young age and spoke about being harassed at school by his teachers as well as other students. Omar's childhood was marked by the occurrence of war and violence in the region. Omar recollected often seeing piles of dead bodies of people he had seen just hours before. He recounted these memories in the therapy sessions with a degree of numbness and acceptance.

Omar continued to experience violence and harassment throughout his school years. The police and his teachers constantly inflicted him with emotional and physical pain. His threshold for pain tolerance increased as he grew older. In his early teenage years, Omar developed a political voice. He was imprisoned as a consequence of his involvement in student politics, and contracted typhus fever in prison. His family felt he had, by his incarceration, besmirched the family name and standing, and blamed him. This precipitated

DOI: 10.4324/9781003380214-15

Omar's suicide attempt just before his fifteenth birthday. A second suicide attempt occurred much later on in life, when he was a grown man. I asked him how he currently felt about suicide, he responded by describing it as "pointless".

He pursued higher education and went on to study engineering in university. While there Omar began publishing political papers. Because of his publications, he was frequently arrested by the police who abused him physically and verbally and tortured him on one occasion.

Omar progressed academically and was able to obtain work but was denied promotion opportunities due to his oppositional political views and his ethnicity. He subsequently moved to the UK, was granted political asylum and settled in Birmingham. He found work and developed a routine; his acclimatisation to life in the UK had begun. A few years prior to our sessions, Omar during a visit to Germany, was stopped by the police on the street and was treated as a terror suspect. This event deeply shook Omar, activating memories of his early years akin to a post-traumatic recall. Omar experienced it as deeply unjust, and discriminatory. This incident further embedded a fear and dislike of authority figures; a dynamic which plays out in Omar's encounters with officials of any capacity.

Presenting problem

When I met Omar, he had stopped working for a number of years and had been living his life in increased isolation. From what I gathered, Omar did not like the company of others. In our first session, he told me how interacting socially was experienced as giving a part of himself away. A part which could be used/misused against him. What brought Omar to therapy was the anxiety and sadness he felt in his daily life. He described feeling "dark, sad and with nothing to live for".

When I read Omar's assessment notes prior to our therapy sessions, I was struck by the amount of conflict and violence that existed in his life. Particularly, Omar's personal experience with conflict. The assessment notes reproduced a picture of a man being questioned, arrested, jailed, tortured and harassed by one form of authority figure or another at every juncture in his life. The traumatic incident of being questioned by the police on the streets of Germany as a terror suspect was the latest episode in his protracted history of conflicts. It had rehashed much of the previous traumas Omar had suffered.

The context and external socio-political events during our sessions created what I will term a "perfect storm" in the therapy room. It was a period when the Turkish government sent troops to a region occupied by Kurdish separatist groups to engage in armed conflict. The events in that region may have provided a somewhat hostile backdrop to the sessions with Omar.

Theoretical framework

The theoretical frame of my work with Omar could be described as post-Freudian and drawing particularly from object relations which situates relationships the primary pulsating driver in human beings (Fairbairn, 1952).

Klein's (1932) developmental schema and how early anxiety is experienced, and managed help explain this position. It can be formulated that Omar's early experiences of growing up in conflict left him needy yet angry at the very object that he depended on and longed for. In the first couple of sessions, Omar gave graphic accounts of his childhood. Klein (1959) sees personal experiences arising out of a constant interplay between the external reality and the inner world of the self. It was probable that Omar's internal world had been shaped by the destruction he witnessed in the outside world. Omar, in a Kleinian sense, 'introjected' the conflict he witnessed in the outside world. It was my hunch that Omar's internal world reflected the scenes he had witnessed as a child.

The harrowing experiences Omar lived through as a child were replete with violence and persecution and were managed by Omar through splitting. Klein (1959) formulated that, infants managed anxieties by splitting their experiences into good and bad ones in order to make sense of an otherwise chaotic world. In this early developmental period, which Klein designated as the Paranoid-schizoid position, there are only good and bad (Klein, 1959). I observed early in the therapy that Omar viewed the world in this black and white manner.

According to Klein's model of the Paranoid-schizoid position, the infant gets rid of the bad experiences by projecting them to the outside world or onto others (Klein, 1959). I felt drawn into that sense of conflict in Omar's life even before our sessions started. A week before our first session, I called him to introduce myself and discuss scheduling. He was quiet and agreed to the time I offered him. He then abruptly asked: "are you Turkish?" Coming from a Kurdish man, the question raised a sense of apprehension in me. Later, I understood that this was Omar's way of putting me on notice that he was sensitive to me, to who I was and to my views. In our very first exchange, when I asked Omar what his previous experience with therapy was like, I felt like he again put me on notice when he said:

"My experience with therapy was horrible. The therapist just sat there with his legs crossed and didn't say anything then he interrogated me. He asked me if I had murderous thoughts against the police that abused me. I said: 'I am not a criminal why would I have murderous thoughts?' Then he asked me that again in the next session. I said we should stop the sessions because this is not professional."

I felt apprehensive once more because I interpreted Omar's story as him telling me that if I did not say the right things, he would fire me just like he fired his previous therapist. Omar's projections marked the undertone of much of our time together. He was a man who looked visibly angry. He looked at me with a furrowed brow and piercing looks in many of the long silences we experienced. At the end of our work together, his projections turned into outright attacks resulting from what he described as my "inability as a therapist to connect with people".

My countertransference

The way countertransference is conceptualised in terms of object relations, or two-person psychology, allows me to think of it as a beneficial analytic tool rather than an impediment to the therapist. Two-person psychology recognises the self as a body that transmits "response to the presence of another" (Bollas, 1999 p. 47). If I think of countertransference within the two-person psychology framework, then it enters the room with me and the client. Not only does it become important for the therapist to understand which state he/she is in relation to the client but also where his/her countertransference lies as it informs, in part, the therapist's understanding of the relational work. While it is easy to consider Omar's intrapsychic processes from an object relations perspective, it is equally important to examine the impact of those attacks on our relationship. They did eventually lead me to withdraw and take a more combative stance against him. Could this have been avoided if I were aware of what was going on from a relational perspective and were able to process my countertransference?

In one interaction, Omar spoke about his experience at a refugee centre. When I asked him about the centre, he replied by saying "I am surprised you don't know where it is". This elicited a sudden feeling of rage in me. Even though I contained myself in the room, I felt like I had been prodded by Omar. In many ways, this, and other similar interactions, led me to take a more combative stance with Omar. Upon reflection, I realised that I may have reacted to the word "surprised" as a former boss often pointed out mistakes in my work to me in a passively-aggressive manner and would say how "surprised" he was that I made such errors. I experienced a similar feeling of being attacked.

In the middle part of our time together, there was a deliberate attempt by Omar to reach out and trigger a reaction from me. First, he asked me what my plans for an upcoming public holiday were. I felt probed and in the vein of being a blank canvas for Omar, I explored his reasons for asking me about my plans. In the following session, the exchange I most dreaded took place:

O: I am interested in your views – as you are a therapist – in what is going on in the region between the Kurdish and Turkish.

AD: Why do you ask?

O: I am interested. As you know, I am Kurdish, and you are Turkish. I am interested in what you think about what is going on.

AD: I remember you asked me if I was Turkish on our phone call. What was coming up for you?

O: I knew from your name. Ali is a Muslim name, and your last name is Turkish.

AD: I see. So, are you interested in my views as a therapist or as a Turkish man?

O: I don't care about nationalities. I am a humanist. I care about your views because your job is to analyse people and I wanted to understand how you see what is going on. But I see that you are not brave enough to share your views with me.

AD: This is your time. I think it is better use of our time to see what is coming up for you.

O: There are horrible things going on in the region and elsewhere in Kurdistan. It's real, it's happening. So, I wanted to discuss it. But you are very reserved and don't want to give anything away.

I felt overwhelmed by a rush of feelings and experienced Omar's questions as hostile. I felt shame from being associated with an oppressive state. I even felt anger at being cornered, by Omar's questions which I absolutely did not want to answer. I would later have an opportunity in supervision to process how I evaded Omar's questions about my views on the Turkish-Kurdish conflict. In the therapy room however, I kept my eyes on the clock while I negotiated around Omar's questions.

The rush of feelings of shame, anger (even rage) and hostility I experienced following Omar's reflections were valuable data, but which I could not make use of in the immediate moment(s). They may have been clues into Omar's internal states, as Grotstein (2018) suggests, that I could reference to inform my reflections. The Kleinian concept of *reverie* as developed by Bion (1967) which referred to the particular attitude adopted by the analyst which was achieved when the analyst abandoned preconceptions, memory and desire (Grotstein, 2018). I do not agree that therapists can abandon memory and preconceptions fully. However, Bion (1967 p. 125) also refers to reverie as a "language of achievement". That language emerges as the analyst waits patiently for the arrival of a fact through the client's material, or from his own unconscious, and hears the language of achievement by turning the material into "intuitive resonance" (Grotstein, 2018). Bion's formulation of the communicative aspects of intersubjective communication between the client and the therapist allows countertransference to be used as a therapeutic tool. Reflecting on our sessions however, I never had the patience (nor the therapeutic experience) to wait to hear in the relational sense what Omar's internal state was communicating. The feelings emerging in me as a result of our interaction, pushed Omar and I further apart. In many ways, the sessions with Omar felt like a tennis match with both of us batting to the other the unwanted feelings. Perhaps the concept of projective identification may help understand the feeling of that tennis match in the therapy room. Ogden (1979) describes projective identification, originally conceptualised by Klein, as a three-part process of ridding of unwanted aspects of oneself, depositing these unwanted parts into the other person and recovering through the other person a modified version of what is deposited (Ogden, 1979). From this perspective, my feelings of anger, rage, shame and frustration may have been feelings that Omar projected and, in turn, received from me in the room.

In our fifth and final session, Omar brought all of the unwanted feelings out and our work came to a halt:

O: I feel like we don't have a connection. This is not working between us. I don't feel like we can communicate. I feel like you are very closed. We cannot seem to connect. You have built sanctions around you, and I feel like the spotlight is on me. It's nothing personal. I am sure you have your training and your code of ethics around revealing yourself. But I cannot see how we can work together when there is no connection between us. Why wouldn't you answer a simple question? It is not my intention to judge you or criticise you for your views? Is it because I am a Kurd?

AD: I understand how you feel. As I said before, this is your space, and this is your time. It is a more useful use of our time to look at what is coming up for you. Even if we look at what it is about me being closed and what that might be bringing up for you.

O: I feel like you are putting all of the burden on me. Like last week when you said that you were getting an energy from me when I was quiet in the earlier part of the session. I felt like I don't have the right to feel energetic.

AD: Absolutely. You have the right. My intention was to reflect how I perceived you and perhaps allow us to process that. How are you feeling now? Are you angry with me?

O: No. It's nothing personal. It's just that I am grateful for the service the centre is providing but it's unfortunate that it is not helpful to me.

After a long silence, I asked Omar if he wanted to say anything. He shook his head and spent the remainder of our last session in silence. He then got up, shook my hand and left the room. That was the last time I saw or heard form Omar. I cannot help but think whether as a result of Omar's projective identification and my inability to separate what belonged to him and myself, I had become Omar's interrogator. The trauma of being interrogated by the police which had been re-enacted with his previous therapist may have played out again in my relationship with him.

Regardless of the countertransferential experience I experienced during my work with Omar, one thing was certain: I kept my views and our differences out of the room which possibly led to the therapeutic alliance being broken between us.

Supervision

The therapeutic journey Omar and I went through during therapy followed an equally curious supervision process. Looking at the supervision process alongside my work with Omar provides a deeper understanding of the relational process and valuable lessons for future supervision sessions.

Much like the therapeutic work with Omar, examining the supervisory process from a relational perspective allows me to situate my part in the process and provides good insight. Heralded by Fairbairn (1952), relational theory sees humans as object seeking individuals from birth where relationships become the basic ingredient of psychic structures. As much as the therapeutic relationship with Omar shaped my work with him in the therapy room, my relationships in supervision were helpful and developmental.

In this regard, it is useful to examine the effect my relationship with my supervisor had on my work with Omar. Looking at the supervisory relationship from a relational lens, is an analytic venture in and of, itself (Rock, 1997). Langs (1994) points out the two levels of communication between the supervisor and the supervisee where the conscious communication is about the client material and the education of the supervisee, and the unconscious communication is about the interaction of the supervisor and the supervisee. My relationship with my supervisor, David, had both dimensions. On the conscious level, we processed Omar's therapeutic material together. This contributed greatly to my therapeutic education. It also helped me formulate Omar's case in order to understand him and to be able to connect with him. The unconscious aspect of my relationship with David in supervision that greatly affected my work with Omar was my perceived authority of David. The supervisory relationship in this sense is one where two subjectivities come together to create a dyadic process (Frawley-O'Dea and Sarnat, 2001). David's authority in keeping the frame in the supervision group coupled with his command of the client material allowed me to feel contained in the group. This of course was a result of what (Frawley-O'Dea and Sarnat (2001) refer to as my authorisation and willingness to be affected by David's authority. They note that "the supervisee and supervisor enter into a relationship through which they participate in the evolution and refinement of the supervisee's uniquely developing craftsmanship" (Frawley-O'Dea and Sarnat, 2001, p. 61). It could not be truer for my experience with David as we explored my developing therapeutic style. It was most evident in how David explained and facilitated discussions in the area of working therapeutically with differences.

After weeks of venting my frustrations, fears and doubts about my work with Omar in supervision, David left me with a remark as I brought my work with Omar to a close: "differences must be brought into the room so they can be worked out". That was exactly what I feared I could not do with Omar. Jafar Kareem, the founder of the Nafsiyat Centre, describes intercultural therapy as taking into account the whole being of the client that includes his or her shared experience in the world (Kareem, 1992). Does taking into account the whole being of the client require recognising or even bringing into the work the differences between the therapist and the client? Peter Cockersell (2019) notes that the overt recognition of differences enables the transferences to be worked through more openly in the room. With the experience and training I have now, I understand how important it is to bring those differences in the therapeutic relationship, out to be explored. I do believe however, that it requires a certain amount of ego strength, self-awareness and even discipline.

Keeping differences out of the therapy room can also have negative consequences, such as reinforcing the power imbalance caused by cultural or political differences. Kareem (1992) wrote: "The very fact of being from another culture involves both conscious and unconscious assumptions, both in the patient and in the therapist. I believe that for the successful outcome of therapy it is essential to address these conscious and unconscious assumptions from the beginning". It may be said that the assumptions that stayed out of the room haunted Omar and myself in our work together. I am sure Omar carried assumptions about me and my views as a Turkish man during a time when there was conflict between Kurdish and Turkish people. My assumptions were about Omar's views of me and my national identity. So, what does Kareem mean when he says that the assumptions might be addressed from the "beginning"? When is the beginning? In the case of Omar, the beginning is possibly the phone call we had, before either of us stepped foot inside the therapy room. In many ways, that phone call stayed with me and Omar throughout our sessions and could have been an opportunity for expressing and addressing the differences. Since the work now at Nafsiyat is time limited to twelve sessions, the therapy requires a level of nimbleness. When the therapist sees an opening to address the differences, they need to take up the opportunity for exploration this offers with the client.

There was also the supervision group which affected and shaped my work with Omar. Informed by the same psychodynamic and relational view of the supervisory process, the supervision group also had a co-created relational space which included its own set of transferences and counter-transferences. The group consisted of four supervisees of which I was the only male (other than David, the supervisor). Bion (1967) noted that the transference is felt to the whole situation and my transference in the supervision group greatly shaped my work with Omar. One of the supervisees, Leyla, was a Kurdish woman whose family had fled the violence in Northern Iraq and Turkey. I felt extremely self-conscious in supervision sessions when I presented my work with Omar. Every time I presented Omar's material in supervision, I felt a degree of guilt and impending doom. I felt as if Leyla was going to be offended with how I worked with Omar. These were some of the most frustrating days I have been through as a therapist as the work with Omar would leave me depleted only to live through the same feelings in supervision a couple of hours later. Upon reflection, the same process that stopped me from bringing my whole self and my differences to the relationship with Omar was at play in the supervision group as well. This phenomenon, first formulated by Harold Searles (1955) as "reflection process", has come to be known as parallel process, where the supervision process plays out one or more dynamics present in the therapist-client relationship (Frawley-O'Dea and Sarnat, 2001). In my case, there were two dynamics that played out in both. First, I felt questioned to the point of feeling probed by the supervision group. This resembled how Omar felt questioned by the authorities, expressed perhaps in my experiences of his questions and of my attempts at adopting a neutral stance with him in the therapy room. This was a major theme in Omar's life that played out in the therapy room. I felt like the group was closing in on me to bring out the differences between Omar and me. This has traditionally been thought as the therapist unconsciously identifying with the client's psychological functioning (Frawley-O'Dea and Sarnat, 2001). Perhaps, I identified with Omar as a victim of some form of questioning that brought out a countertransferential feeling of guilt in me. Secondly, and more drastically, I felt the same differences between Omar and I that I failed to bring into the therapeutic work were also at play in the supervision group between Leyla and I and they surfaced in the same way as they did with Omar. In one supervision session where I explained how I felt exposed when Omar asked me my views about the Turkish-Kurdish conflict, Leyla said she always wondered what my views were and would be interested to know what I thought. I froze in the same way I did in the therapy room with Omar. I may have said a few words about how discussions around these issues were not promoted in school growing up and how my views are still in the process of being formed. I failed to bring the differences between Leyla and I into the supervision group. The feelings in the therapy room and the supervision room were the same and I wonder if the outcome was too. Herbert Hahn (1999) underlines how in supervision, much like in therapy, the importance of how the "here and now" could be used to bring out the projections. Hahn (1999) also notes that supervision is first and foremost a relationship between the members of the supervision group and those relationships can best be fostered through drawing on direct experiences in the group. I feel like I missed an opportunity to bring my feelings towards the differences with Leyla and even my inability to work through those feelings in the group. On hindsight, working through the same blockages in the supervision group may have helped my work with Omar. As much as David touched on supervisee disparities, he could have furthered and deepened these discussions through explorations of his cultural, ethnic and racial location and of the supervisees' intersectional positionalities in the group.

Recommendations and conclusion

The most important lesson I walked away with from my experience with Omar is the value of bringing in and working through the differences. I am not certain if the outcome of our work would be any different had we done so, but the work may have yielded more material for us to process. The same applies to the supervision process. It was a golden opportunity to voice and process the differences and more personal countertransferential feelings in the group. Therefore, I would recommend that supervisees make an effort to bring in the cultural or personal differences arising in the course of the supervision sessions to work through them. Chances are that the same issues may be at play in the therapy room with clients, that is the parallel process. This requires training and also courage, on the part of the supervisees. I would encourage therapists in training and supervisees to cultivate this training and courage throughout their supervision sessions, especially in group settings.

My work with Omar has shown me the value of working through differences and since then I have had many opportunities to process them in supervision. Another Kurdish-Turkish supervisee has since replaced Leyla in the supervision group, and I have been able to bring in many of our differences as material for the supervision sessions. It has been an invaluable experience for both of us, as well as I am sure for the group, as we continue to work through our differences. As a result, my therapeutic work has been immensely enriched by the process.

I also believe supervisors have the unique role to foster an environment in supervision where supervisees are able to bring in differences and other countertransferential material. This can be explicated by supervisors paying attention to subtle clues where these issues may arise or by offering the space for supervisees to express themselves. I benefitted from David being acutely aware of the differences in the room and how they may be processed to the benefit of the supervisees and ultimately, our clients. It may not have been possible to make use of this precious, therapeutic tool had it not been for him allowing us the space and challenging us where needed.

References

Bion, W. (1967). *Second Thoughts*. London: Heinemann.
Bollas, C. (1999). *The Mystery of Things*. London: Routledge.

Cockersell, P. (2019). Intercultural, intracultural psychotherapy. In: Ababio, B., Littlewood, R. (eds.) *Intercultural Therapy; Challenges, Insights and Developments.* London: Routledge.

Fairbairn, W. R. D. (1952). *Psychoanalytic Studies of the Personality.* London, UK: Routledge, 1994.

Frawley-O'Dea, M. G., Sarnat, J. E. (2001). *The Supervisory Relationship: A Contemporary Psychodynamic Approach.* London: The Guilford Press.

Grotstein, J. S. (2018). *But at the Same Time and on Another Level: Psychoanalytic Theory and Technique in the Kleinian/Bionian Mode.* London: Routledge.

Hahn, H. (1999). The good, the bad – and the ugly? In Clarkson, P. (ed.) *Supervision; Psychoanalytic and Jungian Perspectives.* London: Whurr Publishers Ltd.

Kareem, J. (1992). The Nafsiyat intercultural therapy centre: Ideas and experience. In Kareem, J., Littlewood, R. (eds.) *Intercultural Therapy.* Oxford: Blackwell.

Klein, M. (1932). *The Psycho-Analysis of Children.* London: Hogarth.

Klein, M. (1959). Our adult world and its roots in infancy. In: *Envy and gratitude and other works 1946-1963.* London: Vintage.

Langs, R. (1994). *Doing Supervision and Being Supervised.* London: Karnac Books.

Ogden, T. H. (1979). On projective identification. *International Journal of Psycho-Analysis, 60*, 357–373.

Rock, M. H. (ed.) (1997). *Psychodynamic Supervision.* Northvale, NJ: Jason Aronson.

Searles, H. S. (1955). The informational value of the supervisor's emotional experiences. *Psychiatry, 18*, 135–146.

Chapter 11

Call to Adventure
The Pitfalls of a Narrative Structure for an Intercultural Trainee

Hady Kamar

Introduction

At the outset of my counselling training, my cohort and I, were cautioned that we were about to embark on a journey that, if met seriously, would end up breaking us down before building us back up – hopefully, into something resembling a therapist. At the time, this dramatic portrayal of the journey towards becoming a therapist allowed me the expressed permission I had been looking for to situate myself as the protagonist in my own life; along with a narrative through which to reimagine and reshape my life. The narrative received a formal structure when I learned about the utilization within Jungian therapy of Joseph Campbell's universal story template: the "hero's journey," also known as, the monomyth.

Like many others brought up in Hollywood stories, I had been primed to believe one's life should have a *compelling* narrative arc. And my role as a successful member of society is to find and live by that arc. Perhaps the most famous and canonized narrative structure in contemporary Western media is *the hero's journey*. Popularized by the American academic and author Joseph Campbell, the hero's journey concept developed out of Campbell's background in comparative literature and religion. The hero's journey structure goes something like this: A protagonist is thrust out from the mundanity of everyday life into a world of adventure and supernatural wonder. Fabulous forces are encountered, the protagonist overcomes a challenge, and a decisive battle is won. Finally, the hero comes back from this mysterious adventure with the power to bestow boons on their fellow man (Campbell, 2004, p. 28). In his book, *Hero with a Thousand Faces,* Campbell claims this particular narrative structure has been universal across world mythologies. His evidence for this claim relies heavily on the work of Swiss psychoanalyst Carl Jung, who theorised that within the psychological makeup of every human are universal and timeless archetypes with which we develop our personalities (2004, p. 130). Fast forward some years since my training and eventually this identification I had with the drama of the journey had mostly fizzled out. Up until recently, I had assumed my enthusiasm for the hero's journey lost its

DOI: 10.4324/9781003380214-16

energy because I failed to stay present with the unfolding narrative and was instead caught up in the complexities and mundanity of professionalising. Now, reflecting on my early training in light of experience, I recognize fundamental problems with using the Hero's Journey to narrate one's personal development broadly and specifically to the process of professionalising. Campbell's emphasis on assigning archetypes and victory in the face of challenge has been incongruent with the reality of client work as an intercultural therapist as well as obstructive to the supervisory process.

Supervision indirectly provided the first challenges to my fantasy role of "therapist as a victorious hero." Throughout, I was encouraged to explore how my clients' external realities may lead them to consciously or unconsciously take me out of the role I had assigned for myself and into another - perhaps even that of a villain. A client might pass judgment on my character based on observable cultural markers, skin colour, or gender presentation (Agoro, 2019, p. 25). Those judgments may have taken root – for either myself or the client (Kareem, 1988) – even before our first meeting (Kareem, 1988). Therefore, it was important to understand their external reality as that was where the damage came from; and that involved suspending my narrative.

Still, despite my training, it would take time for me to understand the degree to which this narrative was guiding my actions and how it had been embedded into my psyche in the first place. In this chapter, I will use a combination of my own experience in training, along with a critical look into the genesis and impact of Campbell's "hero's journey" on personal and professional development, in order to illustrate why it is critical for supervision – and indeed the training organisation as a whole – to make explicit inquiries into the narrative structures trainees bring on their "journey" toward professionalising.

"Had I Known ..."

Critiques are often levelled at Campbell for employing a limited research scope in determining the universality of the themes comprising the monomyth. Folklorists and anthropologists claim the monomyth suffers from source-selection bias (Segal, 1987; Toelken, 1996) and it overlooks historical and cultural particulars in favour of generalisations (Doniger, 1992 cited in Leeming et al., 2010, p. 125). Dundes (2005, p. 4) notes that Campbell ignores regions outside the Indo-European tradition when claiming universality in myths across cultures – for example, he cites the lack of a deluge myth in sub-Saharan Africa as one example of a myth not present across all cultures. In Campbell's defence, David L. Miller argues the universalising represented within the hero's journey is the result of a method of "comparing the likeness of unlike things (that is, of finding similarity within inherent difference), as opposed to the likeness of like things" (Miller, 1995 cited in Leeming et al., 2010, p. 125).

The selection bias Campbell is accused of has not limited his popularity. Christopher Vogler, author of *The Writer's Journey* – a guidebook for screenwriters utilises the story structure of Campbell's Hero's Journey – strongly asserts Campbell uncovered the unifying life principles embedded in the structure of stories all along (2007, p. xv). Vogler's own work would go on to be hugely influential with the author claiming *The Writer's Journey* not only resonated with screenwriters, but it was also used by teachers, psychologists, advertising executives, prison counsellors, video game designers, and scholars of myth and pop culture (2007, p. xv). For someone born in 1984 – brought up on all types of sci-fi, fantasy, comics, and videogames – this structure has had a major influence on shaping my understanding of how a successful, victorious archetypal *man* is formed. As an adult, it enabled me to formalize my desires associated with entering training and becoming a professional.

I approached my early client work and group supervision as a part of the trial – a fantastical testing ground filled with magic elements of the unconscious, transference, splitting and integration. While imagining the guidance of the archetypal mentors, my placement became an arena within which I could confront the personal struggles that might impede my adventure. Furthermore, being a trainee at an intercultural therapy organisation presented its own challenges. For example, supervision necessitated we reflect on issues such as race, gender, class, and poverty – all of which, for me, reinforced the "alternativeness" of my very own special journey. And to what end? Well, according to the hero's journey, one day I would emerge victorious, as an archetypal Master of Therapy.

Naive as it may seem, in hindsight, this concept of "journey" had been embedded in me unconsciously well before I had been aware of the Hero's Journey. However, unlike Campbell's assertion that the monomyth is a manifestation of constitutional components found in the unconscious, I argue instead it was embedded; in the Fanonian understanding of the collective unconscious. That is, when a group holds a collective unconscious belief, that belief should be understood as culturally derived and composed simply of "the sum of prejudices, myths, and collective attitudes of a given group" (Fanon, 2008, p. 188). It is for this reason I believe among the many dialogues we have in supervision about unconscious motivations, trainees would also benefit from discussing personal narrative structures and how that may affect client work.

The development of "adventure" in Western literature

To understand how one might consciously or unconsciously adopt the Campbellian understanding of journey and adventure, it is important to understand how these concepts originated. Simon Gusman and Arjen Kleinherenbrink (2018) in their book *Adventures Don't Exist* (translated from

German: *Avonturen bestaan niet)* present the thesis that contemporary ideas of personal or professional journey originated in Western literature and that throughout Western[1] literary history the idea of adventure has been regularly reframed to include new meanings. These meanings, they argue, were adapted to fit the historical context of the time. Using this conceptual framework, they argue that the Western literary concept of adventure developed within and alongside societal contexts led to an emphasis on individuality and to developing colonial and capitalist projects. A development they say culminates in today's "system-confirming" notion of adventure that, the attempt to commodify adventure, has led to a culture where adventure is understood to apply to nearly any scenario:

> ... adventure par excellence is rebellious, unorthodox and "anti-systematic". While these days adventure has just as much become "system-confirming". The adventurer goes to a festival, or on a world trip or joins the military, all of which maintain the prevailing social and economic status quo. How can adventure be the bearer of so many contradictions? How can we be stunt-flying millionaires, sweaty backpackers, loyal soldiers, freshmen, young entrepreneurs, experimenting scientists, tripping festival goers and brand-new parents and describe these in adventurous terms? ... You might think there is a common denominator in the game that makes all of this adventurous. Is it maybe the risk factor? Then nightclub porters and test subjects would also be adventurers. Is it the notion of travel? Then coach drivers are the greatest adventurers in the world. Is it perhaps because of great physical or mental effort? Then we would count movers and psychiatrists among the adventurers. By today's definition we can consider all of these adventures - and rightly so. (2018, pp. 71–72)

Gusman and Kleinherenbrink identify Campbell and the popularization of the hero's journey as prime catalysts in what they call the "democratisation of adventure" (2018, p.72). Campbell's emphasis on the hero's journey being both "outward" and "inward," they argue, has opened the arena for almost any act to be considered an adventure – even training as a therapist – so long as it adheres to the "Campbellian circle" (2018, p. 73) of departure, initiation, and return.

Through what they dub the "genealogy of the adventure" (2018, p. 91), Gusman and Kleinherenbrink illustrate the concept of adventure we hold today – particularly the hero's journey – is based primarily on a series of prevailing social contexts within the West and are products of the literature of their times. While the authors admit their reconstruction of a literary genealogy is selective and incomplete, it does, however, provide an interesting overview into literary development in light of prevailing social contexts. They reflect on what a particular literary period's connotations of adventure were and track them forward in order to match those values with contemporary discourse on personal and professional journey. By exploring some of that genealogy here, it will become clear how our contemporary notion of journey – in my case a professional journey – is uniquely tied to European social and political motivations. It will also help provide the groundwork for understanding how the dynamics associated with the "European adventure mentality" can impact work with clients and supervision.

A genealogy of adventure

Beginning with Ancient literature, around 800 BCE to 500 CE, Gusman and Kleinherenbrink write stories of adventure that were primarily concerned with gods and demigods. The mythical stories of characters like Hercules and the king of Uruk are of primal adventurers who are the incarnation of "raw" adventure (2018, p. 75). These are characters whose feats are wholly unreachable by ordinary people and were instead practical models for understanding how to live one's life (Vogler, p. xiv).

After 500 CE, European literature made the shift toward "medieval literature." German academic Michael Nerlich notes it was during this period where the term "adventure" or *aventure* in Medieval French first started to first appear – representing the "highest meaning of human existence" (1987, p. 11) and was motivated by nobility of birth and by religion. The representation of the hero in much of medieval literature is of the chivalric knight who rides out into the wilderness - out of civilization – and proves his mettle through feats of "bravery and courage" (Gusman and Kleinherenbrink, 2018, p. 76). These characters were often of noble background and their stories were meant for us to marvel at the hero's selflessness and bravery and to cheer for them as they returned victorious. The heroes in these stories are not bound to heroism but choose to venture into it. While the chivalric hero would certainly adventure for personal gain – status, land, wealth, marriage, etc. – they would be dishonoured if these came to them without sufficiently proving their worth through conquest. Much like the gods and demigods of ancient literature, the social stations these protagonists occupied were above and outside the reach of the commoner – making them alone worthy of adventure.

Moving forward into the fourteenth century, we see the literary protagonist shift from chivalric hero of medieval literature to the industrious merchant of the Renaissance. We also see a semiotic evolution of the word adventure from referring "to the fate of individuals" to its new meaning where the individual's fate is theirs to conquer (Arnould, 2015). In this shift of meaning, we also see the shift in intention for adventure. Where the medieval hero needed adventure as a means to justify their status, the renaissance hero adventures in order to gain wealth and to improve their station within the social hierarchy. Thus, the journey becomes a by-product of their greater goal; a necessary risk that would have otherwise been avoided were they able to make their riches with less struggle. Jacques Arnould writes of the Renaissance hero and their historical context:

> These men embodied on land and on sea what the mathematicians had been studying on paper: calculation of probabilities and risk management. They no longer saw the world, or human fates, as divine playthings; the world was within reach, offered to the intelligence and enterprise of humans who could become, to quote Descartes, "like [its] masters and possessors" (2015).

The mentality of masters and possessors Descartes describes is the basis for the "morality-free rationales" for the merchant adventurer's "ideology of adventure." An ideology that justifies "exploration, subjugation, and exploitation" (Nerlich, 1988 cited in Beames et al., 2019, p. 3). In other words, the colonial enterprise.

Beames et al., (2019, p. 3) expand on this point:

> Boje and Luhman (1999) explain how Nerlich's ideology of adventure 'makes the industrial revolution and enlightenment possible as a project of capitalism' (para. 2). Nerlich showed how the stories, literature, poems, and plays of the time promoted an 'adventure-mentality' that became 'appropriated in capitalistic commerce and production as adventure-practices' (ibid). Bell (2016) further explains how the cultural production of today's adventurous and heroic individual is located within ongoing 'histories of imperialism and enforced inequalities' (p. 8) … From this perspective, the socially agreed concept of what it means to be adventurous is built on stories, images, and ideas which are tied in with certain dominant cultural forces. Consider for a moment the countless foreign lands (and the people who inhabited them) that were plundered and exploited for others' benefit. In summary, the roots of the word adventure are very much linked to centuries of male capitalist endeavour and colonization. Those reading a book on adventure and society should see that adventures in antiquity, the middle ages, the renaissance, and the industrial revolution were very much influenced by the social norms of their times.

Supervision: A challenge?

Taking a step back into the context of the therapy, one could enquire into how the adherence to this model of journey could be interpreted as a practice of exploitation for personal gain. This line of enquiry did not become apparent as one to follow at any point in my training. This could have been due to the ubiquity and normalization of the adventure-mentality as a culturally recognised benefit within professional settings. It could have also gone unrecognised due to how the "adventure-mentality" can obfuscate genuine inquiry by taking on a moral justification, i.e., depicting the therapist as taking on a monumental struggle against the problems afflicting our clients. I suspect it was most likely because I never saw a space where making mention of this narrative had a place in intercultural supervision.

During my training, I remember this prevailing sense of incongruence between the image I held of myself on this journey and the psychodynamic framework held throughout the organisation. This feeling of incongruence was usually most pronounced after leaving a session of supervision. Ultimately, the conflict was between the linear narrative structure I was employing - where the story required me to assign clients and colleagues archetypal roles - and the psychodynamic and divergent thinking that the supervisory exercise required I be open to. In these instances, I experienced a split between these two positions and in order to maintain the narrative, I would remind my "hero-self" that it needed to take a back seat while I was being governed by the psychodynamic principles of the organization. In other words, no one was going to indulge my fantasies and I would have to wait until I struck out on my own.

As it turns out, in order to manage this incongruence, I would need to engage in a sort of wilful othering of intercultural therapy as a professional endeavour separate from the mainstream therapy where my victorious therapist fantasy had the advantage of precedent. Due to the emphasis placed on dominance and success within the contemporary ideas of journey and adventure, I was inclined to, in a Kleinian sense, create a split, associating intercultural work as a non-advantageous career path and mainstream Eurocentric therapy, providing the advantage. What then did this mean for my clients? Were my clients in effect less advantageous?

Editing the story

The following case study is an example of the way the "ideology of adventure" – with its emphasis on archetypes and success over failure – played out early in my training. My client was a 27-year-old male from Iran who I refer to as L. L came to the United Kingdom and overstayed his student visa and was seeking asylum. At the time we met, he was still waiting on a decision concerning his status. L presented with low mood and depression and said he suffered from an inability to overcome what he considered to be chronic lethargy. After our first session, it became apparent L's sense of self-worth was very low and we explored whether his self-worth and motivation were in any way tied to his current experience of the asylum process. He explained that, due to the instability and lengthy periods of uncertainty, he found himself "wasting" his days away on the internet and gaming. As is often the case with asylum seekers and refugees, the dehumanising and bureaucratic asylum process can have a denigrating effect on one's self-worth; where the individual identifies with the label and sub-citizen position they occupy. However, L would share his political and social alienation began well before he sought political asylum. Prior to arriving in the United Kingdom, L had a major falling out with his father over his political engagement. L's father berated him for always having "weird ideas" and his failures in comparison to his older, more successful and more "realistic" brother. He shared the overwhelming emasculation he felt when after his attempts at participating politically, he found himself needing to be bailed out of jail by his father. An event which led to his father embarrassing him and his mother, as she always did, needing to come to his defence. L explained the contrast between the overwhelmingly critical responses of his father and the overly sympathetic responses of his mother had been the family dynamic for as long as he could remember. Now, struggling to continue with his education in his adopted home (UK), L found himself re-enacting something of his parental-early childhood internalisations.

The "weird ideas" L felt diverged from his cultural upbringing and stemmed from his interests in his major past-times: engaging with leftist politics and reading/watching comic books and films.

With L, I thought I had hit the jackpot in terms of finding a client with whom I felt I could truly relate to and help. We quickly found a common language where metaphors of heroism, villainy, outcasts, adventure and ethics all came into play. L likened himself to the Batman character, privileged (and parentless) existing on the edge of society and acceptability. During our sessions, we would explore the trajectories of these characters and place them in real-life scenarios where we would imagine what positions they would take in politics and social situations. We bought in together to the adventure narrative; him on his adventure toward becoming a successful version of himself and mine as the elder version of him, further progressed on the road to overcoming inadequacies and toward success.

During supervision, we reflected on the way in which the relational approach I had taken with L – appeared to unlock and converge for him energies that were being held internally as separate and split objects. Additionally, the stories of adventure and redemption and the combined investment we placed in them, formed for us a shared model of mind (Lyons, 2020, p431) that contrasted the "foreignness" he felt within his family, his community and in the United Kingdom. The guidance provided by the group allowed me to sensitively manage the intersubjective space forming between us. In particular, navigating the sensitive issue of difference in mine and L's social positioning – e.g. legal status and financial position – which, if unaddressed, could produce a painful decoupling and sense of rejection as the therapy ended.

Despite the positive steps L and I had taken together, all was not entirely well with our work. Halfway through his allotted twelve sessions, L began to miss appointments. Given the material I provided to the supervision group and his history, L's absences were explored via a number of theoretical lenses. For example, as the reproduction of long standing attachment styles whereby L was fluctuating between dismissive-avoidant and fearful-avoidant attachments. *Dismissive avoidant* as the coping mechanism he had developed for managing his disappointments (and being seen as a disappointment) and *fearful-avoidant* as a protection against the intensity of emotions he experienced in therapy. Emotions that may have been eliciting in him feelings attributed to his parents. However, these observations made within the supervision were working off limited information. What I had not mentioned to the group was very early in our work together, L shared with me a sexual inclination toward BDSM pornography. It was a brief mention of something he wanted to speak about, but he felt very embarrassed to bring it up. We agreed to come back to it later on but never did. I had not ignored it because of any discomfort I felt in discussing it or for the sake of sparing him the embarrassment of elaborating. Instead, it was because this line of inquiry was a detour from the established journey narrative he and I identified as being central to his experience. Having the common language of this narrative led us to understand the roles we were to adopt. And while I may have adopted the mentor role, I left little room for his sexual energies to mobilise; essentially re-substantiating his father's belief that L had "weird ideas." Despite our rapport, by not allowing L the space to diverge from the journey into the embarrassing and potentially messy exploration of his sexuality, I may have been re-enacting with him the overbearing expectations and objectification his parents and, in truth, society at large, had subjected him to. Not to mention reinforcing shame around his sexuality and emasculation.

The values of success and dominance that underpin the ideology of adventure governed my work with L. I recall repeatedly thinking to myself as I worked with him that "this could be my niche," "this is how I become successful." I held a mental image of myself travelling down this road, projecting well into the future, on how I could develop this type of practice with this type of client into a successful professional and personal endeavour. Supervision, through editing and omission, allowed me to craft my adventure with L to include the *types* of challenges that would allow this journey to progress within the reasonable boundaries of the narrative. In reality, this adventure-mentality enabled an industrious and exploitative way of thinking whereby the client became for the therapist an object or tool for progress.

It is easy to see in this example how the ideology of adventure, with its roots in dominance, might subversively integrate with the trainee's client work and may be easily missed without prior exploration of the trainee's personal narrative structure.

The positive alliance that forms through mutual collaboration between client and therapist (Bordin, 1979) is oftentimes contingent upon similarity in client and therapist's intersectional identities (PettyJohn et al., 2020, p 318). Throughout each stage of the hero's journey, the adventurer meets individuals who represent different archetypal figures who the adventurer must confront and ultimately integrate into their whole, true selves. In my journey as therapist-in-training, I would, to varying degrees, project roles onto the client and members of the organisation, in order to act as agents in the progression of the Campbellian circle. The allure of the journey brings with it the temptation to deny the client their identities as well as their agency to disrupt the Campbellian circle.

What happens, for example, if the therapist (the hero), from the clients' perspective, represents the villain? In many cases, our social position has an impact outside the scope of our linear, hero-centric journey. Thereby revealing a simple yet pivotal contradiction with employing a two-dimensional model of the therapists' journey. In this respect, intercultural supervision served an important function in my training in that it helped pull the story back into the light; outlining with clarity and contrast that what I believed I was doing with the client had qualities and variables unbeknownst to me. I mean something to someone else and without exploring those meanings, I was going off on my journey – not the clients.

A story that doesn't track

Contemporary shifts in literary narratives involved with platforming alternative voices have provided new landscapes for adventure. Postmodern and postcolonial works have challenged the notion of what constitutes adventure and who determines success and failure. With it comes an investigation into where these preconceptions on success and failure are located in the mind and how they got there in the first place.

The trend of rooting adventure in psychology began to become popular in Western literature around the 17th century. A disconnect formed between adventure and adventurer; whereby the content of the experience did not make the adventure, instead the "form" did (Wanderer, 1987: 21). The hero of this literature may, in fact, complete the Campbellian circle - departure, initiation, and return - without ever venturing outward, but instead making their journey into the inner dimensions of their own psyche. Take for example, Cervantes' 17th-century novel, Don Quixote, where the protagonist, Alonso Quijano, loses his mind after reading too many chivalric romances and becomes a knight-errant to revive chivalry and serve his nation. In these novels the hero is pitted up against their unconscious – a dark region of unexplored landscapes where battles lay in wait between the Id and superego. These stories stress the psychological development of the protagonist *as* the adventure. Campbell would embrace this thematic shift stating, "that myths are of the nature of dream" and "that dreams are symptomatic of the dynamics of the psyche" (Campbell, 2004, p. 237).

The journey as an inward struggle would take a turn with postmodern and postcolonial stories, which questioned the values and motives of our personal

journeys. Where, for example, during the romantic era criminality in literature was represented as pathology, the postmodern narrative proposed that
the mental health of the hero was not indicative of a deficiency of the hero,
but instead represented a referendum on society. As Hassan puts it, with
postmodernism, "the old principles of causality, psychological analysis and
symbolic relations ... the principles on which the bourgeois novel once
comfortably rested, began to tremble" (Hassan, 1967). Where the protagonist
of modernism was *normal* but occupied the paranoid position (to their det-
riment), the protagonist of postmodernism occupied the schizoid position -
becoming critical of normality and going beyond "the pre-coded identity that
the society enforces by the process in which the individual becomes a
"minority" (Daram and Rahmani, 2013, p. 47). This era saw an "emphasis on
diverse and different realities" (Larrain, 1994, p. 289) and distrust of tota-
lising discourses. The postmodern works of the 1990s and 2000s – my
formative era – placed the *marginalized other* at the centre of their narratives
with hopes to de-stigmatise them. Essentially, character struggle is no longer
equated to a character flaw. While this is at once a system non-conforming
break from societal oppression, it also presents the opportunity for one who
might consider themselves outside of the cultural norm to then identify with
an "alternative adventure" into mental health. In my case, my training had
very much to do with this identification. However, when using a postcolonial
lens to view this phenomenon, we begin to see the problematic nature of
taking on a mental health adventure that utilizes the parameters of only a
Western narrative structure.

   Postcolonial theory and art help to shed light on how the concept of hero
and adventure becomes embedded in the cultural consciousness in the first
place as well as in what ways it manifests in the individual. Employing the
critical lens of Edward Said's concept of Orientalism, Said argued that
European knowledge of the "East" was a distribution and elaboration of
beliefs and information which itself constituted, rather than being constituted
by, its object. (Leask, 1992, p. 17). By extension, one could argue that because
the hero's journey's foundations are in the West, that it contains within it
a European view of the "East." In my case, when I fantasized about the
story arc of my journey toward professionalizing, I imagined myself as a
second-generation, Arabic-speaking, former artist, who went through his
own counselling, struggled through issues, overcame his issues, now training
as a therapist, and eventually became the *inbetweener* who performs emotional triage for other Arab*ish* Muslims in the West. In this scenario, even as
the hero, I am orientalizing myself, whereby I place myself outside of the
"occidental centre" (Leask, 2004, p. 17). Occident refers here to the Western
hemisphere that gazes on the East. Nigel Leask, a scholar who specializes in
the topic of Romantic Orientalism in literature, suggests that when considering the body of knowledge known as "orientalism" we must consider that
the *relational* meaning of the word is already an index of its subordination to

an occidental centre (2004, p. 17). This idea has led me to wonder, despite contemporary views on adventure being biased towards success, whether my adherence to this narrative would ever allow me better than second place? Could I ever truly complete the Campbellian circle and become a "master of therapy" if through the use of this model, I am still subject and subordinate to the Occidental centre? Furthermore, how did this unconscious subordination manifest in how I presented my clients in supervision? Could I ever truly internalize feedback regarding power and powerlessness if, because of this narrative, I automatically placed both myself and my clients in a subordinate position?

Real-life stories

These questions regarding the occidental centre have implications beyond simply how one views themselves (and their clients) and push us to interrogate the material impact of the adventure mentality on the trainee. Sunil Bhatia (2018) expands on this material impact of the adventure mentality through the example of the capitalist creation of the "enterprising neoliberal worker" in Indian tech companies. The worker is indoctrinated into the mythologies of the West where they are expected to follow the ideology of Western corporate culture through individual transformation, acquiring new behaviours of increased emotional intelligence, assertiveness, flexibility, productivity, and self-regulation – all while encouraging culturally "American" displays of positivity, extroversion and self-confidence. Language is very similar to the qualities the hero develops on their adventure to self-discovery. All of which, according to Bhatia, constitutes the embrace of a self-orientalizing framework.

Bhatia, cites the use of the Myers–Briggs Type Indicator (MBTI) and Transactional Analysis (TA) as two of the most pervasively used instruments for training purposes in Indian corporations (Vasavi, 2008 cited in Bhatia, 2018, p. 45). MBTI, he says, purports to be grounded in Jungian archetypes. He provides this example to highlight the concrete ways in which specific psychological knowledge and discourses are becoming reframed within new locales. He writes, "The particular Euro-American ideas about self and identity and the *stories* [italics mine] in which these selves find meaning are historically constituted, however now, represent an idealized "global self" or "best global practices" (2018, p. 55).

The profession of psychotherapy too has Euro-American parameters of "global self" and "best global practices." These parameters are set within an industry where professional development is contingent upon a system of transactions between therapist and clients as well as therapist and the industry itself. The trainee develops their craft within the industry of higher education and continuing professional development. While this is not in and of itself problematic, Bhatia's critique encourages us to investigate the historical context and motivators that propel us on our journey toward professionalizing.

Imagine, for a minute, that the journey of the trainee counsellor did not include the trainee being seen as - to use Campbell's words - a "young acolyte" sent out with little resource to work and grow in service of the greater good. If instead, the trainee was thought of as a skilled adult with financial dependents and material responsibilities, would a clinical placement then be able to employ a trainee without monetary compensation? Trainees are incentivized to bank on the promise of a later payoff - an imagined story of the future. This narrative has become increasingly central to our picture of the "accredited" therapist and has created the structures within which we imagine and develop into the therapists we are meant to become. Perhaps we should campaign for, what Patricia Richards calls, an *epistemological decolonization.* Wherein we "challenge marginalization of particular ways of knowing, thinking, and researching" – and I would add, training - which is "rooted in both epistemic and material inequalities" (Richards, 2014, p. 145). The story structure I held had material consequences as I spent a great deal of time feeling vulnerable and unsure whether I could afford to continue. I also believe that I took less chances within supervision because the grounds I stood on were shaky to begin with. I believed supervision was meant to be in service to the client; how could my material concerns *possibly* impact the client?

Concluding remarks

The development of Intercultural therapy is often discussed, in lineage and contrast, with the European cultural and political landscape on which the foundations of psychotherapy were set. This connection of politics and culture co-facilitated the development of societal values and hierarchies, leading to an enterprise of colonial expansion that would ultimately impose those hierarchies and values globally (Gusman and Kleinherenbrink, 2018). Critiques are levied against mainstream psychotherapy for engaging in similar practices which reaffirm inwardly and influence outwardly, values based on the theoretical roots of Western, intellectual traditions. Traditions that are argued to privilege hierarchical, binary, oppositional and white supremacist values (Agoro, 2019, p. 24). Similarly, the narrative structure of the hero's journey is itself a manifestation of the historic interplay between European politics and culture. The emphasis Campbell places on mythologies that promote expansion and dominance has had a great impact on the idea of personal and professional journeys. From an intercultural perspective, the cultural and political privileging of success over failure promotes values antithetical to those espoused by Jafar Kareem in his development of the model. Instead, Kareem asked us to interrogate our assumptions around success, dominance, biases, and equality, not only philosophically, but actively as an integral part of the counselling experience (Kareem, 1988).

The practice of intercultural therapy takes into account the practical external realities that constitute the therapist and the client's social positions. Social positions that intersect and overlap on the micro level of individual experience, reflecting, as social psychologist Lisa Bowleg puts it, "multiple interlocking systems of privilege and oppression at the macro, social structural level (e.g., racism, sexism, heterosexism)" (2012, p. 1267). It tasks the therapist with exploring the conscious and unconscious assumptions held by both the client and the therapist regarding these positions (Kareem, 1988 cited in Acharyya et al., 1989). The therapist is also tasked with considering in what ways their biases are unconsciously enacting unspoken and pre-established power dynamics. Power dynamics may or may not limit a client's ability to agency, self-determination, and choice.

Campbell's monomyth reflects the dominant enlightenment perspective of Western civilisation in which the right to choose has been made primary (Grocott, 2012, p. 12). "Adventure" as we know it is based on the choices we make at any given stage in our lives. What does the hero's journey have to say to those who become stuck in Campbell's "road of trials" (2004, p. 89)? The reality of the matter is that using this concept of adventure as a primary lens through which to view journeys whether personal or professional carries with it a certain amount of delusion and willful ignorance of the many instances of coercion and powerlessness that our clients must endure. I consider myself fortunate that intercultural supervision never shied from this perspective and did not indulge in the fantasy of success and failure. Instead, my experience of supervision was that success and failure were viewed by our group with a tenderness that allowed for the human and their external realities to be considered.

It is for the reasons outlined in this chapter that I believe among the conscious and unconscious assumptions and biases that the trainee is encouraged to explore in supervision, we should add to that list our "embedded story structure." The foundations of how we narrate our progression as therapists and how we interrogate that structure are important to our maturation as intercultural therapists. Indeed, this maturation is not simply a matter between client, therapist and supervisor, but also includes many other layers of the profession of counselling, including the institution within which they studied, the organisation the trainee is working in and the context of the larger career progression. Considering the context and the dominant narrative in the United Kingdom is of success equating with career progression, the intercultural training institution is well positioned to have these conversations with trainee therapists. The material is rich and discussing it within supervision can perhaps go a long way to discover a more congruent and more equal journey for the trainee to consider.

Note

1 The authors define Western literature as prose and poetry coming out of Europe and post-colonization Americas.

References

Acharyya, S., Moorhouse, S., Kareem, J., Littlewood, R. (1989). Nafsiyat: A psychotherapy centre for ethnic minorities. *Psychiatric Bulletin, 13*(7), 358–360.

Agoro O. (2019). Who's being assessed? Post-modernism and intercultural therapy assessments: A synergetic process. In: Ababio, B., Littlewood R. (eds) *Intercultural Therapy: Challenges, Insights and Developments*. London: Routledge.

Arnould, J. (2015). *The History and Philosophy of Adventure*. [online] Public Books. Available at: https://www.publicbooks.org/the-history-and-philosophy-of-adventure/ (Accessed 21 Mar. 2021).

Beames, S., Mackie, C. J., Atencio, M. (2019). *Adventure and Society*. New York: Palgrave Macmillan.

Bell, M. (2016). The romance of risk: adventure's incorporation in risk society. *Journal of Adventure Education and Outdoor Learning, 17*, 280–293. 10.1080/1472 9679.2016.1263802.

Bhatia, S. (2018). *Decolonizing Psychology: Globalization, Social Justice, and Indian Youth Identities*. New York, NY, United States of America: Oxford University Press.

Bordin, E. S. (1979). The generalizability of the psychoanalytic concept of the working alliance. *Psychotherapy: Theory, Research & Practice, 16*(3), 252–260.

Bowleg, L. (2012). The problem with the phrase women and minorities: intersectionality-an important theoretical framework for public health. *American Journal of Public Health, 102*(7), 1267–1273. 10.2105/AJPH.2012.300750

Campbell, J. (2004). *The Hero With a Thousand Faces*. Princeton, N.J.: Princeton University Press.

Daram, M., Rahmani, R. (2013). Beckett's Molloy: Postmodern schizophilia. *International Journal of English and Literature, 4*(3), 45–52

Dundes, A. (1996). Folkloristics in the twenty-first century. In: *Lee Haring Grand Theory in Folkloristics*. Bloomington, IN: Indiana University Press.

Dundes, A. (2005). Folkloristics in the twenty-first century (AFS invited presidential plenary address, 2004). *The Journal of American Folklore, 118*(470), 385–408. Retrieved March 7, 2021

Fanon, F. (2008). *Black Skin, White Masks*. London: Pluto Press.

Grocott, K. (2012). A theological critique of Joseph Campbell's Monomyth as a source for meaning making in American Film. Doctor of Philosophy, Charles Sturt University, Australia.

Gusman, S. W., Kleinherenbrink, A. S. (2018). *Avonturen bestaan niet [Adventures Don't Exist]*. Amsterdam: Boom.

Hassan, I (1967). *The Literature of Silence: Henry Miller and Samuel Beckett*. New York: Knopf.

Kareem, J. (1988). Outside in … inside out … some considerations in intercultural psycho-therapy, *Journal of Social Work Practice: Psychotherapeutic Approaches in Health, Welfare and the Community, 3*(3), 57–71. 10.1080/02650538808413384.

Larrain, J. (1994). The postmodern critique of ideology. *The Sociological Review*, *42*(2), 289–314.

Leask, N. (2004). *British Romantic Writers and the East: Anxieties of Empire*. Cambridge: Cambridge University Press.

Leeming, D. A., Madden, K. W., Marlan, S. (2010). *Encyclopedia of Psychology and Religion*. New York; London: Springer.

Lyons, L. S. (2020). Embracing reality: Mindfulness, acceptance and affect regulation; Integrating relational psychoanalysis and dialectical behavior therapy. *Psychoanalytic Inquiry*, *40*(6), 422–434.

Nerlich, M. (1988). *Ideology of Adventure: Studies in Modern Consciousness, 1100-1750*. Minneapolis, Minn.: U. Of Minnesota P.

PettyJohn, M. E., Tseng, C.-F., Blow, A. J. (2020). Therapeutic utility of discussing therapist/client intersectionality in treatment: When and how?. *Family Process*, *59*(2), 313–327.

Richards, P. (2014). Decolonizing globalization studies. *The Global South*, *8*(2), 139–154.

Segal, R. (1987). *Joseph Campbell: An Introduction*. New York & London: Garland Publishing, Inc.

Toelken, B. (1996). *The Dynamics of Folklore* 2nd ed. Logan, UT: Utah State University Press.

Vogler, C. (2007). *The Writer's Journey: Mythic Structure for Writers*. Studio City, CA: Michael Wiese Productions.

Wanderer, J. J. (1987). Simmel's forms of experiencing: The adventure as symbolic work. *Symbolic Interaction*, *10*(1), 21–28.

Chapter 12

Towards an Intercultural Supervision

Kiros Hetep

It is hoped that supervision will continue to be a place where I can feel relatively undefended about my limitations as a therapist. It is through my congruent vulnerability that I continue to grow and develop as a therapist endeavouring to understand human experiences in part, via intercultural therapeutic principles. The psychotherapist, Jafar Kareem, who was born and raised in India promulgated interculturality in the United Kingdom as a viable therapeutic positioning. He felt that the Euro-centric psychotherapies on offer were failing black and minority ethnic groups (Kareem and Littlewood, 2000). In this chapter, with Kareem's comment in mind, I argue that supervision, which elides the cultural dimension from its supervisory framework, in a large part, excludes the accounts of supervisees and clients from minoritised communities. As a South London, Black British man of Caribbean heritage, I found my place in the world of therapy through my encounter with the intercultural approach applied in supervision; one which acknowledged, recognised me and opened the door for me. This personal story is threaded through the chapter.

I undertook an integrative counselling diploma training and secured during the course, a placement at a therapy centre which provided intercultural therapy to clients from diverse ethnic backgrounds (Kareem and Littlewood, 2000). I fulfilled all the required clinical hours for my training at this placement centre.

Now to my experience of supervision and the stages of my development as an intercultural therapist. Initially, I found group supervision tedious, exhausting and anxiety provoking. The thought of someone critiquing my work in the presence of my peers felt disconcerting. I tried to avoid this discomfort. Reflecting on my training journey, I am now of the view that a trainee and for that matter experienced therapists, in undertaking intercultural clinical work will find the experience of immense benefit to their practice. As a trainee, my placement at the Intercultural Centre began with group supervision. In hindsight, I would argue that group supervision is perhaps more beneficial for the trainee counsellor than individual supervision because of the various relational dynamics it provides.

DOI: 10.4324/9781003380214-17

If the supervisory group is well balanced with a blend of experiences, ethnicities and racial identities, it offers the inexperienced therapist a space for dialogue and exploration of multiple perspectives.

As a trainee therapist, my anxieties in the supervision group were related to feeling observed during case presentations. I noted how discussions regarding the frame such as how a colleague's punctuality or lack of it, could affect the therapeutic and supervision work. In my self-conscious state, I reflected on body language and what mine may convey to my peers in the supervision and also to my clients. In addition, I was reviewing the states evoked in my body as a consequence of certain themes being discussed or named in the supervision. A pre-occupation with time and the clock, an interest in colleagues' presentation, or a detachment from it were much a part of my reflections in the initial (and to a degree still ongoing) weeks of attending group supervision. During that period, I was interested in cognitive behavioural therapy (CBT) and became proficient in Ellis' ABC model of personality (Ellis, 1977) which elaborates a theory about the relationship between thoughts, feelings and client behavioural outcomes. In the supervision group at the Intercultural Centre, I was stimulated by the cultural perspectives and the idea of the therapist benefitting from deepening insights about their own culture as well as their client's. This process of introspection and curiosity in my view, mitigates the dangers of cultural assumptions being made in the supervision and therapy (Kareem and Littlewood, 2000).

As a young, Black, male trainee of Jamaican heritage, the prospect of reviewing Freud and his psychosexual schema of development was unappealing (the placement centre had a psychodynamic underpinning). In addition, the college course curriculum, among its theoretical offering explicated the developmental processes of infants with regard to attachment and separation (Bowlby, 2012). I was worn out by it all. I, therefore, resolved to become an Intercultural CBT therapist in an intercultural psychodynamic placement centre. My plan was to absorb the intercultural principles and ignore the psychodynamics which came with the placement. My resolve had also been encouraged and reinforced by research articles: David, Cristea and Hofmann (2018), Hofmann et al. (2021), and Blane et al. (2013); which positioned CBT (my starting place) as the recommended treatment option for common mental health problems such as depression and anxiety (depression was an area of particular interest for me as a trainee counsellor).

I participated in dialogues in the intercultural psychodynamic supervision group for at least four weeks without any case allocation being made to me. I observed, heard, listened to my peers' present cases from an intercultural perspective. It was important, at this early stage, to work with a supervisor who was black and of African heritage. I referenced his approach. His role, practice, and racial identity were significant. For me, it disrupted a certain negative stereotype and narrative about black men and also about the psychodynamic orientation. I watched and heard this supervisor invite colleagues to share their thoughts and impressions of their clients' cultural dynamics; it was intriguing. The invitation to supervisees to offer cultural reflections personally triggered all kinds of thoughts and feelings. It challenged me to consider my countertransference with regard to race, culture, and to bear in mind its relation to the client's cultural and racial transferences. Kareem states

> from the point of view of the intercultural therapist, I believe that it is the responsibility of the therapist, from the very outset, to facilitate the expression of any negative transference which is based on historical context, and not leave the onus on the patient. The patient may be too needy or too afraid and thus may not recognise the existence of negative feelings.
>
> (Kareem and Littlewood, 2000, p. 23)

Of interest to me regarding this supervision approach was the aspect which encouraged therapists to regularly engage in cultural research and to foster a relatively non-judgmental receptivity about their clients' cultures. I soon realised how these elaborations enriched the therapeutic relationship with my clients. The Intercultural therapist, I begun to comprehend, engages clients in explorations about their cultural and psychological interiorities unencumbered by the therapist's prior cultural knowledge. The therapist in response avoids the error of foisting what they think they "know" about the client's culture onto the client. I now turn to further processes a trainee with limited intercultural therapy experience could consider in the evolution of their competence in intercultural work.

The trainee in their evolution could well make progress by considering their own culture and the meanings they derive from it. If the trainee is unable to explore their own unconscious prejudices with regard to their culture, then working with someone who has a different culture could be detrimental, especially for the client. Another question might be what aspect of the therapist's culture is prized or attractive and a contemplation of the parts she or he finds shameful or dislikes? How did the therapist arrive at these destinations of attraction and shame in relation to their culture? This might be indicative of the trainee's capacity to face and explore difficult aspects of self, culture (and by implication could place limits on similar explorations with clients in therapy). For example, a British-born African Caribbean trainee may be proud of the 100 years of rich cultural and historical development of the Greater Antilles but dislike, distance and gloss over the fact that the culture was derived from its relationship to Africa. A consequence of the tragic and exploitative relationship that European nations had with Africa at the time (Glevey, 2012). Can the therapist face and explore these "difficult" aspects of their history? An intercultural counsellor's personal therapy, in my view, ought to be with a counsellor who is able to facilitate explorations of these cultural historical and racial dynamics, in conjunction with the trainee's engagement in intercultural supervision. As this, in my opinion, can be foundational in the trainee's development.

A number of colleagues have remarked on how difficult it was during their counselling training, to explore race and culture and how this also played out in their supervision and personal therapies. It was as if their colour (and its implications in a dominant white British setting) and culture did not matter, they said. This lack of cultural training in counselling courses has been echoed by a number of commentators (Ellis, 2019; Lowe, 2014). Training providers and trainee practitioners should understand that an exclusive immersion in European psychotherapeutic literature ill equips the practitioner in their understanding and engagement with the diverse ethnic and racial communities in the United Kingdom. Research into the clients' cultural background is helpful. Understanding the difference between individualism and collectivism (Kareem, 2000) and the attendant process of internalisation, contributes to a useful location of the trainee in their therapeutic engagements. Consider now the implications for a trainee – whose inner landscape has a collectivistic leaning, and of this therapist then engaging with a client who relatively speaking has an individualistic view of the world. Can the therapist recognise this and facilitate a working with, as opposed to against (imposing) (Ward, Stephen Bochner and Furnham, 2001)? I was taught that the intercultural practitioner enables the client to describe and inhabit their own cultural frame of reference with an expectation that the practitioner also works in acquiring a basic working understanding of their clients' cultural frame of reference. Culture is dynamic and fluid, the therapist's responsibility is to have an understanding of the current dynamics of the culture of their client and how that plays out in the therapeutic relationship – with the client defining who they are culturally and not have their cultural identity fixed by the therapist's researched knowledge. A client's awareness of the therapist's working cultural knowledge in the therapeutic space but held without imposition – results in what I would describe as an authentic, intercultural therapeutic encounter.

I will now describe two case studies I presented to two different supervisors: one with a supervisor in an intercultural organisation and the other from a non-intercultural setting. The case examples are not intended to be read as an exercise in intercultural supervisor idealisation and a denigration of Eurocentric supervision. My objective is to highlight the importance of considering racial and cultural elements within the supervisory space.

During my intercultural placement, initial discussion, after the allocation of cases to the trainee occur during the supervision. It is an arena which facilitates dialogues between the supervisor, therapist and peers, explicating the potential cultural, cognitive, racial, affective, behavioural and spiritual themes evoked by the client's material. An intercultural supervision attends to the hidden or ignored cultural and racial aspects of the therapeutic and supervision encounters. Now, to the two case examples.

Case 1

Kwame is 38, male, from Cameroon, a refugee, awaiting permanent residence. He has no family in this country, is single and because of his status, is not permitted to earn an income. The client presented to the agency with depression and anxiety.

Kwame began the first session visibly anxious and softly spoken. He spoke about his journey to England. Kwame was forced to flee Cameroon as his political affiliation and activism was in opposition to the government's. He left his mother, siblings, friends, home and culture behind which he said was very painful. Within his home culture, Kwame knew how things worked. In England, Kwame was unsure about most things, including his entitlements, and was unable to work due to limitations on his immigration status. He grappled with the realisation that, for the first time in his life, he was in a foreign environment in which the majority of the people were from different cultures, the dominant culture and racial group being white. It was whiteness, he said, which drew attention to his skin colour. In Cameroon, his blackness was not his focus or a source of unease, however in England, his skin colour had now become a major part of his identity, a negative identity marker. Kwame had no intimate relationships apart from the professional ones with staff at the charity centre where he was being supported with food and a weekly stipend. He described a lack of motivation; felt he had failed himself and his family and was doubtful about making a career for himself. In the first session, Kwame reflected on his experience of being in the waiting area of the therapy centre and his discomfort on hearing two people speaking a Cameroonian language – he said he felt a sudden sense of persecution, exposure and also nostalgia. He did not disclose his nationality to them, but he recoiled into himself. In the first session, Kwame and I agreed to explore themes of alienation, dislocation, depression and low self-esteem as these were the concerns troubling Kwame.

Dialogues in supervision

I brought Kwame to supervision to discuss the case formulation and to explore my associations with the emerging cultural transference and countertransference dynamics (I had become interested in the psychodynamics of therapy). I explored, during the supervision, my countertransference processes in the session with Kwame. There was, I observed a difference in my tone when presenting Kwame in supervision, there was an overemphasis on the fact that he had no means of earning an income, his lack of relationships, social and community engagement and support. My supervisor wondered what I currently thought about my client. After a sigh, I said that his situation seemed hopeless. My supervisor also wondered whether what I had shared might in some way reflect Kwame's inner world, one of hopelessness and despair. In supervision, I discussed Kwame's question after our contracting in the initial session, during which he asked, "Where are you from?" I responded, "Where am I from? I am curious about your question, please say more". He replied, "Were you born in this country?" This is a question that I am frequently asked, and it took a while for me to understand why I was constantly asked that question. Within the black community, this question was always in reference to my background, of origin, of place. What are the implications for my Black British male location and identity? "Yes, I was born here, I wonder what that means to you?" I responded, Kwame then said, "I was just wondering where you are from because you have a certain look". This prompted me to ask, "I wonder how it might feel for you to work with me, a black man who has a certain look?". My client replied that it made him feel more comfortable as he was not in his own country and was unsure of the kind of help, he will receive from somebody of a different racial background. I explored the "feeling comfortable" comment Kwame made. My supervisor encouraged me to consider Kwame's identification or the beginnings of it with me - how that could be helpful but could also raise themes of collusion if not borne in mind. The supervision exploration had ventured into the dynamic field of differences of being black men (supervisor included, within a group of my peers some of whom were white) but with different and shared cultural identities. During the supervision, we wondered about the meaning and feelings evoked by his encounter with the Cameroonians in the waiting area. Could this be listened out for and explored in the therapy? How would he approach the waiting area in his future appointments? Might the waiting area where he met people from his country remind him of his foreignness but also of the reasons why he could not return to his country of origin? We also wondered about my position of authority as a black man in my relationship with Kwame – bearing in mind his historical and political encounters with powerful black men in authority in Cameroon. This dialogue was linked to my relationship with my supervisor – also a black man of African heritage in a position of authority. I realised how useful it was to have such dialogues with my supervisor and peers, it was a modelling and rehearsal for similar explorations with my clients.

Case 2

Kingsley is 18, male, Black British, student, employed part-time. Kingsley presented with depression and anxiety.

Kingsley is of Jamaican heritage, born and raised in London and worked part-time near his home while he continued his studies. Kingsley described feeling lost, he felt he had squandered educational opportunities and being in education at the moment he said was an attempt to appease his mother whom he said was disappointed that he failed to achieve the grades expected of him. Kingsley hated his course but felt persevering would make his mother happy.

What his mother did not understand was how depressed Kingsley had become. Kingsley spoke about previous periods of suicide ideation. He had felt very low in the months preceding, seeking therapy.

I took this case to my supervisor who did not espouse an intercultural approach. My supervisor empathised with Kingsley's feelings and asked how I felt when Kingsley described what had brought him to counselling. Uncertainty was my response. My supervisor said it would be a good place to consider during my next session as exploring the theme of uncertainty may provide Kingsley with a canvas on which explorations about his life direction options could be made. My supervisor asked if Kingsley's father was present in his life, I informed my supervisor that, Kingsley had a fraught relationship with his father. Mother and father had separated when Kingsley was seven years old and his father was present in Kingsley life preadolescence. The contact changed and became infrequent in his teenage years. My supervisor then asked me to be mindful of how Kingsley might relate to me as we both share the same cultural background.

I was encouraged to explore how Kingsley felt as a British-born, African Caribbean black male in this country, what was the current relationship between Kingsley and his mother, and could a mother be harbouring some shame and responsibility for Kingsley's poor grades and emotional health? What did shame mean to Kingsley? My supervisor mentioned that I may be seen as the brother or good enough father in the transference, and to consider its evocations in the therapeutic relationship. I thought this was a useful intervention and I welcomed culture being included in the conversation. My supervisor mentioned that exploring the relationship between Kingsley and his mother may allow a deeper understanding of his attempts to please his mother which could facilitate and authorise an engagement with his own dreams, needs and goals. The interventions were useful and helped provide an effective service for Kingsley, but there were elements and themes my supervisor could have included that an interculturally framed supervision may well have suggested as potential areas for exploration.

Our cultural similarities (Kingsley and I) were helpfully highlighted. I was however not asked to explore how Kingsley may have felt about working with a black man (differences). This may seem trivial to some but in intercultural therapy this question, if appropriately timed, may yield indications of unanalysed areas of prejudice for the therapeutic dyad (client and therapist). I am not suggesting that an absence of cross-cultural/intercultural work renders all interventions ineffective. That is not the case. My objective is to highlight how an intercultural supervision approach facilitates a deeper multi-dimensional acknowledgement of human existence and experience in the therapeutic encounter.

Reflecting on the experience of the supervision I received during my work with Kingsley, I have considered the following: the supervision (and the assessment) could have enabled an exploration of the cultures of Kingsley's father and mother – were they from different cultures? Or seen as being part of an assumed homogenous black Caribbean group? For the reason that cultural contexts may well have shaped and played a significant role in the interactions between Kingsley's parents and Kingsley. Shame could have been explored; as this has been associated with the experiences of some Caribbean and African communities in the diaspora (Arnold, 2012). Kingsley and I explored his location as a young black man in Britain, this consideration enabled him and I to appreciate the tensions and pressures he had internalised – linked in part, to family and in turn to mother's fears and hopes of the structural barriers confronting Kingsley as a black young man in London. I may not have probed this area, had it not been for my intercultural perspective. My intercultural lens helped to better understand Kingsley's mother's experience of arriving in England from Jamaica as a child. Her own mother and father had left Jamaica for England when Kingsley's mother was an infant. Kingsley's mother remained in Jamaica whilst her parents worked in the United Kingdom to "build a better life". They then "sent" for Kingsley's mother when she was nine years old. Kingsley's mother was impacted by the separation from her parents. The effect of the separation of African Caribbean children from their parents has been extensively documented in the work of Dr Elaine Arnold (Arnold, 2012). Kingsley was born when his mother was twenty-two years old. She named her son after her father – who according to Kingsley was an educated hard-working man. Kingsley's parents divorced when he was 16. Kingsley's father remarried and had a son (Kingsley's younger half-brother). His father had struggled to find work during the marriage to Kingsley's mother and he recalled how this was the cause of arguments in the household. Kingsley's mother was the main breadwinner at that time. His father now has his own business. Kingsley's mother still retains her experience of his father as a man who lacked educational ambition, did not pursue higher education and struggled to find work in the initial stages of their marriage. She feared that this lack of ambition and job insecurity might play out in Kingsley's life. This commentary is not intended as an in-depth comparative analysis of the two supervision experiences but is recounted here to highlight how intercultural supervision focuses on the cultural racial issues within the therapy relationship and how this focus is maintained throughout the course of the treatment.

In conclusion, supervision from a non-intercultural framework runs the risk of either consciously or unconsciously sidestepping matters of culture and race. The trainee therapist, when foundationally held within the normative, formative, perspective and supportive (Culley and Bond, 2011) supervision structure, can be facilitated to name and explore, cultural and racial relational issues within therapeutic relationships. My view and experience as a black man of Jamaican descent born and raised in South London, from a working-class background, is that this kind of intercultural supervision enables an experience which engages the whole being of supervisor and supervisee (I am seen, validated and recognised in all my parts). This in turn enhances the work between the client and therapist. It is a cultural, racial relationship matrix of the supervisee(s), client and supervisor in dynamic exploration in the supervisory space.

References

Arnold, E.. (2012). *Working with Families of African Caribbean Origin: Understanding Issues Around Immigration and Attachment* (1st ed.) London: Jessica Kingsley Publishers, pp. 23–39.

Blane, D., Williams, C., Morrison, J., Wilson, A., Mercer, S., (2013). Cognitive behavioural therapy: Why primary care should have it all. *British Journal of General Practice*, [online] *63*(607), 103–104. Available at: <https://bjgp.org/content/63/607/103> (Accessed 18 January 2015).

Bowlby, J. (2012). *The Making and Breaking of Affectional Bonds*. Hoboken: Taylor and Francis, pp.150–188.

Culley, S., Bond, T. (2011). *Integrative Counselling Skills in Action*. 3rd ed. London: SAGE Publications, p. 186.

David, D., Cristea, I., Hofmann, S. (2018). Why cognitive behavioral therapy is the current gold standard of psychotherapy. *Frontiers in Psychiatry*, [online] 9. Available at: <https://www.ncbi.nlm.nih.gov/pmc/articles/PMC5797481/> (Accessed 10 July 2020).

Ellis, A. (1977). *Reason and Emotion in Psychotherapy*. Secaucus, New Jersey: The Citadel Press.

Ellis, E. (2019). Race issues in therapy: Finding our voice across the black/white divide. In: Ababio, B., Littlewood, R. (eds.) *Intercultural Therapy: Challenges, Insights and Developments* (1st ed.). Abingdon: Routledge.

Glevey, K. (2012). *On Being African*. 1st ed. London: Panafed LTD, pp. 38–47.

Hofmann, S., Asnaani, A., Vonk, I., Sawyer, A., Fang, A. (2021). *The Efficacy of Cognitive Behavioral Therapy: A Review of Meta-analyses*. [online] Available at: <https://www.ncbi.nlm.nih.gov/pmc/articles/PMC3584580/> (Accessed 3 September 2021).

Kareem, J., Littlewood, R. (2000). *Intercultural Therapy*. 2nd ed. Oxford: Blackwell Science, pp. 14–38.

Lowe, F. (2014), Introduction. In: Lowe, F., (ed.) *Thinking Space: Promoting Thinking about Race, Culture, and Diversity in Psychotherapy and Beyond*. London: Karnac Books.

Ward, C., Stephen Bochner, S., Furnham, A., 2001. *Psychology Culture Shock*. 2nd ed. Milton: Taylor & Francis Group, pp. 11–16.

Chapter 13

Hidden Realities

Anna Chait

Race is both an empty category and one of the most destructive and powerful forms of social categorisation.

(Rustin, 1991, p. 57)

When I hear the question "Where are you from?" I wonder what is being asked. The question implies the other wants to situate you not only geographically but also on their psychic map. Locate your similarities and differences and decide whether these are to be celebrated or depreciated ones. How to respond is another challenge? Should one do so by simply stating their country of birth? Or their parents? What about grandparents and matters of language, culture, religion, race, and ethnicity? The question of identity is a complex one. Discussions around these issues tend to be defined as if they exist in absolute terms. Furthermore, it would appear that these aspects, for the most part, are excluded in a traditional psychoanalytic approach. It is with these questions and aspects in mind that this chapter arose, highlighting the importance of why, in this day and age, an Intercultural Supervision space is essential; one where such aspects can be explored and thought about in-depth. This chapter outlines the significance of unconscious normative processes (Layton, 2006) and their impact on the interpsychic/intrapsychic life of the individual and their lived-life experience. It emphasises the importance of understanding psychosocial dynamics of inequality, specifically when working with members of Black, Asian and Minority Ethnic (BAME) communities and the dangers when these are not addressed in supervision, becoming split off from the analytic process. A brief description of the phenomenon of Islamophobia is provided followed by a case study of a British/Middle Eastern/Asian female Muslim, illustrating the complexities of a hybrid identity and the interplay between race, ethnicity, culture, sexuality, gender, and religion. We will observe how the patient's identity and self-concept have been shaped by the impact of introjections arising from her experience of growing up in a dominant white Islamophobic world. These aspects are explored within an intercultural supervision space

DOI: 10.4324/9781003380214-18

where the members themselves, each of diverse cultural backgrounds bring their own histories and narratives, creating reflections and insights both through a parallel process as well as the disentanglement of the patient's material, unpacking layers of structural racism and female oppression. Henceforth engendering and creating an intersubjective relational matrix between therapist and patient where aspects of her racial, cultural, religious and sexual identity can be therapeutically explored.

The psychosocial realm

Until not so long ago, psychoanalysis pushed social reality to the margins. Dalal (2001) posits that for the most part the focus of psychoanalytic theory "is from the inside to the outside" (p. 45), thereby highlighting projective processes whilst giving very little emphasis to introjective ones. He states that "objects appear to exist in sociological vacuum" (p. 45). Meanwhile, Keval (2016) links the inner social experience of the ethnic "other" to the process of marginalisation not only in society but also in the psychoanalytic field, stating that: "trainings on diversity are given a refugee status, without a home or receptive container" (p. 75). Layton (2006) echoes this and posits that the very fact that psychoanalytic theory envisages internal constructs only as far as within links to family, specifically the mother and father, enforces "normative unconscious processes" (p. 239). She describes such processes as: "the consequences of living in a culture in which many norms serve the dominant ideological purpose of maintaining a power status quo" (Layton, 2006, p. 240). She suggests that such ideologies are built upon a matrix of binary values such as good/bad, dirty/clean, dominant/submissive, etc., assigning the quality perceived by the dominant group as "bad" onto "other," whilst retaining the higher or more desirable qualities for the dominant group. These not only shape the dynamics of the external world but also the intrapsychic make-up of ethnic minorities or members located on the margins of society. This is highly significant in psychoanalysis, given that at times, both therapist and patient may be functioning within the same dominant discourse, without questioning what this discourse may be.

Psychoanalytically, the infant operates within a paranoid-schizoid position whereby he or she will attempt to rid itself of its bad objects by splitting and projecting these onto the mother who acts as a container (Klein, 1946). Bion (1961) extends this idea to social processes whereby certain groups, racialised categories and the so-called "minorities" become "an ideal container" (Rustin, 1991, p. 62) for hatred and other undesired qualities. Such dynamics ensure that those at the top of the hierarchy can then get rid of anxiety or unwanted aspects by collectively using "other" as a dumping container of such primitive anxieties. Akhtar (2014) posits that in fact such minorities and dynamics are therefore essential for keeping the dominant group in control.

Furthermore, such group projections mean that those who receive them may develop self-reinforcing mechanisms which psychically serve to maintain the dominant ideology and status of power. It is such social discourses, enmeshed within conscious and unconscious dominant ideologies which serve to shape an individual's sense of self and identity. The nature of environmental/social forces becomes highly significant in psychoanalysis, specifically from the viewpoint that the analytic frame is an intersubjective one, borne out of the encounter and interplay of social histories and constructs. As Kareem (1992), the founder of Nafsiyat points out: "neither patient nor therapist is innocent of history or memory" (p. 21). It is therefore important to understand and take into consideration that societal transference and power imbalances may be imbued within the patient's intrapsychic subjective reality, which unless addressed may become enacted within the therapist/patient dyad.

An intercultural framework

Spurling, 2004 points out:

> The client's experience, the make-up of her object relationships and inner world, is a product not only of her membership of her family, but also of a particular culture, ethnic group, social class, gender, sexual orientation and such other (p. 109).

An intercultural perspective accounts for power dynamics and structural inequalities present within a patient's lived life experience and how these may have intruded upon their intrapsychic organisation. For instance, a patient who has had a lived life experience of racial or gender oppression may find it difficult to explicitly voice their concerns. It is therefore essential that such differences are addressed by the therapist. Oftentimes, a traditional supervisory psychoanalytic approach means that the impact of the external/psychosocial world runs the risk of becoming dissociated and split-off from the patient's process. An example to illustrate how such splitting may manifest in the supervisory space follows:

> Joana worked as a therapist within the counselling service of a prestigious University. She reported that her new patient Derek, a British, black male of Nigerian origin had expressed concerns about receiving therapy within the University organisation as he felt some of his issues related to institutionalised racism within the establishment. When Joana brought this into the supervision space, she was advised to think of such issues in terms of the patient's internal object relations to his mother. This guidance was useful, as Derek had an abusive mother with narcissistic, sadomasochistic traits and it enabled Joana to think further about the patient's defence mechanisms. Nevertheless, Joana felt

silenced and restricted regarding the exploration of Derek's lived experience of abuse and its links to the external world. She believed that Derek's experience of abuse from his mother could have been compounded by living within a matrix of institutionalised inequality and structural racism. Given that his commencement in therapy coincided with the death of George Floyd, an African American murdered by a white policeman whilst in their custody, Joana thought that the unfolding of such events could have possibly triggered unconscious feelings of being silenced and annihilated within the University institution, coupled with transgenerational traumatic unconscious memories of colonialism and enslavement. The supervision space seemed to reflect an attempt to disassociate itself from the white oppressor (Moss, 2001) whilst splitting-off Derek's black racial identity and denying it. Given the student's background and narrative, it could have been useful to address the transference in terms of social oppression and issues pertaining to white fragility (Robin D'Angelo, 2018).

Islamophobia

Nowadays, Islam is the second-largest religion in the United Kingdom. Often it seems that the media promotes and engages in propagating a view of Muslims as the enemy (Davids, 2006). In the United Kingdom, Muslims have become the targets of everyday microaggressions and verbal attacks. This behaviour becomes reinforced when prominent political figures, such as Boris Johnson, publicly make derogatory comments about Muslim women. All this has resulted in creating the phenomenon of "Islamophobia." Simply put, the term islamophobia, refers to the hatred, prejudice and fear of Muslims and Islam, resulting in a stereotyping of Muslim communities and individuals (Davids, 2006). The very use of the word "Muslim" in Britain, has become loaded with implicit assumptions which add to a further reinforcement and compliance with dominant unconscious Western ideologies. Not only are such assumptions harmful, but they also create the false illusion that the word "Muslim" refers to a homogenous group, implying that there are no differences amongst those who identify as such. These projections not only serve to dehumanise individuals but also demonise and objectify them. One may view such projections as the creation of a denigratory social object aimed at Muslim communities. Hammer (2006) suggests that the mobilisation of racist thoughts becomes easily available in a racialised society. Indeed, as Akhtar (2014) states, "the word minority is a loaded one" (p. 137), pointing out that such minorities are in fact in some cases larger in numerical quantity than other white groups which are not referred to as minorities.

How do these aspects come into the therapeutic space? The following case illustrates some of these themes which manifested in an intercultural supervision space, in the manner of a parallel process. A parallel process in supervision is whereby the transference of the supervisee and the counter-transference of the supervisor appear parallel to that taking place between the client and the therapist. That is to say, the dynamics present in the thera-peutic dyad between client and therapist, can become manifest in the supervisory space, re-enacted with other members in the group as well as the supervisor. The supervisor and supervisee can thus think about and explore this as a means to gain insights into the patient's inner world, specifically when the supervisee "takes on the client's tone and behaviour to convey to the supervisor emotions experienced whilst working with the client" (McNeill and Worthen, 1989, p. 329).

Case study

The case follows Nadia, a 48-year-old female therapist with dark brown hair and light brown skin and her patient, Zahra a 31-year-old female who identifies as British/Lebanese/ Asian Muslim. The patient was offered 12 sessions of intercultural psychodynamic therapy and was seen face-to-face. Given that there appear to be three phases to the work, the beginning, the middle and the end, the clinical work will be presented as such, although this does not explicitly mean that the process is a linear one.

The beginning

During the initial assessment, Zahra reports she feels conflicted about her own sense of identity. She says she feels guilty and confused about this, adding that although she has been to counselling before, there were a lot of things she was unable to talk about, especially issues regarding her racial identity and ethnicity. Nadia reflects to the client that given the current political climate and issues pertaining to racial inequalities, it was natural to feel guarded. Acknowledging the external circumstances (Lowe, 2014) seems to put the client at ease, who then goes on to tell the therapist that her parents are Lebanese and that her father treats her two brothers differently to the way he treats her, she elaborates by saying that he espoused strict religious views as to how Muslim women should behave. The effect in the room intensifies as she states that she feels ostracised by the Lebanese community, saying she feels Muslim because she had been born that way but often doubts what this means to her. She adds that she had managed to escape some of her parent's demands during her time at university when she had a number of sexual encounters with different men. Later on, she states that when she is with her white English work colleagues, they sometimes make comments alluding to ethnic minorities being uneducated or uncivilised. Nadia notices her own personal reaction to this, as she tries to defend from this thought, thinking "That's not me." Later she recognises it as an attempt to disassociate from the oppressor (Moss, 2001). An attempt to split or ward off her own racial defences and prejudices in the countertransference.

Nadia's intercultural supervision group is comprised of four supervisees, three of them female (one of them Nadia) and one male. The supervisor is male too. All members of the group are of diverse cultural backgrounds, Including the supervisor who is British Black of African heritage. The group represents a well of wealth in terms of diversity. This is significant for as will be observed, the fact that the supervision group is diverse in itself allows for new insights and reflections within an intercultural framework. From the patient's account of her story, Nadia thinks there are a number of complex issues relating to Zahra's conflicting sense of Identity. When Nadia first presents the patient, she refers to her as British/Lebanese. Shena, a member in the group, asks: "Is she Muslim?" Nadia wonders about the question which seems to a be rather closed one. What does this question mean? What unconscious dynamics have been triggered by this presentation? Nadia responds that the patient said she was Muslim because she had been born that way. It occurs to her, that the question is asked by the only member of the group wearing a hijab. Perhaps Nadia's rapid response has been informed by an unconscious assumption that Shena has strict views in regard to what being Muslim means; perhaps Shena fears Nadia will not understand. The supervisor alludes to the fact that one may identify as Muslim for different reasons and that these are not fixed or homogenous. Discussion ensues as to how the word "Muslim" can evoke a series of identifications and disidentifications, a way of life, religious beliefs, choice of clothes, a sense of belonging, different languages, and different nations. The discussions serve to think about how these may reflect some aspects of the patient's internal world and defence systems. The patient may wonder whether she can trust Nadia with matters pertaining to Islamic identity and other aspects of ethnicity and race. Nadia perhaps represents an oppressive Western object in the transference, a symbol of white fragility; an object which demonises and objectifies matters pertaining to the Islamic world. Meanwhile, Nadia wonders about her reaction to her colleague Shena. Had Nadia interpreted the wearing of a hijab as a symbol of strict religious beliefs and if so, what did that unconsciously symbolise? On the one hand, it is as if Nadia feels placed in the position of the Western oppressor whilst at the same time feeling protective of Zahra, fearing the patient will be denigrated if Nadia was to disclose Zahra's sexual behaviour. One may think of these struggles as a process which can inform the therapist of the patient's internal world, mirroring the environment the patient inhabits, that is to say, a Western one as well as an Islamic one. Thereby being pulled between forces of dominant conflicting ideologies, oppressing one another as if caught up in a struggle of defences, fighting against being taken over and engulfed by each other.

In therapy, Zahra talks about times when her mother singled her out over her two older brothers, her mother often blamed and criticised her for her brothers' mistakes. The affect intensifies as she expresses her hate for her, adding that she thinks her mother hates her too. In the transference, Zahra most possibly experiences Nadia as a harsh critical mother. Nadia goes on to reflect that perhaps she feels like she is being scrutinised. Zahra responds by saying that she feels as if Nadia is waiting to find her mistakes and catch her out. Exploration of this internal sense of persecution leads Zahra to insight into how much she criticises and hates her own self. It seems she may have internalised a scrutinising depreciative object one which repudiates her mother as well as herself.

Meanwhile, in her narrative, there are references to being bullied at school for being one of the few Middle Eastern/Asian girls there, the majority being white. Zahra alludes to the white-middle-class teachers who sometimes were nice but other times made her feel stupid and insignificant. Nadia hears this as another reference to how Zahra feels in the room. As the session draws to an end the patient makes a reference to Nadia's name and how to pronounce It. It seems that Zahra's question may indicate a wish to find out about Nadia's own heritage and ethnicity. In supervision exploration regarding the therapists' gender, age, race and accent suggest that these aspects in themselves can become significant in the therapeutic dyad. Meanwhile, Shena puts forward that the wearing of a hijab also symbolises identity. The supervision process points towards visible and hidden aspects of the self. This enables Nadia to think about Zahra's own appearance. Zahra wears Western clothes and Nadia wonders whether perhaps for Zahra being Muslim becomes part of a hidden identity. As the therapist holds these aspects in mind, the patient recounts an experience of being let into a prestigious restaurant despite the fact that she had not booked in advance, she elaborates by explaining that if they had known she was Muslim or Lebanese, she most probably would not have been allowed in. For a more in-depth understanding of how children of colour can be impacted by growing up in a dominant white society, Nadia's supervisor advises her to read a paper by Thomas (1998). He refers to the "proxy self"; a self that protects the black or brown object by projecting a white identity, within a sophisticated mechanism to differentiate between those white people who can be trusted and those who cannot. The "proxy self" not only serves as a means of protection but also as a means of transcending institutional and social barriers. However, it comes with a psychic cost: the shame of hiding. How do these concepts relate to Zahra? Zahra needs to explore aspects of her identity; indeed, she informs Nadia that in her previous treatment, she could not trust her therapist with issues of race. This served as a "cautionary tale" (Ogden, 1992). Before she can do this, a safe space which can contain the dialectic tensions of her racial/ethnic struggle needs to be created. Can Nadia be trusted to hold appropriate boundaries? Can Zahra integrate her British identity without the brown/Islamic object being denigrated? Explicitly referring to the current oppression of ethnic minorities whilst being contained within an organisation in which

Muslim women and other minorities are visible, seems to enable the brown internal object to feel held. Nadia's own gender, age and heritage; an older female with light brown skin, possibly serves Zahra by not having to position her therapist on either side of the white/brown racial split, leaving room for the patient's internal racial object relations to be explored. Nadia begins to understand that Zahra's Muslim identity is intrinsically intertwined with Zahra's racial self. Her narrative becomes full of references as to how much she hates her mother. Nadia's interventions are informed by formulating as to how in unconscious phantasy and in the transference, she is experienced as the attacking abusive mother. Other times, Nadia represents the white-middle class objects, synonymous with a white-dominant hierarchy which can make Zahra feel stupid and insignificant. These objects highlight Zahra's internal world; she counteridentifies with her mother whilst unconsciously repudiating herself for being like her. Meanwhile, the white internal figures are oppressive ones who underestimate and overlook her.

The middle

In supervision, Nadia is becoming increasingly aware of feeling pushed out and being dismissed, specifically by Adan, the only white male supervisee in the group. She feels silenced and uncomfortable at voicing her concerns, "it is as if the therapist were unconsciously trying in this fashion to tell the supervisor what the therapeutic problem is" (McNeill and Walthen, 1980:144). Initially during a process of negative capability (Bion, 1970), it becomes very confusing for Nadia to disentangle how much of what is going on in the supervision group relates to herself and how much relates to Zahra's material. During her presentation, Adan expresses that Nadia does not make sense and she should explain herself in more adequate ways. This leads Nadia not only to feel persecuted by her colleague but also angered by his belittling attitude. She experiences the others in the group as bystanders who observe but do nothing. It becomes increasingly clear to Nadia that there is a feeling of exclusion, one which leads to a sense of humiliation, shame and power-lessness, resulting in a fear of speaking up and a sense of being silenced. Eventually, Nadia feels so provoked that she explodes in a fit of anger expressing concerns about her colleague's white male privilege. The event leads to an unpacking of supervision dynamics, exploring how each member within the group positions themselves in relation to each other. Promoting a deeper understanding as to how such positioning creates a lens which can enable or inhibit the therapeutic process. Nadia's personal frame of reference comes from growing up between two different cultures which conflict and collide with each other, with the non-British object being denigrated over the British one, coupled with a lived-life experience of being silenced by those who occupy a place of normative privilege in British society. Whilst one may agree that such enactment is a reflection of Nadia's own personal history and there exists the inherent risk that she may overidentify with Zahra, it also serves to highlight some of the intrapsychic processes which seem present in the patient's internal world and may be manifest in the therapeutic space. Leary (2000) suggests that "there is an emerging recognition that the particularities of the analyst's personality and his or her person- including his or her race, ethnicity and gender, are always instrumental in evoking the clinical themes and dialogues that develop in the course of the work" (p. 648). In Nadia's case, her lived-life experience not only serves her to understand some of the complex unconscious processes which may be taking place in the transference, including a deeper awareness of hierarchical inequalities but also in evoking certain aspects of the therapeutic work. The fact that the intercultural framework is held by a black male supervisor is symbolic, given that the psychoanalytic field is dominated by white analysts.

Nadia decides to explicitly acknowledge and interpret that there may be power imbalances present for Zahra in the counselling space, offering that perhaps at times she feels she has to hide or feels the need to be something she is not. Zahra's early social experiences had been deeply painful, Nadia sensed that the patient felt so ashamed that she feared being humiliated if these were disclosed. Zahra recounted an occasion in which she had worn a colourful skirt to school, it was a special gift from her mother, and she had felt very proud and pleased with it. However, the reaction she received was unexpected; the white girls made fun of her clothes, she was teased and given a pejorative nickname. Zahra looked down as if to hide her shame and embarrassment. Nadia presented this session in the Intercultural supervision group. Huner, one of the supervisees who had herself lived in a refugee camp as a child, persecuted for being an ethnic minority in her country of origin, brings forth valuable insights regarding issues of silent oppression. Discussions revolve around how the external gaze can become internalised, highlighting the forces of introjective processes. Abbasi (1998) points out that prejudices oftentimes are not so much felt by what is being said but by disapproving looks, in time such external intrusions are etched into the very core of the self.

In the session that followed, Zahra expressed how she felt towards her own family who she described as awkward and inadequate, expressing her sense of rejection towards her parents' traditions. The session moved on to unpack and explore the sense of shame and guilt she experienced for not wanting to be like her mother, implicit within this lay the fact that she was Asian/Lebanese/Muslim. This was accompanied by a sense of betrayal to her family. She felt singled out at home for being the only girl and being treated differently in a position of inferiority. Meanwhile, she recognised a hidden desire to be white, not only because in her internal experience that meant she would not be bullied but also because she experienced white British women as having more internal freedom and privilege. As she tells her story her emotions range from anger to sadness, shame, guilt, fear and confusion.

Joseph (1985) posits that: "the way our patients communicate their problems to us is frequently beyond their words" (p. 453). In Zahra's case, much of the unspeakable is communicated through the intensity of the affect. Given that patients may believe that their own negative affective emotions are bad or dangerous, the ability to tolerate them informs the patient that her emotions can be understood thus Zahra is enabled to engage in a meaningful process (Markowitz et al., 2011).

With the help of supervision, it becomes more evident that Zahra presents with aspects of internal racism: "a paranoid us-them construction involving self and racial other" (Davids, 2011, p.XI). In his paper: "Colonial Object relations," Lowe (2008) describes the process of inter-nalised, black-and-white object relations whereby the white object becomes controlling and dominant over the black (or brown). Zahra's inner world is torn as the external white object has been internalised and controlling of the brown object, whilst the brown object turns against itself. Zahra uses her therapist as a missing object, one which can withstand the dialectic tensions of her racial struggles, not only as a means to explore them but also as a new model which can be taken in, enabling a shift towards a depressive position. Nadia draws on insights gained from the material of other patients presented by her colleagues in the intercultural supervision space. Given that a large number of patients' issues are intersectional, she becomes more aware of how such issues lead individuals to feel under-serving of not only love but also of other basic necessities such as good accommodation and permanent work. The supervision process includes the exploration of which options become accessible to Zahra along with which ones become internally excluded and ruled out. For instance, Zahra states she would like to start her own business by selling beauty products she makes herself, however, she immediately rules out this option by saying it is a stupid idea that would never succeed. A reflection of an internal sabotage mechanism which she has internalised by excluding herself from the possibility of success alongside the denigration of not only her skills and intelligence at making the products but also her own sense of what beauty means.

Female oppression

One of the conflicts in Zahra's internal world was how to think of herself as a modern British Asian woman without pathologising aspects of her Islamic/ Lebanese identity. Nadia wondered why she had not been able to discuss the patient's sexual behaviour within the supervision group. Had the patient internalised certain denigratory attitudes pertaining not only to her colour and ethnicity but also to her female gender and sexuality? Did Nadia feel a need to protect Zahra's "Muslim dignity" and if so, what did that mean? Zahra recounted various experiences when her father had told her she should not behave as white women do. The patient felt that white women were freer to express their sexuality and that she felt she had to hide hers.

The presentation of this material in supervision led to dialogues about how women are placed in relation to men. Specifically, the theme of gender construction and gender performance, whereby gender roles become culturally constructed and enmeshed within normative unconscious processes, determining how males and females should think, dress and interact. It also included exploration as to how Zahra perceived Nadia in the transference. Did she symbolise the white woman who was free to explore her sexuality or was she the judging brown object inherent in her father's narrative? Furthermore, did the therapist symbolise one of those white women her father so strongly disapproved of and did Zahra herself disprove too? The interplay between these intercultural white/brown objects seems to have become deeply entangled in Zahra's internal world. During the supervisory dialogue, Shena reflects that for the most part Muslim female gender roles are very much linked to being married and having children. Huner adds that pre-marital sex or expression of female sexual desire in Islamic cultures is deeply sinful (i.e. Haram). Meanwhile, Adan adds that it is common in the West to portray Muslim women as oppressed by a dominantly patriarchal society and that while this may be true to some extent, there is a tendency in Western ideology to rid itself of misogynist belief systems by projecting them into Islamic cultures, denying its own patriarchal oppressive qualities which lie enmeshed within the structural system. Layton (2004) posits that for the most part, female sexuality is psychosocially constructed within a dialectic binary, whereby the woman is either positioned as a virgin or a whore. Nadia had become increasingly aware of the sense of shame that had been projected onto her during the therapeutic process both in the counselling and supervisory space. The supervisor thus reflects on the weight of the shame latent within Zahra's sexuality which has become so silencing that it is difficult to verbalise. Nadia feels contained and understood in this process and further reflections are made as to the fact that in a large number of Asian/Lebanese/Islamic cultures such as in Lebanon, the sense of shame pertaining to a woman's honour is carried collectively by her whole family not just the individual, these insights help therapeutic process to progress.

Holding these insights in mind, the patient discloses she had had a long relationship with a Muslim man. They liked each other because of their shared values and progressive attitudes. However, after a while, he had become increasingly aggressive and controlling of her. The patient adds that he became sexually abusive, and she felt it was her fault because she had allowed it to continue. Zahra said her sense of culpability was compounded by the fact that she had had a number of sexual relationships before she met him. The therapist stays with the feelings evoked in her which she finds very disturbing. At times, it is difficult to hear some of these things without prejudice towards the male Muslim perpetrator. Exploration of the countertransference in supervision enables Nadia to become aware she is projecting the anger and denigration into Muslim men, along with the brown/ Islamic object they represent. Possibly this prejudice is symbolic of prejudice Zahra experiences from the white Western object against which she feels she has to protect and defend. The process serves to highlight Nadia's own internalised unconscious bias as a result of growing up in the West. It is not until Nadia can acknowledge her own sense of prejudice towards the male Muslim object present in the room, that she can begin to realise that she is also drawn into a complicity with Zahra, who also seems to hold such internal prejudice towards Muslim men, specifically her father whom she has described as espousing strict religious views as to how women should behave. This complex dynamic seems to exemplify how clients: "unconsciously act out with us in the transference, trying to get us to act out with them" (Joseph, 1985, p. 447). It emerges that Zahra is unconsciously trying to defend against her own prejudice of Muslim men, whilst this acts as a denigratory dynamic towards her own self and Islamic/Lebanese/Asian identity.

The end

The ending of therapy is a mourning process (Knafo, 2018), especially in short-term therapy where issues of separation and loss are present from the start (Gabbard, 2009). In Zahra's case, these are intrinsically linked to a sense of loss in identity and to the trauma of the sexual abuse she had suffered. In exploring the ending of therapy such issues were coming to the fore. Nadia had been exploring what emotions were held behind Zahra's tears. Zahra responds by elaborating that after the abuse she felt that not only had she lost her self-worth and identity but also her father who did not believe her. Nadia reflects that perhaps she feels abandoned by her too, there is a deep sense of sadness in the room. Nadia presents some of the aspects of sadness to the supervision group, unpacking the emotions which at times feel uncontainable and overwhelming. The supervision space acts as a holding container in which Nadia can recount her own experience of the session whilst guidance is offered as to how to proceed with the ending. Meanwhile, Nadia's process alerts her that sometimes an ending can unconsciously feel like a death. Nadia links this to Zahra's loss of Muslim identity; a death which has not yet been mourned. Zahra witnesses the impact her sadness and loss have on Nadia enabling a mirroring process, whereby Nadia can hold the disturbance in mind enabling the patient to do this too (Carpy, 1989).

By the penultimate session, Zahra said she did not want to talk about the end. Knafo (2018) posits that when a patient says this, it implies the patient does not want to end. In the last session, Zahra talks more explicitly about the end of the relationship with her abusive boyfriend. She talks about her concerns about new laws regarding migrants, elaborating that she fears what will happen to people like her from ethnic minority backgrounds. She then adds that she feels hopeful that at least the Black Lives Matter movement has now grown in numbers and people are becoming more aware of systemic racism. Nadia reflects back to Zahra by saying that perhaps there is still a sense of loss and exclusion, with aspects of inequality which are still present for her but that perhaps on some level there is some sense of hope that she will connect with her own identity and find a place where she fits in and belongs. Zahra replies that at least now when she feels bad her thoughts feel more manageable and she is better able to understand her internal conflicts.

The session draws to an end.

Conclusion

To date some traditional psychoanalytic approaches, push the social reality of ethnic minorities to the margins. An awareness of unconscious normative processes, the dynamics of inequality and their impact on the intrapsychic/interpsychic world is essential, specifically when working with members of BAME communities. The author suggests that there are grave dangers when these aspects are not addressed as issues of exclusion and marginalisation may become reinforced rather than deconstructed. Intercultural supervision provides a framework where the introjection of such dynamics and their effect on the individual can be therapeutically explored.

Zahra's case presents a number of conflating issues regarding her hybrid identity, highlighting some of the complexities enmeshed within an inter/intracultural matrix. In the initial assessment, the patient informs Nadia that she did not feel comfortable discussing issues of her racial identity with her previous therapist. This served as a "cautionary tale" (Ogden, 1992) alerting Nadia of the need to explore racial aspects of the patient in the supervision space. In so doing other aspects of Zahra's hidden/repressed identity begin to emerge, within this lies the unconscious denigration of herself as a Muslim/Lebanese/Asian female, living within a context where being white occupies a space of privilege. Given that the supervision space itself is diverse, the therapist can begin to understand some of the dynamics at play within Zahra's internal world which manifests in a parallel process whereby dynamics of exclusion, repression, privilege, identification and disidentification become reenactment and henceforth explored. Zahra's unconscious dilemma regarding her identity then moves onto her own sexuality which has been internalised within a matrix of object relations where female desire is both denigrated and envied. Meanwhile, the intercultural supervision framework provides a space where the therapist can process the projections of female sexual denigration and the shame implicit within these. It is not until the conflicting racial/

intracultural/intercultural dynamics in Zahra's world can be held and understood, that she can feel safe enough to disclose aspects of the sexual abuse she had suffered. The final phase of therapy involves addressing issues of loss, linked to issues of the trauma of sexual abuse. Processing the loss symbolises a reparative attempt at disentangling internalised aspects of female sexual denigration together with the mourning of aspects of her Islamic identity. Joseph (1985) points out that: "how the patient uses the analyst informs not only on the transference but also on what the patient needs" (p.447). The therapist's own cultural heritage serves the patient to unpack aspects of the racial split. In the transference, the therapist represents the denigrated/denigratory mother and the brown object implicit within this. At other times the therapist symbolises the white oppressive object which is both envied and admired. The therapist's own cultural history and positioning evokes and brings forth in-depth understanding of the themes which arise in the therapeutic work. The gains of working with members in supervision, whose lived histories arise from diverse contexts and experiences, serve to bring new insights and depth to the intercultural process bringing a sense of holding for the therapist. Meanwhile, the patient uses her therapist as a missing object, one which can withstand the dialectic tensions of her racial/intracultural/ intercultural world, not only as a means to explore these but also as a new model which can be taken in. In the last session, Zahra states that she is now better able to understand and manage her internal conflicts; a new space has arisen, parallel to the intercultural supervisory framework which has formed the backbone and creation of an intersubjective/intrasubjective relational space.

The case evidences the importance of providing a space where supervisees are freely allowed to explore issues related to culture, race, religion, gender and sexuality within an intercultural framework, specifically as it is often the case that these matters feel contentious and controversial. Such Intercultural aspects are inevitably linked to the sociopolitical realm and henceforth the supervisees' psychic positioning within it. In traditional supervisory spaces, these issues are often left unaddressed, leaving the supervisee feeling silenced with a sense of heaviness and shame which will then impact on the therapeutic work. Intercultural supervision ensures that the therapist can provide culturally effective and responsive therapeutic treatment within a framework in which cultural aspects of identity can become integrated into the patient's psychological make-up rather than fragmented, split-off or denied.

References

Abbasi, A. (1998). Speaking the unspeakable. In: Helmreich, A., Marcus, P. (eds.) *Blacks and Jews on the Couch: Psychoanalytic Reflections on Black-Jewish Conflict.* Greenwood: Prager, pp. 133–147.

Akhtar, S. (2014). The mental pain of minorities. *British Journal of Psychotherapy*, *30*(2), 136–153.

Bion, W. R. (1961). *Experiences in Groups and Other Papers*. London: Tavistock.

Bion, W. R. (1970). *Attention and Interpretation*. London: Tavistock Publications.

Carpy. D. V. (1989). Tolerating the countertransference: A mutative process. *International Journal of Psychoanalysis*, *70*, 287–294.

Dalal, F. (2001). Insides and outsides: A review of psychoanalytic renderings of difference, racism and prejudice. *Psychoanalytic studies*, *3*(1), 43–66.

Davids, F. (2006). Internal racism, anxiety and the world outside: Islamophobia Post-9/11. *Organisational and Social Dynamics*, *6*(1), 63–85.

Davids, F. (2011). *Internal Racism: A Psychoanalytic Approach to Race and Difference*. London: Palgrave.

DiAngelo. R. (2018). *White Fragility. Why It's So Hard for White People to Talk About Racism*. Boston: Beacon Press

Gabbard, G. O. (2009). What is A "Good Enough" termination? *Journal of the American Psychoanalytic Association*, *57*(3), 575–594

Hammer, F. M. (2006). Racism as a transference State. *Psychoanalytic Quarterly*, *75*, 197–221.

Joseph, B. (1985). Transference: The total situation. *The International Journal of Psychoanalysis*, *66*(4), 447–454.

Kareem, J., Littlewood, R. (1992). *Intercultural Therapy: Themes, Interpretations and Practice*. Oxford: Blackwell Scientific Publications.

Keval, N. (2016). *Racist States of Mind: Understanding the Perversion of Curiosity and Concerns*. London: Karnac.

Klein, M. (1946). *Notes on some schizoid mechanisms. In Envy and Gratitude and Other Works*. London: The Hogarth Press, 1998.

Knafo, D. (2018). Beginnings and endings: Time and termination in psychoanalysis. *Psychoanalytic Psychology*, *35*(1), 8–14

Layton, L. (2004). *Who's That Girl? Who's That Boy?* New York: Routledge.

Layton, L. (2006). Racial identities, racial enactments and normative unconscious processes. *Psychoanalytic Quarterly*, *75* (1), 237–269

Leary, K. (2000). Racial enactments in dynamic treatment. *Psychoanalytic Dialogues*, *10*(4), 639–653.

Lowe, F. (2008). Colonial object relations. Going underground black and white relationships. *British Journal of Psychotherapy*, *24*(1), 20–33

Lowe, F. (2014). *Thinking Space: Promoting Thinking About Race, Culture, and Diversity in Psychotherapy and Beyond*. London: Karnac.

Markowitz, J. C., Milrod, B. L. (2011). The importance of responding to negative affect in psychotherapies. *American Journal of Psychiatry*, *168*(2), 124–128.

McNeill, B. W., Worthen, V. (1989). The Parallel Process In Psychotherapy Supervision. *Professional Psychology*, *20*, 329–333. Mueller,

Moss, D. (2001). On hating in the first person plural: Thinking psychoanalytically about racism, homophobia, and misogyny. *Journal of the American Psychoanalytic Association*, *49*(4), 1315–1334.

Ogden, T. H. (1992). Comments on transference and countertransference in the initial analytic meeting. *Psychoanalytic Inquiry*, *12*(2), 225–247.

Rustin, M. (1991). *The Good Society and the Inner world: Psychoanalysis, Politics and Culture.* London: Karnac.

Spurling, L. (2004). *An Introduction to Psychodynamic Counselling.* London: Palgrave Macmillan.

Thomas, L. (1998). Psychotherapy in the context of race and culture: An Intercultural Therapeutic Approach. In: Fernando, S. (ed.) *Mental Health in a Multi-Ethnic Society: A Multi-Disciplinary Handbook.* London: Routledge.

Part 5

Ananse(sɛm)

Chapter 14

Ananse(sɛm)
Supervisory Insights from His Shattered Pot of Wisdom

Baffour Ababio

Introduction

Let me begin with a variant of the Ananse folk tale as told by the Akan people of Ghana. In the tale "Ananse and the Pot of Wisdom," we find Ananse the spider traversing the globe with a pot. He supposedly harvests every bit of wisdom, putting them all into the pot. Ananse returns home and proceeds to climb a tree, with the aim of placing the pot in the top branches – accessible only to Ananse. The climb to store the pot is problematic as the pot is hanging on Ananse's chest, impeding his movement. At the foot of the tree, Ananse's child is observing the struggles of the ostensibly wise, experienced parent and offers a suggestion. The child says Ananse's climb would be easier if the pot were slung on his back. On hearing this, Ananse pauses and listens to the promptings of his child, the pot and his unconscious. Ananse realises the folly of the enterprise and flings the pot to the ground, where it shatters. This chapter references and situates its supervisory explorations and discussions within the dynamics of the wisdom pot story.

The first word in the title of this chapter introduces Anansesɛm. This is a reference to folktales or traditional stories, in this case, Akan stories, about Ananse. Anansesɛm is a portmanteau word, the result of two Akan words: *Ananse* means "spider" and *asɛm* can variously mean "matter," "situation," or "trouble." When combined, the resulting expression denotes collections of narratives containing a moral. They are gems of ancient "wisdoms" distilled in a manner to make them accessible to all members of society, no matter their age. Ananse, the central character in these narratives, who is an anti-hero, has the ability to shape-shift but only under duress and no other characters have this power.

The encounter between therapist and client is a complex one, refracting through the personalities of the therapeutic dyad, and within the dynamics of culture, race, coloniality and intersecting identities. There are known and unknown points within the shared socio-cultural space of these relationships. The therapist and client inch towards and away from each other in curiosity,

DOI: 10.4324/9781003380214-20

unfolding awareness, powered by fields of emotions and thoughts. The supervisor enters this matrix with their own wisdom pot of cultural, racial and personal qualities whilst attempting to provide a framework for the supervisee and themselves to process understanding and learning, and to facilitate openness.

The demand on the supervisor can be tremendous, especially the impulse towards omniscience and omnipotence (Tummala-Narra, 2004). This chapter will explore and raise some questions around the economics of power and knowledge and of difference and sameness within the relational supervisory intercultural space. This exploration will highlight the ubiquity of inter-culturality in many interactions and cultures: "the difference [relationally] being a matter of degree" (Thomas, 2004:26). In contending with these processes and the associated power dynamics within the supervision and therapeutic setting, the client's (supervisee's) needs could be overlooked and neglected. An imaginable way through this contention Davids postulates might be the supervisor's adoption of a listening position to the promptings of the unconscious (Davids, 2022). How is attunement to the unconscious coaxed so that the tuning of the inner ear can catch and recognise its com-munications? Bearing in mind this attunement to the unconscious is contig-uous with the supervisor's knowledge, their years of training, experience and authority in interaction with the supervisee who is located as the "junior" partner. A pathway to elaborating receptivity to the dynamic offerings of the unconscious can also be found in Ananse's experiences in the tale of the wisdom pot.

Within the Akan oral tradition, the stories of Ananse are a source of en-tertainment and a conduit for intergenerational transmission of values: a forum for interaction and play. The stories are offered with a caveat that they can be received in full or in part and with the hope that the dynamics of receptivity involve the stories interacting with the subjectivity of each lis-tener. There is an implicit invitation in this caveat for the listener to share with the storyteller, after some reflection, the outcome of the story's cross-fertilisations. The reflections and vignettes in this chapter of stories are offered in the same spirit as the cross-fertilisation caveats tendered in the Anansesɛm oeuvre.

The shattering

There is a space between Ananse hearing his child's voice and letting go of the pot. There is a moment between hearing the message in the child's voice and Ananse's shift in perception of the child as a junior partner to one who could be framed as a junior-senior-equal-collaborating partner in the enterprise. Ananse, the senior partner in the fast-moving shapeshifting scenes of the narrative, feels exposed and inadequate and consequently connects with an experience of also being junior. This is the type of moment that

Beshara (2022) has termed "learnt ignorance." He describes it as a "critical epistemological attitude of knowing that we do not know" (ibid). Ananse letting the pot drop can be read as a moment of insight. There is a realisation that by the very fact of being in the pot, the wisdom was static and calcified and because it was so closely guarded by the characterisation of insecurity and individualism by Ananse, it was sterile. Ananse at once portrays the acquisitive hubris of coloniality operating in plain sight – yet assuming and projecting an invisibility. The smashed pot and the reinstallation of the wisdoms in their multiple sites speaks to restitution and agency. Supervisory spaces subjugated by grabbing coloniality acts to dull understanding and curiosity and to further amplify obstructive dynamics, buttressing "a kind of thinking that we know" (ibid).

I recall attending a seminar during which the presenter produced a thought-provoking psychoanalytic paper. I was unfamiliar with a few of the concepts he shared, which I recognised was because of his perspective as an academic. I wondered about the eminent clinician who had been asked to give a response to the paper. My deliberation about the respondent was in part linked to an identification with him and with the role of Ananse. He may have felt the weight of the pot being in the wrong place as he occupied a cross-fertilised position of subjectivity: listening to the paper, interacting with it and eventually responding to it from this position. When the clinician spoke, he acknowledged his unique location, experience and knowledge and linked it to resonances from the paper but also clarified areas of *not knowing*. I thought by his acknowledgement of "not knowing" he had allowed the pot to drop. There was a collective exhalation – or did I assume this? In any case, the respondent transformed what could have landed as a weighty tome of a paper into prompts, dispersed through the assembled individuals like pollen, to be thought about, pondered and in turn, diffused. This interchange between the presenter and the respondent within the group is evocative of some of the dynamics of the wisdom pot within the supervisory encounter.

The references to supervision stem from my work with training and qualified therapists, in individual as well as in group processes and from my own ongoing experience as a supervisee. I will make these differentiations for clarity in the supervision stories I will recount here. I make reference to "the pot" throughout the chapter: this pot ought to be spoken to, touched, queried and explored. I also invite readers to consider their own pot and its contents. What then does this pot in the supervision symbolise? What does it contain? To what extent have the contents been internalised in, largely, unanalysed ways by the individual (Lowe, 2021)[1]? What might the origins of the contents in the pot be? Might these refer to Eurocentric psychoanalytic concepts of human development; the negotiations of conflicts between drives and societal mores or derivatives of this wherein relationships foreground and define our sense of being human, as in object relations (Gomez, 1997, p. 1)? The pot's contents may include pre-colonial, cultural, political, pre-enslavement, historical, traumatic, geographical, and racial elements and thus present us with considerations about how these realities shape our inner lives (Tummala-Narra, 2004). The supervisor and supervisees in their consultations facilitate spaces where clients can be discussed and heard; this contemplation extends to the hinterlands of supervisor and supervisees. It advances and processes the confluence of conscious and unconscious dynamics. This is, in turn, elaborated through the intersections of the culture and race of all dynamic participants in the supervisory encounter (Kareem and Littlewood, 2006, p. 14).

A number of authors and clinicians, including Mckenzie-Mavinga (2019), Ellis (2019), and Turner (2021) have recognised the pivotal position of the therapist and for the purposes of this chapter, the supervisor in elucidating the intersectional currents at play in the intercultural supervision encounter. The relevance of intercultural supervision can be found in the (unveiled and untold) stories of individuals from racially minoritised communities in the United Kingdom. These narratives unfold in the supervision as explicated by the therapist from their own subjective location. The question is, through which therapist and supervisor lens are these stories heard, retold, (mis) understood or co-constructed? How are the contemporary and historical experiences of positions as the oppressed, oppressor, discriminated, marginalised or privileged, embodied in their varying fluid rearrangements by the protagonists engaged in the supervision?

Global events between the years 2020 and 2022, such as the COVID-19 pandemic and its disproportionate impact on minoritised communities, have been a matter of huge concern, not least in Britain. The murder of George Floyd, sharpened public focus on the much greater weight of injustices on racially minoritised individuals and communities, constraining their inner lives. The forces of injustice, impose dynamics of identification amongst racially minoritised individuals and communities, fostering solidarity, alliances and a pooling of resources to contend with structural inequalities in their lived experiences. These shared experiences may also act to hasten the processes and dynamics involved in getting to know another person from the same or similar community. The desire for understanding, identification and the gravitational pull of empathy between the client and supervisee with shared socio-cultural experiences, could motivate the supervisor to truncate the time taken to get to know the client (and supervisee). This urge, which can lead to misunderstandings, could be decelerated and mitigated by an awareness of the energies present in the pot.

By way of illustration, consider the following case example. I was supervising a group of training therapists when Trainee Subira (a second-generation black British woman of East African parents) presented a case of a black British woman of West African heritage who was using her therapy sessions to process tensions in her relationship with her West African parents. As I listened, I became aware of a rising excitement within me, ignited when

I heard the term "West African." My imagination took flight, propelling me headlong ahead of the supervisee to the conclusion of her presentation; I felt confident of knowing this West African heritage story – *my* story, of deference to elders and parents in this instance – and consequently found myself isolated at the end of the presentation and not in step with Subira and the group. Like Ananse's child, Subira then drew her conclusions and her description of the client was not at all the West African character I had invented. My invention, nevertheless, proved useful as I was forced to ponder my impatience and excitement. In that space and in that shapeshifting moment, it came to me that I had identified with a feature of the client's oppressive West African parents in the transference and countertransference. In my compulsive desire to display the training, experience, and knowledge in my elemental pot, I had temporarily parted ways with the group.

External realities

The reverberations of the Russian invasion of Ukraine war of 2022, have, as *other* wars and incursions, produced varied impacts for different communities and individual clients. Amidst the atrocities and fallout from the war in Ukraine, there have been witness accounts of acts of racial discrimination against racially minoritised individuals. Take Mahmoud, a man of Kuwaiti origin in his early 60s who had been stateless for years, unrecognised in the Latin American country he grew up in. After decades of living in that country, he left with his teenage daughter. They spent about 13 years travelling nomadically en route to mainland Europe and then on to England. Father and daughter's relationship was shaped by their peripatetic life, not by choice but through the imposition of circumstances and structures of discrimination. Tragically, father and daughter got separated before Mahmoud arrived in England; he lost her. He is now in therapy with Yonas, a male, black trainee counsellor who is originally from a country in the Horn of Africa. In a supervision session, the counsellor spoke about Mahmoud in a disjointed and distracting manner – disengaged from the narrative. He referred to Mahmoud's guilt, anguish, his tormented imaginings about the plight of the daughter he lost and then his angry but suppressed outbursts about the war in Ukraine. Despite the horror of the war, "people still have time to discriminate against 'us'," he said. In the supervision group was another trainee supervisee, Ruth, who was a Black, British woman of Central African heritage. As a supervisor, I registered the processes within the group with interest but not with any urgency or desire (Bion, 1967:15) – I declined the invitation and urge to clutch the pot. I allowed it to drop and together with the group, whilst listening to the voice of Ananse's child, sifted through its contents. We heard how Mahmoud just wanted his 'leave to remain' in the United Kingdom to be granted. It seemed to Yonas that Mahmoud was in thrall to his desire to possess the "leave to remain." Yonas spoke about liking

Mahmoud's accent and I silently wondered about this and about the dynamics in the therapy room between Mahmoud and his counsellor, Yonas. Did the counsellor's accent in turn resonate with Mahmoud? And mine with Yonas? Ruth spoke and wondered about the accent – had it struck a rare, homely memory chord in the therapy (and with her in the supervision)? In this state of group reverie, the accent seemed to me like the sound from a favourite, familial ancestral musical instrument recognisable by both Yonas and Mahmoud (and Ruth), unnamed, yet part of the elements which drew them together in their therapeutic (and now us in the supervision) hours. As these thoughts dispersed through the supervision group, Yonas remembered his own journey of migration and his then longing for that thing symbolic of belonging and acceptance, the "leave to remain" permit. How would Yonas and Mahmoud now sit to process Mahmoud's traumas and to contemplate the reverberations of Russia and Ukraine and its dire unsettling implications (of racial discrimination) in their quest for leave to remain, for that internal sense of home? These threads, feelings and thoughts might seem disparate, unconnected. However, to the supervisor and supervisees (and by an indirect extension, Mahmoud) these were indications of a deeply felt group "healing" experience and their connection with "recognition trauma," a term used to describe "powerful feelings associated with awareness of the impact of racism" (McKenzie-Mavinga, 2019, p. 171); it was a communal site of commemoration, of humanising multiple stories, of care, and of emergent resistance and strength. Concerning this, Yarimar Bonilla in her postcolonial chronicles, presents the "memory walks," "take your memory for a walk" or "to make your memory walk" events in Guadeloupe as potentially malleable, cultural, historical, geographical sites and trails to be inscribed upon and historically re-envisioned by Guadeloupeans. For Bonilla, these walks "re-route history," an observation encapsulated by one of her interlocutors, "Didier" who says, "he carefully navigated through each of these [historical] events [and walks] describing them [not as failures but] as part of a larger struggle for autonomy and independence" (Bonilla, 2015, p. 14). My supervisory renegotiated association with the pot, through the voice of Ananse's child and to being junior with the supervisees, re-envisioned and transmuted the consciousness of "recognition trauma" (McKenzie-Mavinga, 2019) into a site of origination, imagination and perception in the supervision.

Ramifications of racial discriminatory acts against the backdrop of war continue to emerge in therapeutic and supervisory spaces in various guises. Sefula, a black, female, qualified psychotherapist of South African heritage brought to supervision the change she had observed since the invasion of Ukraine in her client, Anastacia, a white middle-aged woman who was originally from Moldova. Anastacia spoke about the war and recounted how depressed she had become; her sleep was now markedly disturbed. She recalled the deprivations of her early life, raised by extremely strict parents whose relationship was characterised by domestic violence. As Sefula processed the material in her individual supervision with me, she touched on thoughts and experiences she had been holding in during the therapy with Anastacia. Sefula was withholding her anger and despair over the reports of racially discriminatory acts during the war. Akinwotu and Tondo (2022), writing in *The Guardian,* note how "non-white refugees face violence and racist abuse in Przemysl, as police warn of fake reports of migrants committing crimes." She wondered whether there was space to think about and discuss in supervision how this might be linked to the work with Anastacia. In effect, did she have permission? My response was a yes. I pondered whether she felt I might close down an exploration with a reference to personal therapy.

This permission to speak was also linked to designated restricted senior white management positions and roles in her organisation. At work, she felt, she said, like a "squatter" in systemically constructed domains of exclusion. She could not engage in comments and public discussions involving the invasion of Ukraine (characterised by the Russian government as a "special operation"). She would hold her tongue or smile when she wanted to make a point and felt unable to have multiple conversations. She again wondered whether she could talk about the racism against racially minoritised individuals seeking sanctuary from the war. Could she think about this with me? My response was again a yes. Her story ignited recollections of my personal encounters, when I had smiled to mask the anger, and sense of injustice which boiled within me. I felt revulsed by the memories – the accommodation of indignity and humiliation. It was a compelling moment, both dissociative and helpful as I emerged from that state, observed the fractured pot and reconnected with Sefula's constrictive work experiences.

Subsequently, Sefula accessed an understanding of aspects of Anastacia's dissociative experiences. These experiences were activated when material linked to childhood abuse in Moldova emerged in the therapy. Frawley-O'Dea (2003) describes this as relational and observes: "the relational supervisor is open to considering primary process material delivered into the supervision by way of dreams, somatic states, fantasies, and dissociative experience of the supervised patient, the supervisee, and even the supervisor" (ibid. 360). In the supervision, Sefula engaged with the "pot" she was clutching and shared its contents with me, facilitating a movement in me to loosen my grip, take the lid off my pot and go through its contents in conjunction with Sefula's and Anastacia's. The explorations were varied: they included the impact of racial micro-aggressive attacks on Sefula in organisational settings; Anastacia's experience of childhood abuse and of being white and somewhat marginalised (and raising questions about her internal home) in the United Kingdom along with language, ethnic, nationalistic and class lines; and finally, my unexpressed memories as a professional Black man, negotiating my space, and agency within white power structures. This activated memory was connected to the enduring after*life* of slavery[2] [and coloniality] (Saucier and Woods, 2015, pp. 12–13): it had momentarily taken me away from the supervision space and out of that dissociated place, emerged a consciousness, leading to a sharing with Sefula, the "idea [and prospect of] Black afterlives"[3] (Benjamin, 2018) and consequently, in the explorations, charted a connectivity back to Sefula and Anastacia's, inter-cultural therapeutic relationship in the supervision.

In the earlier sections, I have used stories from my supervisions to describe a way of being with myself, the supervisee and their client in the supervision. I have suggested that a component of the pot's contents is years of training and experience of work in different settings, which instils in the supervisor, a sense of power and authority. In the relatively fluid mutuality of the supervision work, there are moments when the supervisee takes the stage, leads the way and instructs the supervisor. These are junctures to be aware of, cognisant that the unexamined pot can hinder one's perception and openness. It can trap one into the constrictive sterility of one's training and clinical experience if it does not interact with other minds and experiences. These interactive situations are present within the supervision dyad but perhaps amplified in the group supervision context due to the presence of multiple lenses. It is for me, somewhat rooted in the country where I was raised, Ghana, where I observed power, authority and respect being invested in individuals based on age, education and status, to a slighter greater degree than is common in most cultures and societies. With this comes an expectation of a degree of deference from "the junior partner," a dynamic I am mindful of having in my pot. As a colleague remarked, a moment of learning from a supervisee (akin to Ananse's situation with his child) could result in a supervisor distancing themselves or even inflicting a vengeful attack on the supervisee. Ananse could have dropped the pot on top of the child's head, subverting a collaborative learning opportunity.

Language and race

When issues pertaining to racialisation are under review and discussion, how does the supervisor – in this case me, a Black supervisor – conduct the ex-plorations, where the group is comprised of three racially minoritised su-pervisees with Hannah, a racialised white English supervisee, being in the minority? Does it activate an unprocessed wish to expose Hannah to the discomfort generated during explorations of racism in client material? How does that sit with the impulse to protect Hannah, a minority in the supervi-sion group? Yet would doing so thwart Hannah, (her client) and the group's opportunity to gain an experience of processing the anxiety evoked by dis-cussions around anti-blackness and the dynamics of whiteness? Answering these questions (and understanding the nuanced variations of protection, challenging interventions, caretaking and ensuring safety) requires an en-gagement and attunement with *my* pot and its contents, which links back to being a supervisor, who is a mixed-ethnic post-colonial Black Ghanaian/ British in an "audience" setting and the transferential and indeed counter transferential dynamics of my impulses and expectations from the other racially minoritised supervisees in the group. The eminent psychotherapist, writer and teacher, Thomas, shares his experiences of working in a mixed team as follows:

> The situation at Nafsiyat [intercultural therapy centre] is that some therapists are Black, some White and all come from a variety of cultures. We work in this way because we believe that it is possible to work with a mixed gender, culture, and race team. This presents us all with a challenge. Some of us are on the receiving end of racism, and others are from groups with the power to perpetuate racism and others from groups who have previously experienced racism but are now left as inconspicuous minorities, not affected personally by racism. We all have a relationship with racism by the fact that we have a racial identity which has its place in the social pecking order of current racial and cultural supremacy. In a mixed team, discussion and analysis of clinical material is most important since the openness and honesty of its members can help to discover and unlock some of the hidden complexities of race in the countertransference.
>
> (Thomas, 1998, p. 180)

The supervisor's engagement and attention to their own processes must be open and honest, even as it relates to the mixed group of supervisees, client material and associated issues of culture and race. They are tasked not with forcing conversations but with creating an openness to such explorations, making the space safe enough to name and initiate explorations about "elephants in the room." In the documentary *descendant* (2022), the folklorist Kern Jackson has this to say about naming "you name it and once you name it, then all the medicinal [therapeutic] things start to happen, once you name something, you can tell it what to do." In any case the probability of a rupture occurring if racial and cultural issues are left unnamed and unexplored in the supervision is quite high – one or more supervisees might disconnect, leave or feel silenced. The departure of a supervisee might not eliminate the residue of the dynamics left by the unvoiced issue; the remaining group members might not feel safe, which could result in a detraction from the supervisor's functioning as a containing presence. The degree to which a supervisor feels capable of dealing with such issues might be what Symington referred to as the analyst's act of freedom as agent of therapeutic change. He postulated that: "the moment the analyst [supervisor] becomes aware of his or her attitude and is freed from it then the patient [supervisee] perceives it," "my contention is that the inner act of freedom in the analyst [supervisor] causes a therapeutic shift in the patient [supervisee] and new insight, learning and development in the analyst [supervisor]" (Symington, 1983 p. 290, p. 286). The supervisor and therapist's attentiveness facilitates a discernment of the constraining influence of the unexamined pot. They must then connect with their inner liberating space through the voice of Ananse's child to clarify and engage in the shapeshifting co-construction of the therapeutic themes emerging in the supervision. I adduce and understand Akhtar's (2012) term "moral courage" as apropos and as an indispensable module of processing and one that links with an aspect of Symington's "act of freedom."

Carter et al. (2020) draw attention to the understudied area of the impact of racial experiences on whites. The implication for the supervisor rests on their grasp of white racial identity development theory. They posit from studies that the processing of racial experiences by white individuals (as in the example of Hannah being in the minority in the supervision group) is nuanced and influenced by the white individual's racial development status (requiring supervisor knowledge and understanding of the theory and its application) and the attitudes which flow from it. The authors say, "it is likely that some White clients' adverse psychological reactions to race-based incidents stem from tension between their own beliefs in White superiority and the reality that (a) people of color also have rights, (b) individual people of color may sometimes succeed or achieve things that some individual Whites will not, and (c) despite individual experiences, Whites still continue to benefit from power/privilege in the [United Kingdom] [… .].Therefore, if clinicians [supervisors] can help such [supervisees and] clients explore the root of the [incongruous] affect (e.g., people of color should be deferential to Whites), they have a better chance of helping clients alleviate their distress" (Ibid, p. 105).

My comments on the emergence of race and culture in therapy and supervision leads to this next point. That is to register the consistent ongoing currents of intersecting identities in supervision. When the supervisor has a particular proclivity, e.g., race, it heightens a tendency to de-emphasise other identities in the supervisory work. This overlooking of certain client and supervisee identity narratives by a supervisor could frustrate a supervisee. It might be indicative of a supervisor who is out of step with a supervisee's work within the intersections and the broader spectrum of experiences in the lives of their clients. A supervisor's perception of such developmental supervisee shifts could then be held and reflectively linked to the emerging dynamics in the supervision dyad or group, whilst engaging and centering race at the same time. It is sometimes the case that as a supervisor, my vision is guided by my subjective experiences of being Black, mixed-ethnic Ghanaian, British and male. I am however inspired by the promptings of the voice of Ananse's child, conveyed in part through the communications of my supervisees and their clients, to appreciate the increased array of intersections at play in the supervision and therapy. Furthermore, a supervisee or supervisor can subvert the salience of race in a supervision by foregrounding "generalising concerns" (McKenzie-Mavinga, 2019, p. 168). This is a critical space for the supervisor to hold and facilitate – as it could productively advance the exploration of intersecting identities while supervisor inertia could result in the predomination of an anti-black restraining response to Black agency in the supervision and therapy space.

I have commented elsewhere on the place of language in therapy I conducted with a client (Ababio and Littlewood, 2019, p. 43). I highlighted the dynamics elicited by the privileging of English over traditional languages which is part of the internalised colonial edifice in Ghana as an ex-British colony. The probability of the dynamics of this language emerging and re-producing a colonising hold in the supervision cannot be underestimated. Its mutational propensity ranges from privileging the English language ema-nating from a colonialised or dominant interiority to valorising particular accents and linguistically marked class positions. The supervisor/supervisee(s) in such a situation (in their weaponisation of the English language) might tune out (discourage depth exploration of words from other languages) and devalue material from supervisees/supervisor whose English indicates a foreign accent, certain working class or regional-based accents. The supervisor's idealisation of middle-class positions and particular accents may conceal (cultural racism/internalised racism and) the corrosive effect of the supervisor's envy and its detrimental impact on the supervision. This, on a personal note, is associated with the coloniality that wormed its way into traditional Ghanaian structures and bequeathed to local Ghanaian power-brokers and leaders, the oppressive structures of the erstwhile British colonial administrators. The process of engaging reflectively with these cultural, his-torical and political particulars in my pot calls attention to the presence of lingering active internalised remnants of these transmitted pernicious beha-viours. If they were to be left unexamined, they could have an impact on the supervision and therapy space. The supervisor is at their most vulnerable if these elements of their pot are not reflectively engaged with. A thoughtful approach can produce moments of creative collaboration and shifts for the supervisee, client and supervisor.

Similarly, a supervisee's unanalysed race complex (Lowe, 2021) in acti-vation mode could hold sway and overwhelm the supervisee – and in turn, mobilise a "proxy self" which Thomas posits is used by black children as a strategy for surviving in a white-dominant world (Thomas, 1998, pp. 160–161). A supervisee engulfed by their colonial object, might seek to present a proxy self, one that they deem acceptably projects and speaks to Eurocentric themes. A supervisee and supervisor in thrall to these internalised dynamics manufacture a space wherein the narrative of the client mutates and distorts. It is an arena which can actuate racially minoritised supervisees and supervisors to generate and reproduce special "exotic" material, compelled to present evidence of their credentials as "specialised" and culturally competent practitioners. In the competitive quest to present the unfamiliar, reinforced by dubious validations and rewards, these supervisees can, bypass areas of their client's material they deem "ordinary."[4] Mbembe, expounding on Fanon has this to say about these internalised colonial dynamics:

> The represented subject [supervisee/supervisor] always runs the risk of being transformed into an object or a plaything... .... This subject is obliged to take an image that will demand endless struggle. This subject grapples with an image that has been pinned on it, which it labors to rid itself of, whose author he is not.
>
> (Mbembe, 2019, p. 139)

Through self-reflection in their supervision of supervision and a commitment to acts of courage, a supervisor could mitigate these pernicious enacted processes by listening to Ananse's child and by observing the pot through attunement and positioning. This self-reflection involves the supervisor's and supervisee's discernment of their own nuanced subtle shifts, some somatic and visceral. These may include a tensing of muscles (Ellis, 2019), holding of breath, detaching, mood changes (such as fear, annoyance, feeling over-whelmed), an urge to find *the* answer, competitiveness or an inability to remain still, heightened perhaps within a racially and culturally diverse setting. In addition, there may be an increasing inclination to colonise the contributions of others. It might take the form of claiming ownership of colleagues' comments and ideas and a resistance to refer to the source that inspired them, for example, taking over a contribution from a supervisor/supervisee in the group or conversely giving disproportionate attention to those comments. These discernible shifts may well be helpful clinical mate-rial, however, their usefulness emerges only as one attempt to address the pot and the dynamics it generates. The commitment required of the intercultural supervisor and supervisee(s) to temper these detrimental internalised dynamics is what Paul Gilroy characterises as a "tenacious attachment to the overcoming of racial hierarchies, categories and styles of thought"(Gilroy, 2021, p. 110). Furthermore, observing and engaging with the pot permits a creative liberating relatedness. I present the following case examples as illustrative of positionings the supervisor and supervisee may adopt with the pot in the supervision. The first is what I refer to as the case of "I don't want to gloat."

I don't want to gloat

A Pakistani female counsellor who had lived in a European country and was a member of diplomatic circles was seeing a white, male, Portuguese client. They used French in their therapy. The counsellor was Muslim and, in the supervision, described her migration story to the United Kingdom as diffi-cult. She had come from a position of privilege in the European country to a lower status in the United Kingdom and was resourceful in engaging in low

wage jobs and roles to fund her education and secure a professional occupation. The client's partner was terminally ill and the client could no longer
work due to ill health. They were homeless and lived in a temporary, sub-
standard flat. The counsellor came to supervision and presented the case,
elaborating the current dire situation of the client. She then went on to say
a few times: "I don't want to gloat, I don't want to gloat, I don't want to
gloat." Jared Sexton commenting on repetitions says: "To simply repeat a
line, comment, or complaint is, in a sense, to stop oneself from doing
something, to restrain a thought or feeling, to prefer the dominant over the
emergent" (Sexton, 2021, p. 16).

The repetition or refrain from the counsellor after her case presentation
cast a silencing, perplexing and uncertain ambience over the group. As
supervisor, I had no meaningful comment on the tip of my tongue but certainly felt a weight to conjure one up. It was this weight that I reflected on
during the milliseconds of supervision time. I sensed something hesitant yet
tinged with glee in the supervisee's listless tone. It was to her comment and
tone that I threw open an invitation to the group to engage in the process
of analysis. The thoughts trickled in. Was there something about the reversal
of stereotypical racial positioning here? Had this racial reversal engaged any
dynamics in the supervisee linked to an activation of memories of racist
injuries she had sustained? Was the glee emanating from this source? What
about the supervisee's hesitation? Was it linked to a sense of shame evoked by
the realisation of her glee? Her confusion perhaps pointed in part to her
loss of previous diplomatic privilege and to the reversed positioning with
her client: the dynamics of her internalised, unanalysed race complex
(Lowe, 2021) provoked a belief that her role of power and authority was
precarious and not permissible, that she ought to be on the lower rung of the
societal ladder. Through the group processing and authorisation, she engaged
with a shift, which was the permission to uncurb and express herself. She then
explored her gleefulness (of her experience of the client as a white refugee)
and juxtaposed it to the demands she felt the client was making on her. Did
the client feel entitled because of being male and white? The supervisee's
forbidden thoughts emerged as she spoke, the group listening and holding
both her and her client. The supervisee had somehow been trapped on the
treadmill of "not wanting to gloat." However, the group's thoughtful participation enabled something of an act of freedom within her, facilitating (a
shift from her enactment) to a therapeutic, helpful repositioning to her client.

Race in stealth

A white, Eastern European trainee supervisee named Misha was working
with a Bahraini client, who was in her early thirties and had been living in the
United Kingdom for four years at the time of the presentation of this case.
The client's relationship with a black man eight years older than her was

proving problematic as the client's mother was unhappy that her daughter was with a black, British man. They were planning to marry, in part, to regularise the client's immigration status in Britain. The client's parents' marriage had incurred the disapproval of their respective Christian and Muslim communities at the time. Her grandparents' marriage was also interfaith – her mother's disapproval and fear were perhaps linked to this family history as well as race.

This case involved shame and Misha's dawning recognition, evoked by memories of connections she has had with racism and of being perplexed by the emergence of anti-blackness in the client material. Another factor was her sense of not belonging and not feeling accepted in the United Kingdom colliding with her wish to belong. This case occurred in the context of the Brexit referendum in 2016, after which the place of European residents in the United Kingdom became somewhat precarious. It also evoked the therapist's memories of having left her country in Eastern Europe due to armed conflict ignited by ethnic and religious disputes. Misha and her client were each adjusting to their varied locations as minorities in the United Kingdom. The generational issues in the client's narrative were not given sufficient space due, in part, to Misha holding on to unanalysed aspects of her trauma resulting from civil war and the flight for refuge. The marginalised black partner's privilege – his possession of British citizenship and thus ability to regularise his partner's immigration status – was not explored. His racially minoritised status in the therapy was what received amplification and simultaneously suppressed. Misha, in presenting the case in the group supervision, seemed confused, ill at ease and embarrassed. As supervisor, I experienced it as an unsettling feeling, an uneasiness. I was no longer able to hold the sense of ease and solidarity I derive from the sometimes tenuous, alliances between minoritised and other groups suggested by concepts and acronyms such as 'marginalised communities, BAME, racialised individuals, BIPOC, allies'. Anti-blackness intersecting with other factors and the dynamic mirage of jostling for proximity to whiteness had widened the fissures between the groups in the supervision and case material. I wondered initially about the black man in the story; a reflection which elicited discomfort, sadness and pain as well as an incipient anger. Or perhaps, an aggression linked to my professional power as supervisor and to memories of racist incidents; it was bewildering. I recalled the words of a supervisor and mentor who in circumstances such as this recommended the approach of forward exploratory movement by the supervisor into these racially infused spaces with thought, care and courage. I wondered with the group about the client's black partner and me as a Black supervisor and mentioned the unease and discomfort. This resonated with Misha. Her discomfort and unease, she said, masked her attempt to shield me, and indeed herself, from the pain of facing and exploring the reality of anti-blackness in the therapy and supervision. For Misha, it also unveiled the developmental shifts required in engaging with approximations of the lived experience of black precarity and interrogating the contemporary and historical implications of white supremacy in the demanding processes of becoming an ally. This supervision approach incorporated wisdom pot dynamics facilitated in part through supervisor and supervisee racial identity processing, humility, "moral courage" (Akhtar, 2012) and Symington's act of freedom.

Mansa and me

This chapter has explored supervision largely from my perspective as a supervisor. It might now be helpful to comment briefly on my experience as supervisee, with an example derived from work I did in the early, post-qualification phase of my training. My client, Mansa, was a Ghanaian woman who had lived in the United Kingdom for about a decade by the time of her therapy and was still processing her asylum paperwork. She had submitted the application on the grounds of being persecuted for her sexual orientation – she was lesbian. The client had asked for a Ghanaian therapist and for therapy to be conducted in Ga, a Ghanaian language. Mansa seemed pleased about the prospect of being able to work with me in a Ghanaian language. She was living with a Ghanaian family who had provided her with free boarding and lodging. She was originally from the Northern part of Ghana, a deprived part of the country with a population who have histori-cally been discriminated against and her education ended just after primary school. The family she lived with in London shared her religious faith, however, Mansa had not come out to the family about her sexual orientation. She mentioned this at the beginning of our work and requested that her sexual orientation not be disclosed to the family. She emphasised this even after I had rehearsed the confidential nature of our work.

Mansa and I shared some similarities, in nationality and language. Ga was not Mansa's mother tongue, and neither was it mine but nevertheless, it was a Ghanaian language we had in common. We were both Ghanaian and had some differences to work through and so it was, as most interactions are, intercultural. Mansa said she wanted to explore the experiences of her particular socio-economic-class-ethnic position in Ghana and of being an LGBTQ Ghanaian and the ongoing tensions associated with concealing her sexual orientation from the family she was now living with. The work, however, stalled. My invitations and attempts to explore our varying locations within the intersectional contexts of Ghana were not taken up. She found it difficult to explore the area(s) that she stated was of concern and important to her (perhaps for Mansa there was little to be gained from exploring if Ghana's position on these inequities remains unchanged). I took this to my supervisor, who was experienced and knowledgeable. However, she sat with the pot and sought to work through the case on her "own," leaving me stuck in the junior partner position. On reflection, it would have been helpful had my supervisor explored the differing positionalities in the encounter – Mansa's, mine and the supervisor's. It is worth rehearsing the (obvious) point, that the language of my psychotherapy training (supervision and personal therapy) undertaken in London was English, and I was brought up privileging English in Ghana. I speak Ga less fluently and the client's Ga was far superior which may have evoked inadequacy in me. My name, furthermore, is associated with a dominant Ghanaian ethnic group, so Mansa's social transference with regard to Ghana's position on gender, sexuality, ethnic disparity, class and status may have proved difficult to work through. A non-Ghanaian therapist may have provided Mansa with some distance and safety. My supervisor saw a Ghanaian therapist with a Ghanaian client and may have assumed that I (and she, the supervisor) would *know* what to do. The supervisor was astute about themes pertaining to racialisation but not so sure-footed about the permutations of localised cultural dynamics and could/should have engaged the unpollinated/unshattered pot. As my supervisor sat with her pot, I felt excluded from engaging with its contents although this was conceivably an abdication of my involvement in the partnership (an inability to access my Ananse child's voice). The supervision did not translate into an act of freedom (Symington, 1983), and neither did the therapy I was engaged in with Mansa.

Mansa had sought out a Ghanaian therapist and met one she was keen to engage with, but the similarities albeit inviting may have felt too intrusive and familiar, while the relational contextual differences evoked social and cultural transferences and countertransferences which somehow ensnared therapist, client, and supervisor. This work deployed, in part, the use of a "black empathic approach," which Mckenzie-Mavinga in defining says "if therapists have a picture of the clients' ethnic and cultural background it may support their knowledge of the client's experience and ways of coping with racism. Identifying a client's history of oppression and racism and their ways of coping can offer insights" (Mckenzie-Mavinga, 2019:172). The thinking and intervention of the supervisor would have benefitted from drawing on and emphasising "the picture of the client's ethnic and cultural background" (ibid) in Mckenzie-Mavinga's definition due to the permutations and particularities of the case. Could her appellation therefore be expanded to that of a "black, intersectional, cultural, empathic approach"? Turner explicates the application of a modified model in his text on intersectionality (2021). The reader may have their own views about this case and its associated supervisory dynamics. Mansa cancelled sessions after our fifth appointment and dropped out of treatment. I was left with questions and speculations, some of which I have shared here. The questions accompanying Mansa's termination produced and reproduced contemporary instructive stories, which continue to be passed on.

Wisdom pot consciousness

Gordon describes a consciousness which he terms "potentiated consciousness" – one that shifts anti-blackness from a focus on a problematic self to outward movements of critiquing social and racist structures, leading to an engagement with possibilities, options and change (Gordon, 2022, p. 145). The wisdom pot consciousness operates in the interstices of the self and other selves, minds and their co-constructions. It is simultaneously in and out, choreographed through advances into the supervisor's inner landscape and motioning out to the supervisees' and clients' terrain, then further out still into the social, political and cultural. These currents in their responsive resonances reach back into the interiorities of the participants in the therapeutic spaces.

I am reminded of my supervisee, a woman of Yemeni heritage, a qualified experienced therapist, who presented her female client who was in a relationship with an abusive male partner. We reviewed this case during the period of the murders of Sarah Everard and Sabina Nessa, which were both committed in the Southeastern part of England between 3 March 2021 and 17 September 2021, a time when the spotlight was trained on men and violent behaviour. I admonished the therapist for not mobilising certain risk procedures, but she insisted she had conducted an adequate risk assessment. She posed a question that prompted me to examine the pot, asking, "I feel you are being unnecessarily critical of me – I have done what is required and not sure what else I could have done?" My preoccupation with recent tragedies heightened my reflections on patriarchal violence (its implications of legal redress for racially minoritised women). The wish to display performative gender equality to this female therapist resulted in an enactment (a misuse of professional power and propping up patriarchy in the supervision). It was an instructive moment – I *heard* Ananse's child's challenging voice in my supervisee's question. We reflected on what had happened: firstly, to me – in the Symingtonian sense of a liberating act – allowing my training, years of experience and role of supervisor to be metabolised, facilitating this wisdom pot consciousness moment. Secondly, we reflected on what had happened to *me/us* within the prevailing context of violence against women.

This story and the others before it, raise various questions and thoughts. For example, what were the reasons behind my failing Mansa and the test she set for me if she did set one? What of my supervision, and my voice in that story? What of the "I don't want to gloat," scenario, where race, history, class, religion, and gender featured in the transference and countertransference? How best to meet the demands of work in a mixed supervision group where a racialised as white English group member (an evolving ally) was in the minority – eliciting caretaking and (reaction formation) defensive impulses from the racially minoritised supervisor in the company of supervisees of

Nigerian, Palestinian and Indian heritage? How about the press of an internalised coagulated, unyielding colonial language – arousing pretension, envy and denigration in the supervision? Also, the tackling of the unavoidable questions surrounding the typecasting of racialised therapists, obliged, under the arches of racially managed organisations, to generate/mine and reproduce exotic material from the "ordinary" narratives of racially minoritised clients in the supervision space. Additionally, recalling those connected-related moments of group "recognition trauma" (Mckenzie-Mavinga, 2019:171), of pausing and resting, of seeing and caring, of feeling, and acknowledging strength and resistance in the expansive past, present and future. Guilaine Kinouani, in this regard, proposes the authorisation of "Black joy," (by supervisors and therapists) as a "strategic" "deliberate" practise much like "self-care'," which foils and thwarts the inimical micro processes inherent in racialised structures. For Kinouani, "experiencing [Black] joy is central to Black liberation" (Kinouani, 2022:167). The wisdom pot consciousness within these supervision experiences, moments and spaces enables what Gordon (2022) observes about the "potentiated double consciousness" of the racially minoritised individual. Gordon's comments here are applicable to the consciousness inspired by a shapeshifting engagement with the pot. He says "realising that he or she is not a problem but a human being facing problems, the black comes to question the society, which is human-made and therefore changeable. Then with that realisation, the black becomes the Black, an agent of social change. That realisation is born from the contradiction. Realising an avowed universal was false, raises many possibilities to consider. It's not only the Black (e.g., Sefula, Mahmoud et al.) who could emerge but also many other kinds of people [Anastacia, Hannah et al]" (ibid, p. 145).

So, now to the end of my supervision with Anansesem. Did any of these stories speak to you, stir some disagreement or leave you wondering what I meant? Perhaps they may have caused a shaking of the head. They might lead to interesting turns in your practice and, by some curious chance, re-emerge transformed in my practice, to be explored again.

Notes

1 Lowe formulated the concept of the unanalysed race complex – which he posits "resides in the psyche, usually hidden, rarely explored and largely unanalysed. The race complex Lowe said is often repressed but under certain circumstances can emerge and overwhelm the ego and obstruct or disturb its relationship to reality" (2021).
2 "The ongoing effects of racial slavery, but moreover, its continued survival in the matrix of social, political, and economic relations beyond the time of abolition" (Paul Khalil Saucier and Woods, 2015: 12-13).
3 "Black afterlives are animated by a stubborn refusal to forget and to be forgotten" (Benjamin, 2018).

4 "Drawing from animation, theorist daCosta observes the enduring - and mostly troubling - positioning of minoritised characters in problem settings. In deploying "ordinariness" daCosta argues that, "While racial stereotyping is not always obvious, close examination reveals that several forces are at work to ensure that a certain state of affairs is maintained. Worse still this 'condition' ensures that blacks simply do not appear in the right contexts – remaining outside normality [and kept in problem settings]" (dacosta, 2007:7) "Hence blacks, when they 'arrive' within a[n] [animation] frame must do so precisely to fill 'their' problem, performance or entertainment quotas" (ibid: 39).

References

Ababio, B., Littlewood, R. (eds.). (2019). *Intercultural Therapy: Challenges, Insights and Developments* (1st ed.). Abingdon: Routledge.

Akhtar, S. (2012). *The Book of Emotions*. New Delhi: Roli Books.

Akinwotu, E., Tondo, L. (2022). People of colour fleeing Ukraine attacked by polish nationalists. *The Guardian*, 2nd March. Available at: https://www.theguardian.com/global-development/2022/mar/02/people-of-colour-fleeing-ukraine-attacked-by-polish-nationalists. (Accessed 28th March 2022).

Benjamin, R. (2018). Black afterlives matter: Cultivating kinfulness as reproductive justice. *Boston Review*. Available at: https://bostonreview.net/articles/ruha-benjamin-black-afterlives-matter/ (Accessed 15 July 2022).

Beshara, R., Davids, F. (2022). The psychoanalysis of racism and the racism of psychoanalysis. Zoom online seminar. *The Guild of Psychotherapists, London*. 19th February 2022.

Bion, W. R. (1967). Notes on memory and desire. In Spillius, E.B. (ed.) (1988) *Melanie Klein today: Developments in theory and practice, Vol. 2. Mainly practice*. Taylor & Francis: Routledge.

Bonilla, Y. (2015). *Non-Sovereign Futures French Caribbean Politics in the Wake of Disenchantment*. Chicago, Ill: Univ. of Chicago Press.

Carter, R. T., Roberson, K., Johnson, V. E. (2020). Race-based stress in white adults: Exploring the role of white racial identity status attitudes and type of racial events. *Journal of Multicultural Counseling and Development, 48*(2), pp. 95–107. 10.1002/jmcd.12168.

daCosta, C., C.H. (2007). *Racial Stereotyping and Selective Positioning in Contemporary British Animation*. Doctor of Philosophy Thesis. University of Brighton.

Davids, F., Beshara, R. (2022). The psychoanalysis of racism and the racism of psychoanalysis. Zoom online seminar. *The Guild of Psychotherapists, London*. 19th February 2022.

Descendant. (2022). Directed by Margaret Brown and Veda Tunstall. [Documentary film]. Netflix.

Ellis, E. (2019). Race issues in therapy: Finding our voice across the black/white divide. In: Ababio, B., Littlewood, R. (eds.) *Intercultural Therapy: Challenges, Insights and Developments* (1st ed.). Abingdon: Routledge.

Frawley-O'Dea, M. (2003). Supervision is a relationship too: A contemporary approach to psychoanalytic supervision. *Psychoanalytic Dialogues, 13*(3), 355–366. 10.1080/10481881309348739

Gilroy, P. (2021). Antiracism, Blue Humanism and the Black Mediterranean. *Transition: The magazine of Africa and the Diaspora, 132*(131), 110.

Gomez, L. (1997). *An Introduction to Object Relations.* London: Free Association Press.

Gordon, L. (2022). *Fear of Black Consciousness.* UK: Penguin Books.

Kareem, J. (2006). The Nafsiyat Intercultural Therapy Centre: Ideas and experience in Intercultural Therapy. In: Kareem, J., Littlewood, R. (eds) *Intercultural Therapy,* 2nd edition. Oxford: Blackwell.

Kinouani, G. (2022). *Living while black: Using Joy, Beauty, and Connection to Heal Racial Trauma.* S.L.: Beacon.

Lowe, F. (2021) The unanalysed race complex. Zoom online seminar. Institute of Psychotherapy and Social Studies, London. 24th April 2021.

Mbembe, A. (2019). *Necropolitics.* Durham: Duke University Press.

Mckenzie-Mavinga, I. (2019). The challenge of racism in clinical supervision. In: Ababio, B., Littlewood, R. (eds.) *Intercultural Therapy: Challenges, Insights and Developments* (1st ed.). Abingdon: Routledge.

Saucier, P. K., Woods, T. P. (2015). What is the danger in black studies and can we look at it again (and again)? In: *On Marronage: Ethical Confrontations with Antiblackness.* Trenton: Africa World Press.

Sexton, J. (2021). Antidoting. *The Black Scholar, 51*(3), 5–24. 10.1080/00064246. 2021.1932383.

Symington, N. (1983). The analyst's act of freedom as agent of therapeutic change. *International Review of Psychoanalysis, 10,* 283–291.

Thomas, L. (1998). Psychotherapy in the context of race and culture: An intercultural therapeutic approach. In Fernando, S., (ed.) *Mental Health in a Multi-Ethnic Society: A multi-Disciplinary Handbook.* London: Routledge.

Thomas, L. (2004). Supervision of therapeutic work with refugees and asylum seekers. *Self & Society, 32*(5), 25–31. 10.1080/03060497.2004.11083813.

Tummala-Narra, P. (2004). Dynamics of race and culture in the supervisory encounter. *Psychoanalytic Psychology, 21*(2), 300–311. 10.1037/0736-9735.21.2.300.

Turner, D. (2021). *Intersections of Privilege and Otherness in Counselling and Psychotherapy.* Mockingbird, S.L.: Routledge.

Index

Note: Italicized page numbers refer to figures. Page numbers followed by "n" refer to notes.

Muñoz, J. P. 152
Murray, K. 5

Nafsiyat Intercultural Therapy Centre 5,
 15, 253
Nafsiyat Refugee Project 111–122;
 boundaries in community settings
 118–119; community-based
 therapy 111–112; culture and
 identity 112–113; intercultural
 supervision model 119–121;
 language 117–118; supervising
 therapists from Black, Asian and
 minority communities 115–118;
 supervision 112–115
narrative structure for intercultural
 trainee, pitfalls of 12, 202–216;
 "adventure" development, in
 Western literature 204–206;
 genealogy of adventure 206–207;
 real life stories 213–214; story
 editing 208–211; supervision
 207–208; tracking of story
 211–213
National Health Service (NHS) 64, 66
National Statistics 37
Nazroo, J. Y. 4, 38
Neff, K. 131, 132
neoliberalism: racialised 39
Nerlich, M. 206, 207
Newtonian Theory 52
Ng, K. 153
NHS see National Health Service (NHS)
Nichols, E. 48, 49, *50*, 51, 52
Nilsson, J. E. 153
Nobles, W. 38
non-verbal behaviour 98

Obsessive Compulsive Disorder
 (OCD) 80
OCD see Obsessive Compulsive
 Disorder (OCD)
Office for National Statistics Data:
 *Domestic Abuse Prevalence and
 Victim Characteristics* 133
Ogden, T. H. 26, 196, 233, 239
omnipotence 246
omniscience 246
O'Morain, P. 151
oppression 6, 25, 27, 31, 39, 40, 43, 55–57,
 93, 105, 137, 150, 195, 215, 232–235,
 240, 249, 255, 260; female 228,

236–238; gender 229; internalised
 11, 42, 44–52, 115, 149, 152, 164;
 racial 29; reinforcement of 156;
 social 230; societal 212; systemic
 130; transgenerational 130; trauma
 41, 58
othering/otherism/otherness 14, 63, 69,
 72, 74–76, 85, 86n2, 133, 135, 137,
 188, 208
overt racism 31
overworking 43
over-working 164
Owomoyela, O. 59

Paranoid-schizoid position, model of 193
passing as white 147–157; minoritised
 practitioner's voice, supporting
 155–156; prior to training
 148–150; in supervision 153–155;
 in training 150–153
passive acquiescence 43
perfect storm 192
Petrucelli, J. 67
PettyJohn, M. E. 210
physical violence 25, 131
Pierce, C. 45
Pieterse, A. L. 27
Pitcan, M. 32
pluralist supervision approach 175
Porges, S. W. 138–139
Porter, N. 120
post-traumatic stress disorder (PTSD)
 42, 132
potentiated consciousness 261
potentiated double consciousness 262
Powell, D. R. 31
Powell, S. 27
powerlessness 128, 129, 213, 215, 234
prejudice 32, 67, 79, 84, 113, 115, 147,
 150, 152, 156, 157, 180, 186, 187,
 204, 224, 230, 232, 235; internal
 2368; systemic 148;
 unconscious 220
privilege 11, 21, 24, 25, 27, 29, 40, 41, 44,
 45, 46, 53, 55, 57, 63, 65–67, 70,
 79, 83, 137, 152, 156, 173, 187,
 209, 214, 215, 235, 239, 248, 254,
 256–258; male 234; normative 234;
 seductive 148; socio-economic 151
Prochaska, J. O. 147
professional identity 8, 21, 27, 30, 31,
 114, 149, 153, 155